A STUDY IN CHINESE PRINCIPLES OF EDUCATION

北大教育学文库 — 刘云杉 主编

蒋梦麟 著

序

　　北京大学的教育学科具有悠久的历史。如果从京师大学堂1902年建立师范馆算起，我们至今有118年的历史，当然师范教育与教育学科不能完全等同。另一方面，北大教育学科的历史并非连续而未中断的。抗战期间，北大与清华、南开三校先后在长沙和昆明分别组建临时大学和西南联大，教育学科也伴随着这段特殊历史而颠沛流离。联大期间新建的师范学院为云南基础教育提供了师资，对提升当地的基础教育水平做出了贡献。抗战胜利后，1946年三校北归，西南联大的师范学院留在了昆明，发展成为今天的云南师范大学。[①]1949年，教育学科被移出北大，调整到其他院校，于是北大无独立建制教育学科的空白状况一直持续到1980年。1980年，教育学科在北大以高等教育研究室的形式重建，随着国家改革开放政策的实施和对教育事业的重视，教育学科也逐步发展起来。2000年，北大将高等教育研究所和电化教学中心予以合并，在此基础上成立了教育学院，成为综合大学建立教育学院的表率。

　　2020年正好是北大教育学科重建40周年、教育学院建立20

[①] 据曾任西南联大师范学院院长的黄钰生介绍："师院建院时，将原北大教育系、南开哲学心理教育系的教育组及云南大学教育系师生划归联大院。"见黄钰生：《回忆联大师范学院及其附校》，载西南联大北京校友会编：《我心中的西南联大：西南联大建校70周年纪念文集》，清华大学出版社2008年版，第268—272页。

周年。为了庆祝学科重建的不惑之年，我们正在做三件事情：一是整理和编纂北大教育学科从建立以来百余年的发展历史，以《学堂兴 师道立》这本书的形式呈现出来；二是邀请师生撰写求学问道的回忆启示录，辑成《学术之道》文集；三是把历史上北大学人撰写的教育研究方面的著作和教材，有选择性地进行影印，汇为"北大教育学文库"出版。本序是对上面第三项工作的一个说明。上述第一和第三项工作在商务印书馆的支持下进行，第二项工作在北京大学出版社的协助下开展。

　　对于北大教育学科发展历史以及我们正在开展的工作，我想做如下两点说明。第一，北大是现代中国高等教育的产物，北大的办学实践本身就是一部大学教育学术史，这方面的研究已有丰硕的成果。例如，在华东师范大学教育系编选的《中国现代教育文选》[①]的作者群中，就包括曾在北大任教和任职的多位学者，如蔡元培、陈独秀、鲁迅、李大钊、胡适、梁漱溟、江隆基等。此外还有一些学者，他们的研究工作具有较强的专业性，其重要性仅为业内所知，但他们的工作同样值得进行回顾和总结，这是我们开展此项工作的重点。第二，就教育学科而言，其学科边界比较模糊，所以北大研究教育问题的学者或者发表过教育论著的学者，绝不仅仅限于教育系和师范学院，而是遍布多个学科，比如社会学、哲学、历史学等，自然形成一个多学科的格局，这个特点对于我们认识教育规律十分重要，因此，这些论著都在我们的收录范围之内。

　　我们选印的教育著作和教材，已经有数十年甚至上百年

[①] 华东师范大学教育系编：《中国现代教育文选》（修订版），人民教育出版社1998年版。

的历史，再版这些学术著作有什么价值呢？它们有没有过时呢？我想分别从历史和超历史两个方面讲一下我们的想法。首先，从历史方面看，这些文献是中国教育学科现代化过程的真实写照，作为一种学术的历史呈现本身是不会过时的。中国教育学科的现代化至今仍然没有完成，可以说，过去的研究工作是我们今天研究工作的前奏，我们今天的研究工作是过去研究工作的续曲。其次，从超历史性方面看，过去的学者与今天的学者一样，都试图透过教育活动的表象去认识抽象的规律，这些规律会超越特定的历史阶段和范围，具有恒久性和普遍性。

对于超历史性，最近读了一些材料，稍有心得，允我多写几笔。早期的北大教育学科是在一批学贯中西的学者手中建立起来的。他们大多接受过程度不一的中国传统教育，也有不少人留洋接受过西方教育，他们用在西方大学习得的理性思维去审辨中国传统的教育实践，中西古今的融通性和对比感十分强烈，对于中西文化制度下的教育特征及其价值有着独到和真切的感受，其思想的广度和深度不在今人之下。这些特点反映在他们的学术著作和行动中。比如，蔡元培先生刚到德国留学时就发现，德国的教育"在课程上，重推悟不重记诵；在训育上，尚感化不尚拘束"[①]。蔡先生在德国留学时，主修心理学、伦理学和美学，他对于教育的理解和所采取的行动指南，主要基于他对中西两种文化观下教育的理解。1916年，他长校北大时，就采取"无论何种学派，苟其言之成理，持之有故，尚不达自

[①] 蔡元培：《辛亥那一年》，载高平叔编：《蔡元培全集》第七卷，中华书局1989年版，第109页。

然淘汰之命运，即使彼此相反，也听他们自由发展"①的治校方针。他聘请胡适来北大任教也是因为其"旧学邃密"和"新知深沉"。②

　　再如，与蔡元培先生相似，蒋梦麟也接受过中西教育。留学美国时，他从农学转到教育学，还接受过哲学和历史学教育，对于中西文化有着同样深刻的理解。在《西潮》一书中，他讲到一个有趣的例子。有一天，他和杜威、胡适在北平西山看到一只蜣螂推着一个小小的泥团上山坡。它先用前腿来推，然后又用后腿，接着又改用边腿。泥团一点点往上滚，快到坡顶时忽然滚回原地。蜣螂这样反复多次，一次次地尝试，又一次次地失败。蒋梦麟和胡适都不约而同地赞叹这个小虫的恒心毅力。杜威却说，它的毅力固然可嘉，但其愚蠢却实在可怜。蒋梦麟写道："这真是智者见智，仁者见仁。同一东西却有不同的两面。这位杰出的哲学家是道地的西方子弟，他的两位学生却是道地的东方子弟。"③ 蒋梦麟通过这个事例想要说明中西文化之间的差异，从而揭示更深层次上的不同，这个不同表现在官觉世界和理性世界，"知易行难"和"知难行易"两种对知行关系的不同认识，道德宇宙和理智宇宙，"学以致用"和"为知识而知识"两种不同的学用关系。在上述二分类中，中国偏向于前者，而西方偏向于后者，造成了两种不同的知识体系和认识论特征。无独有偶，与杜威几乎同期访问中国的英国哲学

---

① 蔡元培：《我在教育界的经验》，载高平叔编：《蔡元培全集》第七卷，中华书局1989年版，第200页。
② 蔡元培：《我在北京大学的经历》，载高平叔编：《蔡元培全集》第六卷，中华书局1988年版，第350页。
③ 蒋梦麟：《西潮·新潮》，岳麓书社2000年版，第256—257页。

家罗素也提出,"西方文明与众不同的优点就是科学方法,而中国文明的最具特色的长处就是对人生归宿的合理解释"①。其他学者,如梁漱溟等,都对中西文化及其知识观有着深刻的认识,今天读他们的作品仍然深受启发。总之,中国的现代化,中国教育的现代化,就是吸收西方文化以改造自身文化的过程。"我们将在儒家知识系统的本干上移接西方的科学知识。儒家的知识系统从探究事物或大自然出发,而以人与人的关系为归趋;西方的科学知识系统也同样从探究事物或大自然出发,但以事物本身之间的相互关系为归趋,发展的方向稍有不同。"②教育学者未必像哲学家那样深切关注中西文化对于知识的影响,但是这种中西比较观肯定会在其著述中有所反映,这种反映一定是深刻和深远的,是其超历史性的表现。

参与此项丛书选编工作的几位同事告诉我,在收集和整理学科史料的过程中,他们不断有"惊喜"发现,我们的先辈做了很多令人叹为观止的学术工作,有些是开创性的,过去我们对此知之甚少。学术既有历史理解的一面,也有历史局限性的另一面。对于历史理解的一面,正像章学诚所言,"不知古人之世,不可妄论古人文辞也;知其世矣,不知古人之身处,亦不可以遽论其文也"③。对于历史局限性的一面,需要我们采取去粗取精、去伪存真的态度和方式予以加工和改造。有鉴于此,我们希望读者在阅读过程中,可以处理好历史与现实之间

---

① 〔英〕罗素:《罗素论中西文化》,杨发庭等译,北京出版社2010年版,第89页。
② 蒋梦麟:《西潮·新潮》,岳麓书社2000年版,第253页。
③ 章学诚:《文史通义·文德》,中华书局1961年版,第60页,转引自罗志田:《变动时代的文化履迹》,复旦大学出版社2010年版,第9页。

的关系。

我们选印了三本著作作为本套影印丛书的第一辑,其中既有过去已经出版的,也有首次刊布发行的。这三本著作分别是:蒋梦麟的 *A Study in Chinese Principles of Education*(《中国教育原理》),陶孟和的《社会与教育》,姜琦和邱椿的《中国新教育行政制度研究》。如果条件允许的话,我们今后还会把这项工作继续进行下去。学术是公器,套用社会学家戈尔茨的话,我们现在所做的事情,不是研究北大的教育学科,而是在北大研究教育学科。

北京大学教育学院院长　阎凤桥
2020年9月20日于燕园

如何想象中国古代的教育世界
——蒋梦麟《中国教育原理》导读

陈洪捷

蒋梦麟（1886—1964），原名梦熊，字兆贤，号孟邻，浙江余姚人。清末秀才。早年先后就读于绍郡中西学堂、浙江省立高等学堂。1904年入上海南洋公学。毕业后自费赴美留学，1909年入加利福尼亚大学农学院，后转入社会科学学院主修教育学，1915年进哥伦比亚大学研究院继续学业，师从杜威。1917年获博士学位，同年回国，受聘为上海商务印书馆编辑，任江苏省教育会理事。1918年加入中华职业教育社。1919年参与创办新教育改进社，担任《新教育》杂志的主编。五四运动后，代表蔡元培校长主持校务，任北京大学总务长。1927年一度离开北大，任浙江临时政治会议委员，并兼浙江省教育厅厅长、国立第三中山大学（今浙江大学前身）校长，1928年任教育部部长。1930年回北京大学，任校长。抗战全面爆发后，为国立西南联合大学轮流主持校务的三常委之一。1945年9月辞去北大校长之职。1949年赴台。1964年在台湾逝世。著有《过渡时代之思想与教育》（1933）、《西潮》（1947）、《新潮》（1967）等；著述被辑为《孟邻文存》（1954）。

蒋梦麟的博士论文题目是 A Study in Chinese Principles of Education（《中国教育原理》），完成于1917年。关于蒋梦麟的博士论文，通常认为有两个版本，一是1918年版，二是1925

年版。1918年版扉页上标明出版者是"商务印书馆",但此版没有版权页,也没有任何商务印书馆的出版信息,应该不是正式出版物。至于所谓的1924年版和1925年版其实是一个版本,只是在扉页上标明"1924",而在版权页中写的是"中华民国十四年二月",而且标明是"初版"。

关于蒋梦麟博士论文的1918年版本,查《张元济日记》得知,1916年8月29日载"蒋君梦麟有博士学位,提出论文,欲托本馆印刷。印价约千元,由本馆代垫,由介绍人立约担保"。看来商务印书馆答应为蒋梦麟"印刷"论文,即"代印",而非"出版"。《张元济日记》1918年1月30日载"蒋梦麟来信,自本年一月,每月由薪水项下拨一百余元,还去年所借之千元。即复一信,原信送交会计室许笃斋,有知照单"。显然,1918年版本是商务印书馆为蒋梦麟代印的版本,非正式出版。那么,蒋梦麟为什么要花钱让商务印书馆"代印"其论文呢?

据说哥伦比亚大学有规定,在本校攻读博士学位者必须出版博士论文,并赠送哥大图书馆100册,才能被授予学位。所以蒋梦麟在博士论文完成前一年(1916)就联系商务印书馆"代印"博士论文,并在扉页上标注了"商务印书馆"字样。但问题是,蒋梦麟的博士论文前言所署时间是1917年8月,而蒋梦麟1917年6月已毕业,并获得博士学位。商务的"代印本"标注的出版时间是1918年。据此可以做如下推测:蒋梦麟在1917年6月毕业时,虽然未能提交出版的博士论文,但由于提供了与商务印书馆签订的"出版合同"之类的证明,并允诺1918年提交100册成书,所以1917年就获得了博士学位。第二年,即1918年,论文才印刷完毕,并寄往哥伦比亚大学。相关具体细节,尚有待考证。

以上是关于蒋梦麟博士论文出版情况的说明。

蒋梦麟博士论文的题目虽然是《中国教育原理》，其实研究的内容是中国古代的教育思想。全书分六个篇章，首先是导论，包括两章，论述中国生活和思想以及教育总貌。第一部分是遗传与教育，包括两章，综述中国古代的思想和教育；第二部分讨论学习观，包括四章，分别论述了知识、科学、知识中的相对价值和学习的基本要素；第三部分是教学观，包括两章，分别论述基础教育的方法和教学的基本要素；第四部分是论述道德教育的理念，包括两章，分别论述道德论的种类和道德教学的基本要素；最后是结论，包括三章，分别讨论中国文化的问题，个人、社会与国家，科学与艺术教育。总体来看，本书从西方教育的角度对传统中国的教育思想进行了梳理和中西对比性讨论，并对中国传统教育思想发展的方向进行了讨论。

这本书虽然很早就在国内出版，但知名度并不高。或许由于是用英文出版的，受众面因此受到影响。但无论影响大小，该书无疑是中国学人用西方的理念来研究中国古代教育思想的早期著述之一。如蒋梦麟自己所说，这是中国教育思想的拓荒之作。该书对中国教育史学的发展具有重要价值，对研究蒋梦麟的教育思想更是意义重大。

本书从现代教育的视角梳理了中国古代的教育思想，并构建了一种中国古代教育思想的体系，其贡献不可忽视。但在建构中国古代教育思想体系的过程中，如蒋梦麟自己也说，他虽然有所警惕，但肯定无法完全避免用现代的观念去解读古人的思想。他虽然只是一笔带过，但这一点却非常重要。由此可以提出一个问题：我们能否抛开西方主导的现代视角，去想象中国古代的教育世界？

清末民初，在西学涌入之时，中国知识界对西方的科学技术采取了拿来主义，照单全收，原因很简单，"声光化电"及"坚船利炮"都是我们所没有的，只好虚心"拿来"。而在人文社会科学方面，情况有所不同。西方的人文社科知识在"坚船利炮"的陪伴下，一时所向披靡，学习西方的人文社科知识已成为不可避免的选择。

但说到借鉴西方的人文社科知识，中国知识界面临如何处理中西关系的难题。有人想把"中体西用"原则坚持到底，抵制西方的文科之学，但更多的人则试图用西方的知识来"消化"中国的传统知识，尝试采用西方的知识系统，来重新建构自己的传统知识。在这些开明人士的脑子中，或许有"自古有之"的自豪感，或许也有跟上世界潮流、重建中国知识体系的责任感。所谓"整理国故"的主张，即按照西方的知识范式来整理中国传统的知识，就是这种观念的一种体现。在这一理念指导下，中国学者们用了大约30年的时间，建立起了包括历史学、哲学、教育学、经济学等学科的现代中国人文社会科学体系。

蒋梦麟的博士论文《中国教育原理》无疑是现代教育学科体系的组成部分。他自己说，中国古代的许多思想与西方的教育思想有很多共同之处，但是不够系统，散见于不同的著作之中，应当将这些零散的教育思想给予明确的表述，使其系统化。而建构系统的模板和参照，当然是西方的。

用西方的观念来重新认识和理解中国固有的教育思想，并为其建构一种思想体系，这当然是有意义的工作。而且外来的视角能够让中国人发现许多我们日用而不知的东西，也看到自己的长处和问题。而且，只有在此基础之上，西方人才有可能看懂中国的教育，我们也才能与西方的学者一起讨论教育的问题。

在清末民初的时代背景下，这一做法和思路是完全可以理解的，也是有必要的。但是，西方的教育学思想和教育学理论，是在西方的历史实践的基础上产生的，所以这种理论在根本上具有一种西方性。如果用这种西方的概念和系统来"整理"中国的传统，难免会失去我们对于古代知识和制度原本面貌的敏感性，甚至扭曲我们对本来面目的认识和想象。

蒋梦麟在中国思想中发现了大量的关于"教"和"学"的内容，于是就直接将其等同于教育范畴的概念，并进而进行中西的对比。当然，汉语中的"教"翻译为教育或教学，似乎是没有问题的。但是，儒家本来就主张德政，是一种教化学说，充满了"教育"的元素，如果从这些"教育"元素出发，那么整个儒家思想就可以被视为一种教育学说。但儒家的思想及其"教育"元素，与我们所说的教育是否对等，能否对等，这是需要讨论的。

比如关于"教"的含义，许慎的解释是"上所施，下所效也"。这里的"上"姑且理解为"统治者"或者"父母"，"下"理解为"百姓"或"子女"，但从这里很难看出与"教育"或"教学"的关系，"上"与"下"显然不能简单地定义为"教师"和"学生"。"施"与"效"的关系应该是一种通过模范效应施加影响的关系，而"施加影响"是一个广泛的社会行为或政治行为，不能局限在教育情境之中。我们当然可以用西方的education或teaching来解读"教"字，并由此来构建所谓古代的教育体系。这种"对接"思路，可以让我们识别出许多中国古代的"教育"元素，而且还能进一步构建出古代的"教育"体系。但这一做法，无异于将"教"这一中国的概念从原本复杂的社会实践中割裂出来，安放在一个所谓"教育"的器皿之中。这也就成为我们想象古代教育的出发点。

在古代，"教"和"学"应该更多的是教化行为、政治行为或社会行为，是"建国君民"的措施，注重"教以人伦"具体化。这些概念肯定包含有教育的元素，但显然不能等同于教育。如果将二者等同，那么我们要么会无限放大教育的功能，把很多内容附加到教育上面，要么会把古代的有关思想和制度仅仅看作是"教育"，忽视其原本的含义。所以说，我们如果用现代教育或教育学的视野来解读这种"教"，显然是有问题的。

如果说蒋梦麟这一代学人无法抵挡当时的历史潮流，不得不用西方的概念和教育框架去理解中国的传统知识，建构中国过去的教育思想，那么我们今天能否基于中国社会自身的逻辑去重新认识中国过去的教育，回到中国过去的教育现场，想象中国古代的教育世界？这是我们需要回答的问题。

A STUDY IN CHINESE PRINCIPLES OF EDUCATION

BY

MONLIN CHIANG. PH.D.
ACTING CHANCELLOR, NATIONAL UNIVERSITY, PEKING

THE COMMERCIAL PRESS, LIMITED
SHANGHAI, CHINA
1924

PREFACE

In presenting this volume to the public, the writer presumes that no apology is needed, as the book is primarily a pioneer study of Chinese principles of education, and a first attempt to articulate the Chinese thoughts on education which are found here and there in the voluminous works of many a Chinese thinker, to interpret the more or less vague statements in clearer language and to weave the scattered thoughts into a related whole. The unorganized and fragmentary writings of the Chinese philosophers contain so much aphoristical statements, which are little supported with detailed discussions and which, therefore, have many shades of meaning, that they allow much room for various interpretations. The writer is oftentimes really at sea to know what they precisely mean, and, therefore, he must acknowledge frankly that it is unavoidable, no matter how careful he is, a certain amount of modern ideas has probably been read into them.

While the materials used in this book are taken from the original Chinese sources, the method employed in organizing and systematizing them is more or less Western. After the scattered ideas have become better articulated and put in a better historical perspective, the writer begins to realize that much of Chinese thoughts on education of olden times are decidedly modern, and that the educational theories as advanced in those days still show unmistakable signs of continuous development and progress.

While writing, the writer has kept several points in mind. First, in choosing materials, only those which have direct or indirect bearing upon the present-day problems are selected. It is hoped that to study the past is not for its own sake, but to make plain the educational theories of to-day in the light of the past. Secondly, in arranging the materials, the historical sequence is kept as far as possible, so that the influences of one idea exercised upon the other can be traced. Thirdly, whenever an opportunity presents itself, the writer is always ready to make a comparative study of different schools of thought and also of Chinese and Western ideas. The value of making comparative studies on any subject cannot be overestimated. Fourthly, the writer realizes that thoughts on education lose their significance if detached and isolated from the general trends of thought. The different chapters are so arranged that when we desire to discuss a particular topic on education, the chapter preceding will serve as a background.

The first chapter is devoted to a general account of Chinese ideals of life and an outline of the development of Chinese thoughts, so as to furnish a background to Chinese education ; and the second chapter, to a discussion of the general scope of Chinese education in order to furnish a bird's-eye view of the subject. It is hoped that these two chapters may help the reader to understand the subsequent ones better. For the same reason, the discussion of moral theories (Chapter XI) precedes that of moral training (Chapter XII), and the problem of knowledge (Chapter V) precedes the method of learning (Chapter VIII).

The problem of knowledge is a study of general methodology. Its study is indispensable to an understanding of not only philosophy, but also methods of teaching and learning.

The problem of science (Chapter VI) is a study to find out why China has not developed modern science. For modern Western civilization owes so much to modern science that its absence from China may explain much of China's perplexities.

The chapter preceding the last is a discussion of modern Western ideas of the individual, the society, and the state, in comparison with the Chinese ideas. A few suggestions have been made as to what should be reconstructed, or preserved, and what should be introduced.

The last chapter is a discussion on the science and art of education as modern educational theories and practice have furnished us. It is intended to focus the problems raised in the preceding chapters on the present-day problems of education.

In preparing this volume, the writer has received help from several quarters. For the inspiration to write this book and for the selection of its title, he is indebted to Professor George Dayton Strayer. The writer owes a more extensive debt to Professor John Dewey and Professor W. H. Kilpatrick, who have read the manuscript and have offered many valuable suggestions; and also to Professor Paul Monroe who has given invaluable advice and constant encouragement during the whole course of writing. The writer is also greatly indebted to Mr. J. Barrett Botsford, who has read through the entire manuscript and has suggested a number of changes.

M. C.

New York City,
August, 1917.

CONTENTS

INTRODUCTION

CHAPTER		PAGE
I.	Background of Chinese Education	1
II.	General Scope of Chinese Education	31

PART I

HEREDITY AND EDUCATION

III.	Human Nature	37
IV.	Nature and Nurture	45

PART II

PRINCIPLES OF LEARNING

V.	The Problem of Knowledge	51
VI.	The Problem of Science	67
VII.	Relative Values in Knowledge	78
VIII.	The Fundamental Elements of Learning	83

PART III

PRINCIPLES OF TEACHING

IX.	Method of Elementary Education	93
X.	The Fundamental Elements of Teaching	107

PART IV

PRINCIPLES OF MORAL EDUCATION

XI.	Types of Moral Theory	127
XII.	The Fundamental Elements of Moral Training	132

CONCLUSION

XIII.	Some of the Problems of Chinese Culture	153
XIV.	The Individual, Society, and the State	169
XV.	Science and Art of Education	184

INTRODUCTION

The sages from the Eastern sea have the same mind and reason as the sages from the Western sea; the sages of centuries ago have the same mind and reason as the sages of centuries to come.—*Loh Shang-san.*

INTRODUCTION
CHAPTER I
BACKGROUND OF CHINESE EDUCATION

Education is the method of life and thought, and life and thought are the contents of Education. A general survey, however inadequate it may be, of the life and thought of a people seems to be necessary in order to understand the Education of that people. As our main thesis in this little volume is Education and as the limit of time and space would not allow us to make a thorough study of ideals of life and thought of the Chinese people, it is necessary to limit our attention here to giving a general idea with a view of furnishing some sort of background.

I. IDEALS OF CHINESE LIFE AND MEANING OF INSTITUTIONS[1]

As the sphere of the topic is wide, covering as it does a period of some twenty-five centuries, it is hardly possible here to present a general account of the development of ideals of Chinese life and the development of Chinese institutions. However, it is not impossible to present, before the Western world, a few controlling ideas of life and institutions characteristic of the Chinese people.

1. *Life and Duty.* One of the most fundamental ideas of the life of the Chinese is duty. To live is to fulfill the duties of life. One must attain the supreme good — *summum bonum*. How may one attain the supreme good? The individual is required to perform to the utmost his duties of life. If he is a ruler, he must perform his duties of being benevolent to the utmost degree. If he is a state official, he must perform his duties of being loyal to the sovereign to the utmost degree. The duties of a father are to act according to the principle of parental kindness; of a son, according to the principle of filial piety; of a member of the state, according to the principle of truthfulness. Starting from these

---

[1] The views expressed in this section are based on the general acquaintance of Chinese classics, philosophy, and history.

as the foundations of life the idea of the supreme good is to be extended to all the activities of life. Thus, a teacher must do his utmost to fulfill his duties relating to teaching; a student, to study; a carpenter, to his work; a soldier, to war; a musician, to music; a farmer, to farming; *ad infinitum*. As a farmer he is not only a farmer, he is also a member of the state in his capacity of son or maybe father; he must act according to the principles of truthfulness and filial piety or parental kindness.

2. *Happiness and Duty*. The fulfillment of duties is the only way to happiness. The Chinese view of happiness is socialistic rather than individualistic. The final aim is to maintain peace in society, in the state, and among the states. But peace cannot reign in the state unless each member fulfills his duties. "If every man loves those whom he should love and respects those whom he should respect, peace will reign in the world."[2] The mutual devotion of the members of the family and state is the path to peace, order, and prosperity. The individual cannot be happy unless the state has attained this happy condition. The individual devotes his life to duties in order to secure peace for the state and the state in turn, by means of peace, order, and prosperity, gives opportunities to the individual to live a peaceful and contented life.

Moreover, it is not only that peace, order, and prosperity make people happy, the devotion itself is happiness. Do we not feel happy when our parents love us and we love our parents, or when we are truthful to others and others are truthful to us? No happiness is permanent unless it is connected with duty.

3. *Life and Meaning of Institutions*. Institutions grow in the life of a people. They are the expressions of life. All the institutions in China are permeated with the idea of happiness through, and in, duty. The home is the place where the parents devote themselves to the children and the children to the parents. The state is the place where the sovereign and the ministers devote themselves to the people and the people to the ministers and the sovereign. The school is the place where the principles of these mutual devotions are taught.

---

[2] *The Works of Mencius*.

The Home is a prototype of the state. The father may be likened to the sovereign of the state and the rest of the members to the people or subjects. On him is laid the responsibility to look after the interests of all the members of the family. In return, the members of the family must show due respect to him and recognize his authority.

The State is based upon families. Unless there are well ordered families, there will be no well governed state. As in the family, the sovereign must love his subjects as the father does children and the subjects devote themselves to the sovereign as children do to their father. But if the sovereign does not take an interest in the people or subjects or acts contrary to the principles of benevolence, the people have the right to take up arms and overthrow him. This idea is so strong in the Chinese mind, that historians use two different terms for the overthrow of a dynasty. If the sovereign is benevolent and a party tries to overthrow his sovereignty by force, it is called *pun-ngih* (叛逆), meaning rebellion or treason. If, on the other hand, the sovereign is unscrupulous and unbenevolent and the people try to overthrow his sovereignty by force, it is called *keh-men* (革命), meaning revolution or "change by will of Heaven."

The people are the master and the sovereign is the honored servant. If he is benevolent, he is the father of the people; if not, their enemy. "If the sovereign looks upon the people as dust and garlic seeds, the people will look upon him as their common enemy." [3] " Heaven sees through what the people see; Heaven hears through what the people hear." [4]

The function of the state is to secure peace, order, and prosperity for the people. It exists for the people and not for the sovereign. A state makes war against other states only for two reasons. The first is to attack a state whose sovereign is unbenevolent and cruel and thus causes suffering among the people, and thereby to deliver the people from misery. The second is to defend the state when attacked by its neighbors. Once in a while,

---

[3] *The Works of Mencius*, Book 5, Part 2, Chapter 3.
[4] *The Book of History*, Tai Sze.

a sovereign makes war upon other states simply for the sake of selfish aggrandizement. But he is always complained of by the people of his time and denounced by historians afterwards. The modern practice that a large and powerful state has the right to swallow up the lesser and weaker states is certainly contrary to the idea of the Chinese people.

The School has always been a state function.[5] Mencius told us of establishing schools in this way: "The people are bestowed by their birth with good virtue. But if they are well fed and clothed and live leisurely without education, they become birds and animals. The sage was aggrieved with that. Therefore, he made Chi Minister of Education and ordered him to teach them the proper human relations—the mutual devotion of parents and children, of the sovereign and ministers, of the husband and wife, of the youths and elders, and of friends." [6]

Again Mencius said: "To establish schools [here Mencius told the different names of schools and their meanings used at different times] is to teach the people human relations. If the ideas of human relations are well developed by the sovereign and the ministers [by teaching the people through schools], the people will love each other." [7]

We have thus far discussed the fundamental ideals of the Chinese life, happiness through, and in, duty; and the institutions, the home, state, and school, where these ideals are expressed. We do not mean that these are the only ideals, but they are the foundations of Chinese life, upon which rest the further activities of life.

Before passing on to the next topic, "Development of Chinese Thought," let me point out that in the Chinese life and institutions there is a unity all-pervading—life consists of devotions, and institutions are the places where these devotions are expressed.

II. Development of Chinese Thought

The ideals of life and the institutions we have just discussed are what may be called Confucian. As Confucius inherited the

---

[5] P. W. Kuo, *Chinese Education*, N. Y., 1914.
[6] Mencius, quoted by Tsu-tse in *The History of Elementary Education*, Book I.
[7] *The Works of Mencius*.

ancient Chinese civilization, the development of the Confucian ideas is but a continuous development of the ancient Chinese civilization. Moreover, the Confucian school is of a continuous existence and no other schools in China ever enjoyed prosperity together with continuity such as the Confucian schools did. If this school is not the only school, it is the representative school in China. Again, this school has a great faith in education and has become the stronghold of Chinese education. To the Confucian scholars, the state and school are one and inseparable. They are equally interested in education and state affairs.

The Confucian statesmen are teacher-statesmen and the Confucian teachers are statesmen-teachers. When in the service of the government, they carry out their policies, and when out of the service of the government, they spread their ideas. With these two mighty weapons in their hands, we can imagine how powerful they are.

The Confucians are, however, by no means without their rivals. The history of the Confucian school is full of vigorous intellectual battles and wars with its rivals. Mencius fought with all his strength the teachings of his contemporaries. The later Confucians fought continuously the teachings of Buddha and of Lao-tse (老子).

Four Great Epochs of Chinese Thought. In the development of Chinese thought, there are four distinct epochs, which may be arranged in chronological order as follows: A. The Creative Period. B. The Period of Restoration. C. The Introduction of Hindu Philosophy with the Rise of Hedonism. D. The Renaissance of Confucian Thought. To these four great epochs, we may add the epoch now in making, namely, The Introduction of Western Philosophy. In making this epoch, which concerns not only the problems of four hundred millions of the Chinese people, but also the problems of the world at large, and which may be of interest, therefore, not only to the Chinese themsevles, but also to the world, the duties are fallen upon the intellectual leaders of modern China.

In presenting the general outline of the development of Chinese thought, we have to confine our discussions mainly to social philosophy, of which educational theories and practice form an integral part, and which is a direct background of education. Philosophy other than social must be omitted. Again, in our discussions of social philosophy, we shall dwell upon the general trends of thought instead of the systems of particular schools.

A. *The Creative Period* (ante-Chin (先秦) period) may be marked by the year 2357 B.C. as its beginning. This is the first year of the reign of Emperor Yao (堯) who has been taken by Confucians as a wise sovereign and, together with the subsequent emperors, Shun (舜), Yu (禹), Tang (湯), Wen (文), Wu (武), and Prince Regent Chow Kung (周公), as seven sages whose accumulative achievements are the foundation of Chinese culture upon which Confucius built his edifice of learning. From 2357 B.C. to 1078 B.C., the year of the death of Chen Wang (成王) to whom Chow Kung acted as prince regent, we may call the period of growth of Chinese civilization. From 519 B.C., the first year of the reign of Chow Chin Wang (周敬王), under whose reign Confucius lived, to 221 B.C., the year of the founding of the Chin (秦) dynasty, we may call the period of culmination. This latter period we here call the creative period of Chinese thought. The man who gathered together all the learning that ancient China had produced and organized them into some sort of system is Confucius (551–478 B.C.). He himself admitted that he simply systematized the accumulated wisdom of the ancients and did not add anything to it. Therefore in Confucius, the past scattered experiences of the ancient Chinese crystallized into some sort of unity, which is now known as Confucianism, or teachings of Confucius.

Confucius was born in 551 B.C., and died in 478 B.C., nine years before Socrates was born (469–399 B.C.). He traveled through the different feudal states and, as his teachings failed to exercise a strong influence over the feudal lords, in his later years he devoted himself to learning and teaching. He had three thousand followers, among whom were seventy famous disciples. Thus he sowed the seeds of Chinese culture, which, in spite of some of its shortcomings, molded the character of the Chinese people in later ages.

Confucius was a typical Chinese thinker. He was thoroughly a practical man. To him conduct is the criterion of knowledge. On him, the later Chinese thought is based. His chief interest lies in the practical conduct of men. The virtue of men is benevolent. To carry out benevolence is to start with filial piety or love of parents. On filial piety human relations are based. Hence, to attain the supreme good is to carry out to the utmost degree the mutual devotion between the sovereign and the people, the parents and the children, and between friends. If these devotions are carried out to the utmost degree, there will be happiness in the family and peace and order in the state, and among the states. This philosophy, which holds the view that life and institutions are based upon practical moral conduct, may be called politico-ethical. Two leading thinkers of this school are Mencius (孟子) and Sin-tse (荀子).

Opposed to it, we find the philosophy of Lao-tse (老子) and Tson-tse (莊子), both of whom advocate that life must he based upon the naturalistic tendencies, not upon the social or moral systems, and certainly not upon the so-called practical conduct. This we may call the naturalistic school. For the sake of conducting inquiry, we may classify the other schools according to their main interests, such as the Economico-ethical school, which holds the view that good morals are to be based upon the material welfare of the people; the Humanitarian school, which advocates that human society is possible only upon the basis of universal brotherhood or universal love; the Penal school, which holds the view that peace and order in the state is to be secured by severe penal laws.

1. *The Politico-ethical School.* This school, as we have pointed out before, is a continuation of the ancient culture and founded by Confucius, whose main interests have already been discussed. We now come to two leading thinkers who belong to this school; namely, Mencius and Sin-tse.

Mencius was born more than a hundred years after the death of Confucius and died in 282 B.C. He was almost a contemporary of Aristotle (384–322 B.C.). In his boyhood, he was under the good influence of his wise mother, whose method of teaching this prodigious child has been ever since regarded by the Chinese as a model. Mencius studied under Tsze-Sze (子思), grandson of Confucius. Having finished his study, like Confucius, Mencius traveled among the different feudal states, which were then fighting against one another, each trying to swallow up the other, and likewise, as his teachings failed to reach the hearts of the feudal lords, in his later years he, together with his disciples, wrote *The Works of Mencius*, to which China owes her democratic idea of the state and organic view of education. The foundation of the state is benevolence and righteousness. Benevolence starts from the instinct of commiseration, and righteousness starts from the inner knowledge of shame and dislike. By the development of the instinct of commiseration and the inner knowledge of shame and dislike we have what is called benevolence and righteousness. According to the principles of benevolence, the sovereign must love his people; according to the principles of righteousness, the government must be based upon justice.

Now if the sovereign is unbenevolent and unrighteous, the people have the right to overthrow him. "If the sovereign looks upon the people as dust and garlic seeds, the people will look upon him as their common enemy."[8]

Mencius held the view that human nature is absolutely good.[9] But this good nature of man must be nourished and developed or else it will be starved. Hence education is to nourish and develop the nature of man. Directly opposed to Mencius is

Sin-tse, who held the view that human nature is absolutely bad. This opponent of Mencius was born more than fifty years after Mencius. Although both belonged to the Confucian school, and honored Confucius as the greatest sage, Sin-tse denounced Mencius as one who knew only the vague principles without any definite scheme to carry them out.[10] Since the nature of man is bad it follows that what is good is made only through the effort of man. If you let every man do according to his nature, society will be in disorder—each fighting for his selfish interest and grabbing whatever he can. Therefore education and politics are needed to preserve order in society.

Politics is to be based on two things: (1) schemes for carrying out the principles of propriety, and (2) justice; in other words,

---
[8] See Note 3 anterior.
[9] Meaning of Good and Bad, see Chapter III on *Human Nature*.
[10] *The Works of Sin-tse*, Chapter VI on *Erroneous Teachings of Twelve Philosophers*.

social system and penal laws. Social system is to regulate the relations of men and therefore it is moral. Penal law is to suppress crimes and protect law-abiding people and therefore it is jural.

Education is to be based on the effort of man. By continuous effort, he conforms his nature to the principle of propriety, the social standards or systems. " A crooked wood can be straightened by making it conform to a straight line ; a dull metal can be sharpened by constant grinding; therefore the superior man, by extensive study and constant reflection, attains the state of enlightened mind and proper conduct."[11]

In education, Sin-tse is different from Mencius in that the one regarded education as the natural development and the other as the artificial means. In politics, Sin-tse based his ideas on moral systems and penal laws ; Mencius, on the other hand, on moral principles.[12]

2. *The Humanitarian School.* The Confucian system of social relations according to the principles of propriety is based upon the relations between the father and son, the sovereign and state official, the husband and wife, between brothers and friends The humanitarian school was opposed to these social relations. Me-tse (墨子), the founder of the school, claimed that if a son loves his parents, he would like to see that other people also love them. But unless he loves the other people's parents, just as much as his, he cannot expect them to love his parents. If each family only loves its own members, the result will be quarrels among families. If a sovereign loves his people, he would like to see that the sovereigns of the other countries would do the same. But unless he loves the people of the other countries just as much as his, he cannot expect them to love his people. The lack of

---

[11] *The Works of Sin-tse,* Chapter 1, *Education.*
[12] It is to be noted that Sin-tse deviated from the tradition of the Confucian school by advocating that the ideal state is to be worked out at the present and in the future. Mencius, on the other hand, sought the model of the ideal state in the past. The progressive idea of Sin-tse was unfortunately misunderstood by his pupils, Han-Hui-Tse (韓非子) and Li Sze (李 斯), and led to a radical measure carried out by Chin-Sze-Huang (秦始皇), first emperor of the Chin dynasty, by burning all the ancient literature in order to prevent the scholars from looking towards the past.

this mutual love is the cause of war, and peace can only be preserved by this mutual love. If love is based upon the relations as advocated by the Confucian school, there will be disturbances in society and wars among the nations. The only method to universal peace is universal love—love for all men.[13] The Confucian school returned the attack by saying that if, according to Me-tse, the people should practice universal love—love for all men alike—they would neglect their own parents. Thus, men would become animals.

3. *The Naturalistic School.* Here we come to a school whose thought, in a certain sense, is un-Chinese. The fact is that Lao-tse (老子), the founder of this school, was a native of southern China. Lao-tse was a contemporary of Confucius, although he was much his senior in age. Instead of taking the politico-ethical problem as the center of interest, Lao-tse inquires into the problem of nature. His system is founded upon what is called *tao* (道). According to the politico-ethical school of northern China (Confucian) *tao* means the inviolable way or path in accordance with which the conduct of nature and of man travels. Therefore to seek for *tao* is to seek for inviolable natural, political, or moral laws. What Lao-tse meant by *tao* is, on the other hand, the abstract ideal for nature. Therefore, to seek for *tao* is to inquire into the origin of the Universe. Now the Universe exists in the state of nature not conformed to the so-called human ideals, yet nevertheless, it does exist. The Universe does not exist according to the categories of human thought. Applying this principle to human society, Lao-tse called it *teh* (德), or virtue. According to the northern China thinkers, *teh* means the true essence of man, such as benevolence, righteousness, wisdom, and the like. On the other hand, what Lao-tse meant by *teh* is the essence of man in the state of nature, uninterfered with by artificial moral categories and free from the restraint of social institutions.

---

[13] *The Works of Me-tse*, Chapters XV and XVI. There was a school which advocated that the way to peace is for men to love themselves only and not others. This radical individualism resembles closely the social ideal of the naturalistic school and, for lack of space, we shall not discuss it here.

Therefore, the ideal society for Lao-tse is the natural state where men live together without social ties such as moral codes and institutions. " Abandon the so-called benevolence and righteousness, people will return to parental kindness and filial piety."[14] " When laws and regulations multiply, the world will be full of robbers and thieves."[15] Only when it comes to the perfect natural state free from social restraint, " people will be well fed and well clothed, satisfied with their modes of living and enjoy their social customs ; . . . cocks crowing and dogs barking peacefully, people will live without interfering with one another till old age and death."[16]

This ideal of naturalistic society of Lao-tse comes very much closer to the modern ideal of radical-individualism. The man who possessed the same trends of thought as Lao-tse is Tson-tse (莊 子). Tson-tse was a contemporary of Mencius, though neither one knew the other. His naturalistic trend of thought may be represented by quoting the following passage :[17] " What is right is not to lose the true nature of man, . . . what by nature is long is not superfluous, and what by nature is short is not insufficient. Therefore, although the neck of a duck is short, if you make it longer, you are to hurt its nature ; although the neck of a stork is long, if you make it shorter, you are likewise to hurt its nature. What by nature is long cannot be shortened and what by nature is short cannot be lengthened. . . . Perhaps benevolence and righteousness are not from the nature of man ! If so, why are the benevolent men so much worried about nature ? . . . What is made square or round by rules and compass is devoid of its nature, . . . and likewise, to conform man's mind to the principle of propriety, . . . benevolence and righteousness, is to deprive him of his true nature. This is a natural state in the world : . . . what is round in reality, is so by nature and not by means of compass ; what is square in reality, is so by nature and not by means of rules ; what is stuck together in reality is so by

---

[14] *Tao Teh King* (道 德 經), Chapter XIX.
[15] *Id.*, Chapter XVII.
[16] *Id.*, Chapter LXXX.
[17] *The Works of Tson-tse*, Chapter VIII.

nature and not by means of glue; what is restrained in reality is so by nature, and not by means of ropes and bandages; ... why shall we stick and bind the world together by means of glue, and ropes and bandages such as benevolence and righteousness?"

4. *The Economico-ethical School.* From the politico-ethical trends of thought of the northern school, the social philosophy of which is based upon practical moral principles and conduct, and the naturalistic trends of thought of the southern school, the social philosophy of which is based upon radical-individualism and natural state, we now come to another trend of thought of the central school. This school was founded by Kwan-tse (管子), prime minister to Duke Hwan of Hsi (fifth century before Christ), through whose statesmanship the dukedom was raised from poverty to wealth and prosperity. Kwan-tse based his social philosophy upon the materialistic welfare of the people on which moral principles are to rest with penal laws as supplementary to moral principles. The fundamental ideas of this school may be presented by quoting the following passages: "When there is plenty of wealth in the country, afar people will come; when there is plenty of developed land, there they will stay. If the barns are full, people will observe the principles of propriety; if clothing and food are plenty, they will discriminate honor from disgrace. . . . In governing the state, there are four cardinal virtues (四維) [principles of propriety (禮), righteousness (義), frugality (廉), and shame (恥)] to be observed. If not the state will collapse . . . giving office to the virtuous, the state will be in tranquillity; cultivating the five kinds of grain (五穀), there will be plenty of food; raising mulberry trees (for silkworms) and fiber plants, and the six kinds of animals, the people will be wealthy; laws to suit the will of the people, they will obey the commands of the above; let the people make what they can do best, tools and other articles will be plenty; severe in penal laws and punishment, the people will keep themselves away from doing evil; rich in rewards, the people will overcome their difficulties [in doing things]."[18]

---

[18] *The Works of Kwan-tse*, Chapter I.

As this school was founded much earlier than the Confucian school, we find that Mencius and Sin-tse were both influenced by it. In spite of his belittling Kwan-tse, Mencius at the same time held the view that to enrich the people is the first step to a benevolent government.[19] Sin-tse, as we have seen somewhere else in this chapter, like Kwan-tse, held the view that penal laws are necessary to supplement moral systems.

5. *The Penal School.* Influenced by Kwan-tse's penal side of social philosophy, Shan Yang (商鞅) founded the penal school. Born in an aristocracy and fond of studying penal principles, he afterwards became the prime minister to Duke Siao of Chin. Through his statesmanship, the dukedom became rich and strong. His basic idea in politics consists of three elements. The first is penal law, by means of which the social order is maintained. The second is confidence, through which the people will obey the commands of the government. The third is state authority, by means of which the government will be in position to carry out effectively its policies. Although Shan Yang founded the penal school, it was not crystallized into a system until the time of Han-Hui-Tse.

Han-Hui-Tse (韓非子), like Shan Yang, was born in an aristocratic family, and like him, was fond of studying penal laws. Together with Li Sze (李斯) he studied under Sin-tse, who, as we have seen before, was one of the leading thinkers of the Confucian school. Han-Hui-Tse's social philosophy is almost entirely based upon the principles of penal law. Severe punishment and heavy reward are the sole means for maintaining social order. Unlike Kwan-tse and Sin-tse, both of whom held that penal laws are to supplement moral laws, Han-Hui-Tse put penal laws above everything else. Instead of taking moral law as the foundation of penal law he held the principle that penal law is the source of all governmental activities. Who is to make the penal laws ? — The sovereign who has the absolute power in the state. There is no freedom for anybody except the sovereign. In Han-Hui-Tse, we find the extreme specimen of the idea of absolute despotism.

---

[19] See Chapter X, *The Fundamental Elements of Teaching*, paragraph to Note 35, while under that chapter quotations are given to illustrate Mencius's method of teaching; but the contents may serve our purpose here.

The Close of the Creative Period. When Han-Hui-Tse presented his views to Chin-Sze-Huang, the king was very much in favor of him and wished to intrust him with the government. But Li Sze, together with whom he had studied under Sin-tse, accused him before the king. He was then imprisoned and murdered by Li Sze in the prison. However, when Li Sze became prime minister to Chin-Sze-Huang, he actually put into practice the penal principles of Han-Hui-Tse and helped the king to establish an absolute monarchy. By this time, the Kingdom of Chin, through the work of several generations, had swallowed up one after another all the other feudal states. China was thus unified and was for the first time in history an empire in its real sense. Through the suggestions of Li Sze, Chin-Sze-Huang, the emperor, ordered all the books to be burned in the whole country, with a few exceptions, and put to death four hundred Confucian scholars. In the year 228 B. C., by a mighty stroke of the will of a single man, all the literature of ancient China was turned into dust.[20] Thus the creative period of Chinese civilization came to a close. With the founding of the Chin dynasty (秦), it marks the beginning of imperialism and despotism, with the disappearance of feudalism, and it marks the end of intellectual development of ancient China.

An empire founded purely upon the basis of penal laws and ideas of a state entirely devoid of historical sense could not live long. Only after a few years of the founding of the Chin dynasty, rebellions broke out here and there and finally a new dynasty was founded upon the débris of the dissolute Chin. With the founding of the Han dynasty (漢) we come to another epoch of the development of Chinese thought. The Confucian school was a historical school, which emphasized the historical experience of the race and attempted to solve the problems of the time by means of past experience. The penal school was a non-historical and radical school, which emphasized the present situation and attempted to solve the problem of the time by revolutionary methods entirely

---

[20] See Note 12 anterior.

devoid of the sense of historical development. The Confucian school, while having sound principles, lacked an adequate working plan.[21] On the other hand, the penal school, while having an adequate working plan, was erroneous in believing that severe punishment and heavy rewards are the foundations of the state. Consequently, the Confucian school failed to solve the problem of the time, and the penal school, while it succeeded temporarily, also failed in the end. However, the penal school achieved one thing, namely, the founding of an empire; and taught the thinkers a lesson, that is, that the state cannot be formed on the basis of penal laws alone. With the Han dynasty, the leading thinkers and statesmen had to face the problem of reconciling two opposite ideas of the state. And naturally, in order to study the problem, historical experiences could not be neglected. Hence, a study of the past was necessary. Here we come to a new period.

B. *The Period of Restoration.* As the ancient records had been destroyed by the first emperor of the Chin dynasty under the influence of the non-historical and radical school, the scholars had to work for the restoration of the ancient literature. Ancient records were then gradually excavated from their hidden places.

Work of Excavation. Famous scholars appeared here and there, and each had specialized in a certain branch of Confucian learning. Through the effort of the generation of patient scholars, the lost records were discovered, systematized, and commented upon. China owes to these scholars the restoration and preservation of the ancient literature, without which the further development of Chinese civilization would be well-nigh impossible.

Ascendancy of the Confucian School. Presently the balance was tipped on the other end. The Confucian school, which was suppressed with other schools during the Chin dynasty, came to the supreme position of great influence and honors hitherto unheard of. Wu-Ti (武 帝) (140–86 B.C.) of the Han dynasty was the first sovereign who made the Confucian school a kind of state religion. The teachings of Confucius were regarded as infallible. The

---

[21] A government purely based upon moral principles alone without adequate means could hardly be maintained. Sin-tse pointed out the defects of the Confucian school as represented by Mencius by denouncing him as one who only knew the vague principles without any definite scheme to carry them out. See Note 10 anterior.

other schools were suppressed. Thus the freedom of thought enjoyed by the scholars of the ante-Chin period was narrowly limited.

General Trends of Thought. As the most important contributions of this period were the restoration of the ancient literature and commentaries written on the texts thereof [22] and little original ideas were contributed towards the later development, we shall limit ourselves here to a very brief discussion of the general trends of thought during this period.

Two important tendencies in thought during this period must be noted. The first was the discussions on cosmology in relation to human society. The second was that all the schools, while dominated by the main ideas of their respective schools, were eclectic in thought.

1. *Ethico-cosmological Tendency.* The leading thinker of the earlier period of the politico-ethical school was Ton Tson-shu (董仲舒). While his chief interest was politico-ethical, he emphasized the idea that there is a close relation between Heaven (or natural phenomena) and Man. Human relations as held by the politico-ethical school are based upon the relations between Heaven, Earth, and Man. The father of mankind is Heaven. Heaven creates and nourishes everything in the Universe. Therefore the idea of Heaven is ever-benevolent. Heaven creates Man by means of filial piety and brotherly love. Earth nourishes Man with clothing and food. Man carries out the Heavenly Idea by means of the principles of propriety (social system) and music. Therefore Heaven, Earth, and Man together form the moral universe.

2. *Eclectic Tendency.* While Ton Tson-shu's idea of ever-benevolence of Heaven is influenced by the humanitarian school of Me-tse, the distinct eclectic tendency was found in Yang Hsiung (楊雄). His system of social philosophy is based upon the naturalistic idea of Lao-tse and the politico-ethical idea of Confucius. To quote him: "The right way [*tao* or truth] is the way of Yao, Shin, and Wen [sages honored by Confucian schools].[23] Confucius was divinely intelligent."[24] "Heaven is noninterference. . . .

---

[22] Without these commentaries, many of the ancient records would be well-nigh unintelligible.
[23] *The Works of Yang Hsiung*, Chapter IV.
[24] *Id.*, Chapter VII.

I adopt Lao-tse's idea of *tao* (道) and *teh* (德) [truth and virtue], but reject his idea of denouncing benevolence, righteousness, and principles of propriety." [25]

Although Yang Hsiung belongs to the eclectic school, his chief interest was politico-ethical. On the other hand, we find that Huei-Nan-Tse's (淮南子) interest was centered upon the naturalistic school. To quote him : " The sovereign must adopt the policy of noninterference, . . . if the policy of interference is adopted above, disturbances will prevail below. . . . Without interference, the sages attain easily the state in which peace prevails. . . . They carry out benevolence without effort, win confidence without uttering a word ; gain without seeking ; and accomplish without action. Natural, virtuous, and truthful, the sages are exemplified by the world as the voice followed by an echo." [26]

While the two tendencies noted above characterized the thought of the period, it was but an echo of the philosophers of the creative or ante-Chin period. Meanwhile, Hindu philosophy was introduced during the reign of Min-Ti (明帝) (A.D. 58–76) of the later Han dynasty (後漢).

C. *The Introduction of Hindu Philosophy with the Rise of Hedonism.* In the year A.D. 65, the eighth year of the reign of Min-Ti, the emperor sent an embassy to India to study Buddhism. It returned with Buddhistic classics together with two Hindu monks. This marks the beginning of foreign influence upon Chinese thought.

Causes for the Spread of Hindu Philosophy. As the scholars began to tire of the commentary works on Confucian classics, the people began to be suspicious of the Confucian teachings owing to the crimes committed under the disguises of the Confucian principles, and the general mass began to tire of this world on account of continuous wars and general disturbances prevailing in society ; it was the psychological moment for the spread of Hindu philosophy. The ideal state of Nirvana, where perfect peace reigns, was very attractive to the people who had been tired

---

[25] *The Works of Yang Hsiung*, Chapter IV.
[26] *The Works of Huai-Nan-Tse*, Chapter IX.

of this miserable world where wars and pestilence were daily occurrences and from which they were anxious to escape. To thinkers, this type of new thought, which is much more than the practical trends of thought of the politico-ethical school, was quite palatable as their mental food. In spite of oppositions offered by the Confucian scholars, Hindu philosophy was spreading like flames, and no conservative forces could ever check it. When mixed with the philosophy of Lao-tse, it gave an impetus to a new kind of thought which may be called Hedonism.

Causes of the Spreading of Hedonism. The chief cause was the chaotic conditions prevailing in society during the Wei (魏) and Tsin (晉) dynasties (A.D. 220-419). The Hedonists adopted the principle of noninterference (or nonaction) of Lao-tse as their fundamental doctrine and borrowed pessimistic elements of Buddhism and fatalistic elements of the Confucian school as supplements.[27] Their chief aim was to satisfy their sensual desire by indulgence in licentious pleasures. Thus, in order to escape this miserable world, the Buddhists were endeavoring to seek the ideal state, Nirvana, and the Hedonists, on the other hand, gave up themselves to sensual pleasures as long as their natural life would permit.

However, this sort of condition cannot forever exist. Since there is life, man must live. Hence, the social problems must be solved. Here we come to another period of the development of Chinese thought.

D. *The Renaissance of Confucian Thought.* As the Confucian school embodied the original civilization of ancient China, it fundamentally suits the social life of the Chinese. It was but a matter of time, therefore, for the thinkers to return to the Politico-ethical school.

Period of Anticipation. During the Tsin dynasty (A.D. 265-316), the Huns gradually began to be strong and aggressive and during the Later Tsin (A.D. 317-419), they overran the whole of China. The country was split into many warring factions and China became the battle grounds of the Huns for more than two

---

[27] Tsai Tsin, *The History of Chinese Ethics*, Shanghai, page 27.

centuries. Upon the débris of the much-torn country, in A.D. 589, Wen-Ti (文帝) founded the Tsai (隋) dynasty, which lasted only for twenty-nine years. When the Tang (唐) dynasty arose (A.D. 618-907), China was rebuilt upon a solid foundation. Under the reign of Tai-Tsong (太宗) (A.D. 627-649), through the able statesmanship of the Confucian scholars Wei Tsun, Fon Yuan-lin, and Tu Su-huei, peace and prosperity once more reigned in the country. These three scholars were the former students of the great Confucian scholar Wen-Tsong-Tse of the Tsai dynasty. Historians tell us that the country was in such a prosperous condition that during the fourth year of the reign of Tai-Tsong the price of rice was very low, not a single case of punishment by death occurred throughout the whole country, nobody would keep anything found on the streets, and people slept with doors unclosed. The emperor was said to have claimed that it was the result of the government based upon the principles of benevolence and righteousness.

Tang Poetry. During the reign of Yuan-Tsong (玄宗) (A.D. 713-756) literature and poetry reached their zenith. The poets of the Tang dynasty achieved such a splendor and beauty in their work that they held an envious position in the history of Chinese literature.

The Birth of a Great Confucian Scholar. During the reigns of Teh-Tsong (德宗) (780-804 A.D.) and Hsien-Tsong (憲宗) (A.D. 806-823) lived a great Confucian scholar Han Yu (韓愈). While as a product of his time he was essentially a great essayist and did not contribute anything new to Chinese thought, he was well versed with the Confucian classics and the philosophers of the ante-Chin period. What he did in anticipation of the revival of Confucian learning was his advocacy of Mencius and vigorous attacks made upon Hindu philosophy and the philosophy of Lao-tse.

After the downfall of the Tang dynasty at the beginning of the eleventh century, China was again the battle ground of the warring factions among the Tartars, Mongols, and Chinese leaders themselves. The country was torn to pieces for half a century. In the year 960, a new dynasty—the Sung (宋) dynasty (A.D. 960-1276) emerged from the débris of the much-torn country, under which China was again restored to peace.

Period of Culmination. During the reign of Zen-Tsong (仁宗) (A.D. 1023-1063) scholars of first-rate intelligence arose. Hu Hsien, Sun Fu, and Chow Tun-yi were the pioneers of the new era of intellectual development of China. Then came the elder Ching-tse (程子) and younger Ching-tse, brothers, who began to formalize the thought of the great epoch. It was not until the reign of Siao-Tsong (孝宗) (A.D. 1163-1189) that the thought of the period was crystallized into a system. The man who accomplished this great work is Tsu-tse (朱子). Opposed to him in views on cosmology and method of knowledge was Loh Shang-san (陸象山), whose thought was not fully developed until the time of Wong Yang-min (王陽明) of the Ming (明) dynasty (A.D. 1368-1644).[28] Of Tsu-tse and Wong Yang-min we shall hear a good deal through the course of our discussion. What we attempt to do here is not to discuss the different systems of the individual philosophers, but the general tendencies of thought during the renaissance of Confucian learning.

Causes. There are several causes for the rise of the new Confucian schools. First, as we have mentioned before, the scholars got tired of the commentary work started during the Period of Restoration, and their mind turned towards a new direction. Secondly, they were stimulated by Hindu philosophy, which is something more than the over-practical philosophy of the Chinese.[29] Thirdly, the social and political problems of the time demanded the attention of the leading thinkers.

Problems. How to govern the state (治國) is the main problem of the time. To develop self (修身), or to cultivate the person, is the first step towards the solution of the problem. Hence, how to develop self is another problem. To seek knowledge (致知) is the first step towards the cultivation of the person. Hence, how to seek knowledge is another problem.

---

[28] The fundamental issue is the method of knowledge and the cosmological issue is only transitory.

[29] For a good account of the influence of Hindu philosophy and the philosophy of Lao-tse upon the thought of the philosophers of the Sun dynasty, see Kayanagi, *History of the Philosophy of the Sun Dynasty*, in Japanese, Chapter XVIII.

To Seek Reason (窮 理). Since knowledge is the first step towards the solution of all the problems, the last problem of the three afterwards became the main issue. What is it that constitutes the essence of knowledge? The answer is that it is reason (理) which constitutes the essence of knowledge. Reason is the universal weapon by means of which all politico-ethical problems are to be solved.

Method of Knowledge. How to seek reason is now the problem that occupies the main attention of all the scholars. This very issue splits the scholars into two opposite camps and causes many philosophical controversies for five centuries to follow. As this problem will be discussed in some detail in Chapter V, The Problem of Knowledge, and Chapter VI, The Problem of Science, we are not to dwell upon it here.

Two Warring Schools. The two warring schools are commonly known as Ching-Tsu (程 朱) and Loh-Wong (陸 王) schools. The one emphasizes subjective reason and analytic or deductive method; the other, on the other hand, emphasizes objective reason and synthetic or inductive method. The detailed discussions are to be taken up in the two chapters above-mentioned.

The Close of the Period and the Intellectual Tendencies Under the Manchu Dynasty. In one sense, the intellectual development under the Manchu dynasty is but a continuation of the renaissance period; in another sense, it is a reaction against that period. It is a continuation because the scholars simply discussed the philosophies of the two warring camps without advancing new theory. It is a reaction, too, because the scholars went back once again, as did the scholars of the restoration period, to the commentary work. As a natural result of long continuous battles of the two warring schools, there appeared the eclectic school, which tried to make a compromise. Theis eclectic tendency begot another tendency which was encyclopedic, for eclectic methods demand a wider sphere of knowledge and the latter demands an encyclopedic knowledge. Hence we have three tendencies of the intellectual development under the Manchu dynasty (A.D. 1644-1912).

Eclectic Tendency. This may be represented by Huang Tson-hi (黃宗羲), the author of the *History of Philosophy of the Sun and Yuan Dynasties and of the Min Dynasty* (宗元學案, 明儒學案). To make a compromise of the two warring schools, he said that although the rival schools had different centers of interest, yet their differences were only a matter of emphasis, and it was unfortunate that the meaningless quarrels should becloud the real issues.[30]

Huang Tson-hi himself possessed an encyclopedic knowledge. He not only wrote on history of philosophy, but also on music, history, astronomy, mathematics,[31] political theories, and literature and poetry.[32]

Encyclopedic Tendency. The encyclopedic tendency is of old origin. Confucius himself possessed an erudition of an encyclopedic knowledge. Tsu-tse also possessed a vast knowledge of such different branches of knowledge as music, history, literature, and different schools of Chinese philosophy, Hindu philosophy, etc. During the reign of Chun-Tsu (成祖) (A.D. 1403–1425) of the Min dynasty an encyclopedic library, *Yun Lu Tai Tien* (永樂大典), which, as claimed by the *London Times*, "easily ranks as the biggest literary undertaking in the world, having had over 2,000 scholars engaged in its compilation, a total of 917,480 pages, and 366,992,000 characters."[33] However, it was not until the reign of Kanghsi (康熙) (A.D. 1662–1723) that the first systematic encyclopedia was compiled. This encyclopedia consists of 10,000 books in 1,628 volumes.[34] Since then, hundreds of libraries, con-

---

[30] See Chapter V, *The Problem of Knowledge*, paragraphs to Note 16.

[31] Huang Tson-hi oftentimes said that the principles and method of calculations of triangles had been known to China in the eleventh century before Christ. The Western people got these from China after the Chinese people had lost them!—*Tao Hsieh Yuen Yuan Lu* (道學淵源錄), Volume 79, page 11.

[32] *Tao Hsieh Yuen Yuan Lu*, Volume 75.

[33] The *London Times*, weekly edition, January 9, 1914, Volume 38, No. 1932.

[34] The original sets of this great work may be found in the Library of Columbia University and the Library of Congress.

sisting of either different kinds of special subjects or genera works, have been published.[35]

In the year 1716, a complete dictionary of the Chinese language was published under royal patronage. This is known as the *Kanghsi Dictionary* (康熙字典), the materials for which were widely gathered from previous works of like nature.

Philological Tendency. As a reaction against the Sun philosophers whose main thesis was the search for reason, the scholars of the Manchu dynasty saw in them the tendency of deviation from the Confucian classics, which were generally regarded as the source of truth.[36] Since the source of truth is in the Confucian classics, only by means of the truth are peace and prosperity to be attained; the problem is how to get the truth. The logical question is how shall we understand the Confucian classics properly? The answer is this: The ancient language, by means of which the Confucian classics were written, is different from the modern language. If we want to understand the ancient language, we must devise adequate means to study it. What are the means? Let us quote the methods of three great scholars: " The pronunciation of many of the words contained in the ancient classics has been unknown to us ever since the Han dynasty. Therefore, the language handed down to us has been misunderstood ever since. The scholars, unable to understand the language on account of its evolution, pronounced the words according to the modern way. . . . It is no wonder, then, that the old language is becoming more and more unintelligible and the new interpretations are becoming more and more self-contradictory. Therefore, according to my opinion, if we want to study the language properly, we must first verify the pronunciation of the words."—*Ku Yen-wu* (顧炎武) (1612-?).[37]

---

[35] This kind of publication started much earlier than the period under our discussion.
[36] Any Confucian school when making attacks upon its rivals, always claimed that the doctrines of their opponents were contrary to the teachings of Confucius and its own doctrines were from the true teachings of the Master.
[37] *Letters to Li Tsze-teh, Collections of the Classical Commentaries of the Manchu Dynasty*, Volume IV.

"The classics contain the truth which is communicated to our mind by means of language. The language is composed of the words. Therefore the learner should study the words in order to understand the language and by means of the language, he may understand the truth. When I was seventeen years of age, I determined to seek truth. But I knew that we could not find it anywhere but in the six classics and the teachings of Confucius and Mencius, and could not understand their language unless we studied first the meaning of the words. For several decades I have continued to study (the words and by means of them the language of the classics). Now I am convinced that by studying according to this method, we shall see the true light of the rise and downfall of dynasties and the progress or declining of society. The philosophers of the Sun dynasty denounced the method of studying the classics by means of etymology and systematic commentary and despised the study of the words and language. Yet they tried to seek truth in the classics. To me this may be likened to crossing a river by giving up the ferryboat."—*Tai Tun-yuan* (戴東原) (1723-1777).[38]

"When I was young, my energy was spent in the preparation for the civil examinations. After I secured my degree, again my energy was consumed in studying poetry and belles-lettres. It was not until my middle age, that I began to study the classics in a serious manner. . . . In view of a proper study of the classics, I devised three methods, as follows: 1. Rectifying the punctuation. 2. Verifying the meaning of the words. 3. Finding out the rules for the "borrowed words" in the ancient language. If we accomplish the etymological work according to the above system, our work for seeking the truth is half done."—*Yu Cho-yuan* (俞曲園) (?-1906).[39]

Thus to study the ancient classics, the methods are these: (1) A study of the pronunciation of the words. (2) The meaning of the words. (3) The meaning of the sentences. (4) A proper punctuation and (5) the proper meaning of the

---

[38] *Letter to Tuan Yu-sai, The Works of Tai Tun-yuan*, Biography.
[39] *Chun Chin Pen Yi*, Preface.

borrowed words." In addition to the above five factors, an inquiry into the authenticity of certain classics is made. This is important because after the Chin fire (秦 火), the Han scholars (漢 儒) were said to have forged some of the classics. Therefore the sixth factor is (6) the verification of the classics—to separate the goats from the sheep, so to speak. Based upon the above logic and the method of tackling the problem, the scholars of the Manchu dynasty set themselves to work. If the reader would examine 2,830 odd books of the collections on the commentary of the classics, he would be amazed to find how scholarly, systematic, and hair-splitting are their works and how patient and hardworking those scholars.[40] During the reign of Ch'ien-lung (乾 隆) (1736-1796), a quite complete philological dictionary was compiled by Tuan Yu-sai (段 玉 裁), a student of Tai Tun-yuan, known as Tuan's *Philological Dictionary.*

Value of the Work. Their work, however, has achieved valuable results as far as the Chinese language itself is concerned. For through their patient and scholarly work, the origins and meanings of the Chinese words are well defined and verified. So far as the truth that they professed to discover is concerned, and so far as we can judge by the result, they have contributed very little, if any, original thought to knowledge. For in order to understand the meaning of ancient philosophy, it is not sufficient to study the philology of the classical language alone, but also to study the whole system. Besides, we can understand the ancient teachings only through the light of our own experience.

Speculative Commentary and Its Value. The scholars of the Manchu dynasty made vigorous attacks upon the commentary work of the Sun philosophers on the ground that their work was speculative. However true that may be, the speculative method,

---

[40] Yuan Yuan, *Collections of Classical Commentaries of the Manchu Dynasty,* 1,400 books, 1829.

Wong Shien-chien, *Continuation to Collections of Classical Commentaries,* 1,430 books, 1888.

Total number of the two collections, 2,830 books, nine times more than the commentaries hitherto produced. See *Commentaries on the Thirteen Classics,* 346 books, 1746.

so far as to judge by the result, has procured just as much valuable contributions to Chinese philosophy as the philological method. For interpreting as they do the classics through the light of their own experience the Sun philosophers have in fact created something new instead of a mere conformation to the ancient teaching. Besides that, the Sun philosophers were creative thinkers, while on the other hand, the scholars of the Manchu dynasty were too busy working on etymological problems and had not enough time left for vigorous thinking.

But the work of the scholars under the Manchu dynasty has paved the way for the introduction of Western thought. For eclectic tendency means tending to open-mindedness; encyclopedic tendency means demanding a wider scope in the field of knowledge; and philological tendency means the exact use of language which is an instrument for clear thinking.

Summary

The history of Chinese thought is a continuous development. The ante-Chin period, which we call here the creative period, was marked by vigorous intellectual activities. There were three distinctive trends of thought. The southern school, which held the principle that institutions were but hindrances to peace and order in society, was naturalistic or anti-institutional. This school was in a way un-Chinese. The central school, which held the principle that social order was to be maintained solely by means of penal laws, was penal or jural. The northern school, which held the principle that moral laws were the sole foundation of society, was politico-ethical. China was then in the stage of feudalism. The different feudal states were waging war against one another. The southern school tried to solve the problem by means of the abolishment of social institutions; the central school by means of imperialism based upon penal laws; the northern school, imperialism based upon moral systems—*li* (禮) or principles of propriety.[41] The radical individualism of the southern school could not be worked out. The moral idea of the northern

---

[41] Imperialism in sense of a centralized government and unified country.

school failed to solve the problem on account of lack of adequate means. The penal idea of the central school solved the problem when the Chin dynasty, the first empire in the real sense of the word, was founded.

There is one important point which demands our attention here. The northern school, or politico-ethical school, was a historical school and tried therefore to solve the problem by past experience. The central school, or the penal school, was non-historical and revolutionary and tried to solve the problem by devising means to meet the present situations. The problem was temporarily solved with the revolutionary method by founding the first great empire. But the revolutional school went too far, for it tried to destroy its opponents by burning all the literature of the ante-Chin period and butchering the scholars of the historical school. Thus it closed its eyes to the past accumulated wisdom of the race. In the meantime, the people rebelled against the high-handed methods of the government based upon severe penal laws. The empire fell to pieces in a few years. This titanic disaster, which happened to Chinese literature and almost destroyed Chinese civilization, caused such an everlasting shock upon the Chinese mind that the Chinese scholars could not get over it for many a century to follow. The temporary success followed by the ultimate failure of the non-historical method brought the Chinese mind back towards the historical school. By going to the other extreme, the Chinese mind has been ever since looking towards the past instead of the present and the future.

When the Han dynasty arose, the social problems were solved in two ways. Politically, it was inperialism based upon a moral system and supplemented by penal laws. Intellectually, it was eclectic in method. This eclectic tendency has been ever since working either consciously or unconsciously in the development of Chinese thought.

When the scholars tired of the commentary works started in the beginning of the Han dynasty, and the people in general tired of living in the miserable world where war and pestilence prevailed, Hindu philosophy was introduced into China and in the meantime Hedonism was born.

Failing to solve the social problems, the people tried to escape from the world either by seeking Nirvana or indulging in licentious pleasures. But since there is life, people cannot very well escape from the world. Hence social problems must be solved. Thus it leads to the renaissance of Confucian learning.

Starting from the problem of governing the state, it was later on developed into the problem of knowledge. The scholars were then busy in seeking reason, the essence of knowledge. Thus a new gate to intellectual development was opened. The problem of knowledge split the Confucian schools into two warring camps. The quarrels continued till the beginning of the Manchu dynasty.

Tired of searching for reason, the scholars under the alien dynasty turned to a historical study of the ancient learning. While the Confucian school was taken as the central figure, all the other schools existing since the ante-Chin period were studied and scientifically commented upon by means of philology, especially etymology. The great cyclopedic movement attained its zenith under the patronage of Emperor Kang-hsi (康 熙). The great *Chinese Encyclopedia*, which consists of 10,000 books in 1,628 volumes, was compiled in the reign of Kang-hsi. Meanwhile, Western influence was gradually coming in. To-day Western influence gained such an ascendancy in China that it first revealed itself in a sweeping change of the state school system and was followed by a radical change of the form of government. The new era for China has begun.

III. Introduction of Western Thought

A Comparison with Introduction of Hindu Thought. The introduction of alien thought into China is not new. As we have seen before, China borrowed Buddhistic philosophy from India, when she began to feel the insufficiency of her own ideas. It was first introduced as a means to reach perpetual life. Then it was taken as a refuge for distressed people. Finally it was studied as philosophy. As the Chinese mind is essentially practical and her philosophy is mainly directed to social problems, Hindu thought, while good as mental food for idealistic thinkers, is super-social and, therefore, fundamentally different from the general social ideals of the Chinese. Stimulated by Hindu philosophy, and as a reaction against it, to a certain extent as an assimilation of it, the philosophers of the Sun (宋) dynasty attempted to solve the social problems of the time by founding a new politico-ethical system.

Similarly, Western thought was introduced when China began to feel the insufficiency of her own ideas. It was consciously introduced because she found that her own ideas were insufficient to meet the social needs and particularly inadequate for national defense. In sending students to study in Western universities, China is simply following the plan adopted in the Tang dynasty when students were sent to study in the Hindu universities.[42]

There is, however, an important point of difference. As we have pointed out before, the Hindu thought is fundamentally different from the practical social philosophy of the Chinese. On the other hand, Western thought, so far as social problems are concerned, is fundamentally the same as Chinese thought, for both Western and Chinese thought are directed towards the solution of social problems. Hindu philosophy led the Chinese to search for an ideal state—Nirvana; while, on the other hand, Western ideas will help China to solve her social problems by means of modern science, art, engineering, and social institutions.

The Problems. The fundamental problem at the present time is identically the same problem that Chinese scholars, philosophers, teachers, and statesmen have been trying to solve from time to time as new sets of conditions arose, that is, how to govern the state. As soon as this question is raised, we are plunged into a complicated situation and are confronted with intricate problems. For the sake of handling our discussions, we are to present in Chapter XIII, on The Individual, the Society, and the State, the following six essential points, which will fundamentally affect Chinese thought and consequently Chinese education:

1. The Greek idea of life.
2. The Roman idea of the law.

---

[42] An interesting account of the life of India may be found in I Ching's *A Record of the Buddhistic Religion as Practiced in India and Malay Archipelago* (671–695 A.D.), translated by J. Takakusa, London, 1896.

3. The Christian idea of God.
4. Science and the modern method of knowledge.
5. The modern idea of the individual and society.
6. The modern idea and method of democracy.

With the traditional respect for knowledge, undaunted spirit in searching for truth, and endless patience and unlimited capacity for hard work, as personified by the Chinese scholars, we hope and sincerely believe that China will be able to solve her all-important problems.

CHAPTER II
GENERAL SCOPE OF CHINESE EDUCATION

In the study of the education of a nation, the author considers it advisable to go back to a study of the underlying trends of thought of that nation. Education would be meaningless if detached and isolated from national life, ideals, and thought. In the chapter preceding, we have discussed briefly the national ideals of life, the meaning of institutions, and the development of thought. In his perusal of that chapter, the reader has in general become acquainted with the background of Chinese education or such at least has been the hope of the author. In this chapter he is to have a general survey of the educational ideals and method.

1. THE MEANING OF EDUCATION

What does education mean—"What Heaven (Cosmos) has conferred is called nature (性); an accordance with this nature is called *tao* (道), path or truth; and to impart *tao*, or truth, is called teaching (教), or education."[1] This definition of education of the Confucian school is handed down to the Chinese people through Tse-Sze (子思), grandson of Confucius and teacher of Mencius, in his book on *The Doctrine of the Mean* (中庸). What Heaven (Cosmos) has conferred is, in the modern sense, natural law, which is inviolable and unchangeable. Since it is inviolable, what man can do is to find out the law according to which nature is at work. This natural law discovered by man is called *tao*, or truth. Education is to impart truth discovered by man in accordance with nature.

Source of Tao, Truth or Path. Heaven or Cosmos is the source of all truth. When it reveals itself in the physical universe, it is called *tao*, truth or path of Heaven. When it is revealed in man, it is called *tao*, truth or path of man.

---
[1] *The Doctrine of the Mean*, Chapter I, Section 1.

Tao of Heaven and Man. An inquiry into *tao*, truth or path of Heaven (天之道), belongs to the sphere of metaphysics, which we shall not attempt to discuss here. What directly concerns us here is an inquiry into *tao*, truth or path of man (人之道). The discussions on human nature, however, also belong to the sphere of *tao* of Heaven, because when we consider the Universe, man is but a part of it. With the discussions on human nature, we are on the threshold between *tao* of Heaven and that of man.

Virtue and Tao of Man. *Tao* of man reveals itself in human relations (人倫)—the relations between the sovereign and minister, the parent and child, the husband and wife, between brothers, and between friends. This is called the universal *tao* (達道), truth or path of man.[2] The relations between man and his fellows, as we have just pointed out, are not only the natural orders of human relations, but are inborn in man. This inborn nature of man is called *teh* (德), or virtue. Virtue functions in wisdom, benevolence, and courage. These are called the universal virtue of man (達德). How are they to be attained? Confucius said: "To be fond of learning is the way towards wisdom; to practice with vigor is the way towards benevolence; and to possess the feeling of shame is the way towards courage."[3] When virtue is unfolded, the proper relations of men will be attained. Therefore, education is chiefly concerned with the development of the virtue of man. *The Great Learning* tells us that education "is to develop illustrious virtue" (明明德). How is this to be done? Confucius formulated a scheme of education to solve this problem.

2. THE SCHEME OF EDUCATION[4]

In *The Great Learning*, Confucius formulated his great scheme of education. According to his view, personal culture (修身) is the foundation of all education. "From the sovereign down to the mass of the people, all must consider the cultivation of the person the root of everything." The development of the person

---

[2] *The Doctrine of the Mean*, Chapter XX, Section 8.
[3] *Id.*, Section 10.
[4] The rest of this chapter is based on *The Great Learning* unless otherwise noted.

is the foundation for the well-ordered family and the well-governed state.

Personal Culture. How is one to cultivate the person? In order to do this, we must first have well-balanced minds. This means that all our feelings must be harmoniously adjusted. We must not be under the influence of passion, terror, indulgence, sorrow, or distress. Any of these influences will upset our mental state. The well-balanced mental state can be attained only through sincerity in thoughts. This means that we must " allow no self-deception." When our thoughts are sincere, we hate or love in a proper way, " as when we hate a bad smell or love what is beautiful." How can our thoughts be sincere? As a preliminary step to this, we are required to have proper understanding. If we can see the truth of things and affairs, our thoughts will be sincere.

The Problem of Knowledge. How can we have proper understanding or see the truth of things and affairs? It is possible only when we go to investigate things and affairs.[5] Thus the investigation of things and affairs is the beginning of knowledge. This problem will be fully discussed in Chapter V, The Problem of Knowledge.

From the above discussed, we may say that the successive steps of education for personal culture are (1) the getting of knowledge, (2) the assimilation of knowledge, (3) sound judgment, and (4) the well-balanced mind. After the problem of personal culture is solved, Confucius continued on to take up the problem of education for the family and the state.

Family. As the individual is the foundation of the family, Confucius emphasized the necessity of the cultivation of the person before taking up education for the family. The family is the foundation of the state. Before taking up education for the governing of the state, therefore, we must educate the family first. " It

---

[5]According to Chen Su-sai (湛若水), " the investigation of things and affairs " and " to attain proper understanding " are but one process—method of knowledge. By means of this, it is to study thoughts, mind (in emotional aspect), the cultivation of the person, and the things and affairs relating to family and the state.—*Sen Hsieh Keh Fu Tun* (聖學格物通).

is not possible for one to teach others, while he cannot teach his own family." A well-ordered family depends upon filial piety, brotherly love, and parental kindness.

The State. The next step is education for the governing of the state.⁶ In the family, there are filial piety, brotherly love, and parental kindness, all of which a well-ordered family must have. From the family, the Confucian school drew a parallelism for the state. The sovereign should be served with filial piety; the elders and superiors, with brotherly love; and the multitudes should be treated with parental kindness.

In commenting on education for governing the state, Tsangtse (曾子), a disciple of Confucius, author of *The Great Learning*, discussed the essential elements of the state: virtue, people, land, and wealth. Benevolence and righteousness are the essential virtues to the state. Of benevolence, *The Great Learning* says, " Never has there been a case that when the sovereign loves benevolence, the people do not love righteousness." Of righteousness, it says, " In a state, gain is not to be considered prosperity but its prosperity will be found in righteousness." Of wealth, it says: " There is a great course for the production of wealth. Let the producers be many and consumers few. Let there be activity in the production, and economy in the expenditure. Then the wealth will be always sufficient." Of the relation of wealth and people, it says, " The accumulation of wealth is the way to scatter the people; and letting it be scattered among them is the way to collect people."

The World. Confucius had world peace in view.⁶ His method of bringing about world peace is to have the state rightly governed first. "There are nine laws for governing the state and the world right: the cultivation of the person, the honoring of men of virtue and talents, affection for the relatives, respect for the great ministers, the kind and considerate treatment of the whole body of officers, the dealing with the mass of the people as children,

---

⁶ It should be understood that what Confucius meant by the state was the feudal state and the world the Chinese world. Nevertheless, the principles are the same to the modern world.

the encouragement of the resort of all classes of artisans, hospitality towards the men from a distance, and the kindly cherishing of the sovereigns of the states. . . . If the people are treated with parental kindness as children, they will be encouraged to do what is good ; if the resort of all classes of artisans is encouraged, production of wealth will be rendered ample ; if men from distant lands are treated with hospitality, the people from all quarters of the world will love to stay ; and if the sovereigns of different states are kindly cherished, the whole world will be brought to revere the state (which observes the nine laws)." Then *The Doctrine of the Mean* continues to discuss the ways of applying the nine laws. Regarding the treatment of the strangers, it says, " Escort them on their departure and meet them on their arrival ; commend the good among them and show compassion towards the incompetent." As to cherishing the sovereigns of the different states, it says : " Restore families whose line of succession has been broken ; revive the states that have been extinguished ; reduce to order the states that are in turmoil and support those which are in peril ; entertain the envoys with liberal treatment. "[1]

The system of education as designed by Confucius begins with the individual, then the family, the state, and finally the world (修身, 齊家, 治國, 平天下). With the individual, the mind is the first thing to be considered ; with family, the individual ; with the state, the family ; and with the world, the state. Therefore, personal culture is the most fundamental element in the whole system of education.

3. The Aim of Education

The final aim of education is to attain the supreme good (至善), *summum bonum*. What is the supreme good ? According to *The Great Learning*, it is defined in accordance with the duties of the social relation of the individual. As we have seen in the chapter preceding, for a sovereign, the supreme good lies in benevolence ; for a minister, in reverence ; for a son, in filial piety ;

---

[1] *The Doctrine of the Mean*, Chapter XX, Sections 12, 13, and 14.

for a father, in parental kindness ; for the relation with one's fellow men, in good faith. Therefore in the fulfillment of the social or moral function of man, lies the supreme good. Here we find the difference between the Aristotelian idea of *summum bonum* and the Confucian. Aristotle, in answering the question raised by Plato, " What is the highest good, the end of life ? " arrived at the conclusion that it lies in the function of man, which is an activity of soul in accordance with reason.[8] Aristotle emphasized the rational nature of man ; Confucius, his moral nature.[9]

4. The Problem of Education

Since the supreme good lies in man's moral nature, or his relation to his sovereign, minister, parent, son, and fellow men, education is to develop one's moral nature in relation to his family and state.[10] As we have seen before, the well-governed state depends upon the well-ordered family which itself depends upon the well-cultured person. It is but natural that education aims to train the individual not only in morals, but also in politics. Hence the chief problem of Chinese education is what may be termed politico-ethical. This is the fundamental problem of Chinese education upon which the later development of education is based.

---

[8] Rogers, *Student History of Philosophy*, pages 110, 111.

[9] In the twelfth century, Loh Shang-san began to claim the supreme importance of the rational power of man. But it was not until the sixteenth century when Wong Yang-min definitely advanced the theory that the supreme good means the fullest development of the rational power of the mind. " The supreme good means the development of the mind to such an extent that it reaches the purest stage of reason."—*The Works of Wong Yang-min, Dialogues*, Section 4.

[10] Mencius told us that the function of the school is to teach human relations—the mutual devotion of parents and children, of the sovereign and ministers, of the husband and wife, of the youths and elders, and between friends—see Chapter I, Note 6.

PART I

HEREDITY AND EDUCATION

The tendency of man's nature to good may be likened to water flowing downward.—*Mencius.*

The work of nourishing the mind may be likened to the work of nourishing a grain of seed in which life lies latent.—*Tsu-tse.*

PART I
HEREDITY AND EDUCATION
CHAPTER III
HUMAN NATURE

Education is the science and art which deals directly with Man himself. The subject matter of education is man. Therefore we must inquire into his real nature—who he is and whence he comes or to what he owes his very existence. The Chinese philosophers would admit *a priori* that to Heaven man owes his existence. Chow-tse (周 子) said: "What is conferred by Heaven is called Divine Law. What man or thing receives from Heaven is called nature."[1] When we say human nature, we mean what man receives from Heaven. Confucius did not discuss human nature at length. He said simply that "by nature, men are alike; by practice, they become different."[2] It was not until Mencius who took up the great issue that human nature is good. Opposing him it was Sin-tse (荀 子) on the one hand who held that human nature is bad, and Kaou-tse (告 子) on the other hand who held that human nature is neither good nor bad.

Meaning of Good and Bad. Sin-tse defined "good" as that which tends towards "maintaining peace and order [of society]" and "bad" as that which is "dangerous and causes disturbances [to society]."[3] This definition can be taken safely as common ground of Chinese philosophers. To use modern terms, we may say that what is good is social, and what is bad is anti-social.

Human Nature Is Good. "When the Duke Wan of T'ang was Crown Prince, having to go to Ts'oo, he went by way of Sung, and visited Mencius." "Mencius discoursed with him how the nature of man is good, and, when speaking, always made laudatory

---
[1]*Chin Sze Lu*, Book I.
[2]*The Confucian Analects*, Book, XVII, *Yang Ho*, Chapter II.
[3]*The Works of Sin-tse*, Chapter on *Human Nature*.

reference to Yaou and Shun, the two wise emperors of ancient time."[4] These wise emperors were recognized by the people as benevolent and righteous men. Why were they so? Mencius would answer that because benevolence and righteousness are inborn,[5] and that they had acted in accordance with human nature.

Human Nature Is Neither Good nor Bad. Opposing him, the philosopher Kaou held that benevolence and righteousness are made through men's effort. I can do no better than to quote from *The Works of Mencius* :[6]

The philosopher Kaou said: " Man's nature is like the *ke* willow, and righteousness is like a cup or a bowl. Fashioning benevolence and righteousness out of man's nature is like making cups and bowls from the *ke* willow."

Mencius replied : " Can you, leaving untouched the nature of the willow, make with it cups and bowls ? You must do violence and injury to the willow, before you can make cups and bowls with it; on your principles you must in the same way do violence and injury to humanity in order to fashion from it benevolence and righteousness ! Your words, alas ! would certainly lead all men to reckon benevolence and righteousness to be calamities."

The philosopher Kaou said : " Man's nature is like water whirling round in a corner. Open a passage for it to the east, and it will flow to the east ; open a passage for it to the west and it will flow to the west. Man's nature is indifferent to good and evil, just like water is indifferent to the east and west."

Mencius replied : "Water indeed will flow indifferently to the east or west, but will it flow indifferently up or down ? The tendency of man's nature to good is like the tendency of water to flow downwards. There is none but this tendency to good, just as all water flows downwards.

" Now by striking water and causing it to leap up, you may make it go over your forehead, and, by damming and leading it,

---

[4] *The Works of Mencius*, Book III, *Tang Wang Kung*, Part I, Chapter I, Sections 1 and 2.
[5] *Id.*, Book VI, *Kaou Tse*, Part I, Chapter IV, Section 7.
[6] *Id.*, Chapter I, Sections 1–3.

you may force it up a hill ; . . . but are such movements according to the nature of water ? It is the force applied which causes them. When men are made to do what is not good, their nature is dealt with in this way."

Mencius's Organic View on Human Nature. The fundamental difference of the two ideas seems to lie in that Kaou-tse took *good* as an outer conformity, while Mencius saw it from the viewpoint of inner growth. According to Kaou-tse, good is an artificial invention of man. We get good from nature just as we make cups and bowls from the *ke* willow. According to Mencius, the good is nothing but the natural growth from the nature of man. Let me illustrate this by quoting a passage from the words of Mencius :[7]

"The trees of the New Mountain were once beautiful. Being situated, however, on the border of a large state, they were hewn down with axes and bills ; . . . and could they retain their beauty? Still through the activity of the vegetative life day and night, and the nourishing influence of the rain and dew, they were not without buds and sprouts springing forth, but then came the cattle and goats and browsed upon them. To these things is owing the bare and stript appearance of the mountain, which when people see, they think it was never finely wooded. But is this the nature of the mountain ?

"And so also what properly belongs to man ; . . . shall it be said that the mind of any man was without benevolence and righteousness ? The way in which a man loses his proper goodness of mind is like the way in which the trees are denuded by axes and bills. Hewn down day after day, can it—the mind—retain its beauty ? But there is a development of its life day and night, and in the calm of the morning, just between night and day, the mind feels in a degree those desires and aversions which are proper to humanity, but the feeling is not strong, and it is fettered and destroyed by what takes place during the day. This fettering takes place again and again, the restorative influence of the night

---

[7] *The Works of Mencius*, Book VI, *Kaou Tse*, Part I, Chapter VIII, Sections 1–3.

is not sufficient to preserve the proper goodness of the mind; and when this proves iusufficient for that purpose, the nature becomes not much different from that of the irrational animals, which, when people see, they think that it never had those powers which I assert. But does this condition represent the feelings proper to humanity?

"Therefore, if it receives its proper nourishment, there is nothing which will not grow. If it loses its proper nourishment, there is nothing which will not decay away."

From this we may know that according to Mencius the good is the outcome of the nature properly nourished; and the bad, the outcome of the nature with lack of proper nourishment. The nature of man *per se* is absolutely good. What we see bad in the nature is because we neglect to nourish it. "If men do what is not good, the blame cannot be imputed to their natural powers."

Human Nature Is Bad. Directly opposed to this naturalistic view of human nature, we have Sin-tse, contemporary of Mencius, who held that the nature of man is absolutely bad. He traced up the distinct egoistic tendencies in human nature. He said, when proving that human nature is bad: "Men were born with selfishness. Acting according to this, there were quarrels among men for the selfish end without due regard to modesty and complaisance. Men were born with dislikes and hatred. Acting according to these, there were cruelties and harmfulness among men, and faithfulness and truthfulness were lost among them. . . . Therefore, men must need the influence of teaching and of the moral truth of propriety and righteousness in order to act properly. From this, we can see clearly that the nature of man is bad. What is good in him is through his making. For example, the *sze* wood, which is crooked, must be straightened through the artificial process of cutting, pressing, and steaming, before it becomes of any use. The metal, which is dull, must be sharpened through the process of beating and grinding, before it becomes a useful tool. It therefore follows that the nature of man, which is bad, must be harnessed through the process of teaching and of moral training in propriety and righteousness, before the social order can be maintained. . . . Those who have gone through the proper instruction, profound learning in the arts and sciences, and training in the moral truth of propriety and righteousness are the superior men. Those who run wild according to their own nature and passion, love ease and dissipation, and disregard the principles of propriety and righteousness are the inferior men."[8]

Thus Sin-tse trusted man's future in the hands of man himself. Nature can and must be conquered by man's effort. It is man himself that created this moral world. Nature has nothing to do with it; nay, man must suppress his nature in order to create this moral world. As with Mencius, education is of absolute necessity to human happiness; so it is with Sin-tse. But with the latter, the power of education seems to be omnipotent. Man can do whatever he wants to do. With the former, education has power only where it is in accordance with the nature of man. Man must use his effort, but only in the direction where the law of nature works.

A Dilemma. While we cannot deny that there are certain tendencies in human nature which are selfish and antisocial, yet we can by no means deny that the effort which man uses to create this moral world has its origin in the nature of man. If, according to Sin-tse, human nature is absolutely bad, then where does this effort of man in creating this moral world come from? Does this effort of man not come from man himself, and hence, from the nature of man? On the other hand, if, according to Mencius, human nature is absolutely good, then where do these selfish and antisocial native tendencies come from? Is it all due to the lack of proper nourishment to the nature of man? This is the dilemma that the Chinese philosophers had to face.

Human Nature Is a Mixture of Good and Bad. Several centuries later, Yang-tse (楊子) tried to compromise these two opposite views by holding that " the nature of man is a mixture of good and bad." " Developing the good elements of the human nature, we will have a good man. Developing the bad elements of the human nature, we will have a bad man. . . . Therefore,

---

[8]Sin-tse, *On Human Nature,* 荀子性惡篇.

the superior man must be diligent in learning and firm in conduct."⁹

Human Nature Is Hierarchical. This eclectic view of human nature did not settle the problem. Han Yu (韓 愈) took up the problem again. He divided the nature of man into three classes— the upper, the good; the middle, a mixture of the good and bad; the lower, the bad. " The upper class is purely good. The middle class can be directed either to be good or bad. The lower class is incurably bad. . . . Mencius said that nature is good; Sin-tse said that nature is bad; and Yang-tse said that nature is a mixture of the good and bad. There were cases that the good turned into bad, the bad into good, and the mixed into either good or bad. The reason is that all these cases belong to the middle class of nature. These philosophers only saw the one and neglected the other two classes. . . . Then, are both of the upper and lower classes of nature unchangeable? The former may be improved through learning, and the latter may be restrained from doing harm with force. Therefore, the upper may be educated and the lower may be restrained. But the respective classes to which they belong cannot be interchanged according to Confucius."¹⁰

Nature, Intelligence, and Heredity. This hierarchical view of Han Yu was derived from the idea of Confucius who stated that " there are only the wise of the highest class, and the stupid of the lowest class, who cannot be changed."¹¹ Ch'ing-tse (程 子) attacked Han Yu's view by saying that he confused intelligence with human nature and his classification therefore was of human intelligence and not human nature. While he saw the difference between intelligence and nature, Ch'ing-tse advanced his theory that the individual differences were due to the inheritance of man, and not to his nature. To quote his own words: " From his birth, man derived from nature his inheritance which through the operation of nature's law may be either good or bad. But there were no two elements so opposing in the nature of man. One may be born good and the other may be born bad. These are all due to

---
⁹*The Works of Yang-tse,* Chapter on *Personal Culture.*
¹⁰*Han Yu, On Human Nature, Chinese Encyclopedia.* Volume 46, *Essays on Human Nature,* Part I, Page 1.
¹¹*The Confucian Analects,* Book XVII, *Yang Ho,* Chapter III.

the inheritance of the individual. Of course, the good is from the nature of man, but we cannot deny that the bad is also from it. It is the *reason* [rationality] of the human nature that differentiates the good from the bad. The nature of man is the overlord of the inheritance. When the inheritance is pure we will have the good; when it is impure, we will have the bad."[12] In some other place, Ch'ing-tse said : " The intelligence is ingrained in the inheritance. The latter may be either pure or impure. The wise man possessed the pure inheritance ; while the stupid, the impure."[13]

Quantitative View on Human Nature. Thus, the nature of man, according to Ch'ing-tse, is above the qualitative differences of good and bad. It is the inheritance of the individuals which has these differences. Tsu-tse (朱 子), the follower of Ch'ing-tse, while admitting that nature is above the qualitative differences, had somewhat different interpretation of the inheritance of the individuals. He took the quantitative view of inheritance instead of the qualitative. He said : " Heaven gave the same *reason* [rationality] to all men when they were born, but they received a different inheritance. Nature may be likened to the water in the river. If you take a spoonful, you will get a spoonful ; if you take a cupful, you will get a cupful. . . . The capacity of the vessel used is different, and therefore the amount you will receive is proportionately different. The difference in the capacity of the individual determines the difference in the amount of *reason* [rationality] he receives."[14] Several centuries later, Wong Yang-min (王 陽 明), in discussing the nature of man, expressed the same view. He said : " The inheritance of the individual men may be likened to the vessels, and the nature of man may be likened to the water. One may get a tank of water ; the other, a tub ; and still the third, a jar of it. The inheritance of the individual men may either be pure or impure, strong or weak ; but the nature of man is ever one."[15]

[12]*Chinese Encyclopedia*, Volume 48, *General Discussions on Human Nature*, Part II, Page 15.
[13]*Ibid.*
[14]*Id.*, Page 10.
[15]*Chinese Encyclopedia*, Volume 50, *General Discussions on Human Nature*, Part IX, Page 36.

Summary. From the various theories of human nature we have discussed above, we have the several stages of interpretations of the nature of man. In the first stage, we find that the existence of such a thing called human nature was recognized, and what is meant by human nature is that which man receives from Heaven. The second stage is characterized by the inquiry made into what human nature is. Is it good or bad? Mencius said that human nature is absolutely good; Sin-tse said that it is absolutely bad; while Kaou-tse said that it is neither good nor bad. And later, Yang-tse advanced the theory that human nature is a mixture of good and bad. Han Yu divided the nature of man into three classes: namely, the upper, which is good; the middle, which is a mixture of good and bad; and the lower, which is bad. In the third stage, the philosophers began to differentiate the intelligence of man, which is particular to the individual men, and the nature of man, which is universal to mankind.

CHAPTER IV

NATURE AND NURTURE

General View of the Problem. While the various Chinese philosophers held that there is something which is inborn in man, yet they emphasized the power of education to develop and improve this inborn nature. With the exception of Sin-tse, who believed that the nature of man is bad and thereby regarded as omnipotent the power of education which entirely controls the destiny of man, the Confucian school as a whole held the view that, although the nature of man is good, the human nature would amount to little without education to direct and develop it.

Education to Add Something to Nature. Confucius said that he was not one who had been born in possession of knowledge, but he was one who was earnest in seeking it.[1] Confucius believed that it is through learning that men are able to secure knowledge. Therefore, all through one's life, he must devote his time towards seeking knowledge.[2] Confucius saw the importance of nature, but he held that it is education that makes improvements on nature. To quote the conversation between Confucius and Tse Lu (子路): In his visit to Confucius, Tse Lu was asked what he would like best. He replied that he would like to practice using a long sword. Confucius said: "This is not what I wished to ask you. I mean that one who possesses a natural ability like you, if added to learning, is unsurpassable." Tse Lu said, "Learning does not add anything to natural ability." Confucius said: "A piece of wood may be made straight by setting a mark line on it and cutting it accordingly with an ax. Likewise

---

[1] *The Confucian Analects*, Book VII, Chapter XIX.
[2] The Master said: "Is it not pleasant to learn with a constant perseverance and application? Is it not pleasant to have friends coming from distant quarters? Is he not a man of complete virtue who feels no discomposure though men may take no note of him?" — *Id.*, Book I, Chapter I.

a man may be made sagacious through education. If one receives an education and is diligent in inquiry, whose original nature can escape from being improved upon?" Tse Lu said: "There are bamboos growing on the South Mountain, which are by nature straight; if you cut them down and use them to make arrows, they are good for piercing the leather. From this we may infer that what is the use of learning?" The Master replied, "If you take a piece of bamboo, fix a few of the feathers on one end and sharpen the other end, would it pierce the leather better?" Tse Lu bowed before Confucius and said, "I am willing to receive your instructions."[3]

Tse Sze (子 思) held the same view as Confucius. He said that education must be added to the original nature in order to strengthen it. Tse Sze said to Tse Shan (子 上): "Beh, I used to engage myself in deep thinking, but I could not make much progress. When I studied, I began to understand truth. I used to raise myself on my toes expecting to see farther, but did not succeed. When I ascend the high mountain, my horizon was greatly extended. Therefore, likewise, to the original nature, learning must be added."[4]

Education to Develop Nature. Mencius, the advocator of the theory that human nature is absolutely good, also believed that education is indispensable to the growth of man's inborn nature. He compared the growth of man with that of a tree. According to him, it is a pity that men know how to nurse a tree and yet neglect to nurse themselves. To quote him: "Anybody who wishes to cultivate the *tung* or *tse* [names of the trees] . . . knows by what means to nourish them. In case of their own persons, men do not know by what means to nourish them. Is it to be supposed that their regard for their own persons is inferior to their regard for a *tung* or a *tse?* Their want of reflection is extreme."[5]

Although the nature of man is good, yet, if education is neglected, men are not far different from beasts. Mencius said:

---

[3] *Chinese Encyclopedia*, Volume 83, on *Learning*, Book I, Page 10.
[4] *Id.*, Page 12.
[5] *The Works of Mencius*, Book VI, Part I, Chapter XIII.

"Now men possess a moral nature; but if they are well fed, warmly clad, and comfortably lodged, without being taught at the same time, they become almost like beasts."[6] Indeed, Mencius had so much faith in education that he put it above politics.[7]

Tsu Tze compared education with the nursing of a grain of seed. Man's potential power to grow may be likened to the potential power of seed. The potential power of seed will lie latent or remain undeveloped without the proper method of nursing it. So it is with man. To quote him: "The work of nourishing the mind may be likened to that of nursing a grain of seed in which life lies latent. The growth of seed depends upon watering and fertilizing. If you say that there is seed and it will naturally take root and send out buds, you will be disappointed. When you have a good thought in your mind and let it alone, it will remain static day after day, and year after year. There will be no progress. It is just like a grain of seed without being fertilized and watered."[8]

The Limit of Education. We have now had enough proofs to say that, with the Confucian school, while it recognized the forces of nature, it at the same time recognized the importance of education without which the nature of man would remain undeveloped and it would result in the wanton waste of human energy. Now let us ask a question whether the Confucian school held that the power of education is omnipotent or has it its limitations? Can education make a man as he is desired, or must it give its way to nature when individual differences occur? Let us examine how the Chinese philosophers would answer it. First let us see what the Master himself would say. Confucius gave recognizance to the existence of differences in the individual endowment. Education at its best cannot create natural endowment. The great men are born great.[9] Those whose talents are

---

[6] *The Works of Mencius,* Book III, Part I, Chapter I, Section 8.

[7] "Good government does not lay hold of the people so much as good instructions."—*Id.,* Book VII, Part I, Chapter XIV, Section 2.

[8] *Chinese Encyclopedia,* Volume 85, *General Discussions on Learning,* Book III, Page 47.

[9] *The Confucian Analects,* Book XVI, *Ke She,* Chapter IX.

below mediocrity cannot be taught up to the highest standard.[10] Those who are made through education are to be classified as mediocre. In short, educaton cannot get more than what nature gives. Wong Yang-min gave a very good illustration of the limitation of education on account of the differences in individual capacities. He took gold ore as an example. The uncultured man may be likened to the gold ore that is mixed with copper and lead. The cultured may be likened to the pure gold that has been extracted from the ore. The amount of gold contained in the different ores is not equal. Some contain more and others contain less. We cannot get more gold than is contained in the ore. It is the same with the education of man. The function of education is to get from the individual to the fullest extent what his natural endowment can give. To quote him: " Men become sages when they reach the stage of being purely rational. Gold becomes pure when the ingredients have been thoroughly taken out. The natural ability of the sages is different, as some have greater ability than the others. This may be likened to a quantity of gold which is different in different ores, some containing more gold than the others. . . . The natural ability of the sages is different. But they are the same as far as their rationality is concerned. When men are rational, they all are sages, irrespective of their ability. When gold is pure, it is pure irrespective of its quantity. . . . Gold is called pure gold because of its purity, rather than its quantity. Men are called sages because of their rationality, not their natural ability."[11]

Growth Is Natural. Education has its limitations because nature itself is limited. Where the limit of nature is, education cannot go beyond. But the method of education is far from being perfect, and, therefore, it is far from reaching nature's limit. It is often the case that when the method of education *is wrong, nature* takes the blame. We often hear a teacher blaming a child's stupidity, when he really ought to blame his own stupidity in his

---

[10] The Master said, " To those whose talents are above mediocrity the highest subjects may be announced. To those who are below mediocrity, the highest subjects may not be announced."—*The Confucian Analects*, Book VI, *Yung Yay*, Chapter XIX.

[11] *The Works of Wong Yang-min, Dialogue*, Section 125.

teaching method. Oftentimes the teacher checks the growth of a child when he is seemingly helping it. Mencius's metaphor of a man "helping" the corn to grow is quite to the point. To quote him: "Let not the mind forget its work, but let there be no assisting the growth. Let us not be like the man of Sung. There was a man of Sung, who was grieved that his growing corn was not longer, so he pulled it up. Having done this, he returned home, looking very stupid, and said to his people: ' I am tired to-day. I have been helping the corn to grow long.' His son ran to look at it, and found the corn all withered. There are few in the world who do not deal with their growth as if they were assisting the corn to grow long. Some consider the work of development no benefit to them; so they do not weed their corn. Others try to assist the growth; so they pull out the corn."[12]

Tsu-tse emphasized the fact that education must be in accordance with nature. He compared the growth of knowledge with that of a plant. There are natural steps which a plant takes, in its process of growth. First it sends out buds then branches and leaves; next come blossoms and finally fruit. Any attempt to help it grow by "pulling" when the time has not yet come will be detrimental to its proper growth. So it is with knowledge.[13]

Forces of the Environment. When we discuss education, we have to keep the two-sided views, namely, biological inheritance and social inheritance, or in other words, nature and nurture. We have the individual on one hand and his environment on the other. The same individual will respond differently when the environment changes. Mencius held that all things which are the same in kind are like one another.[14] The variations among the same kind are caused by the environmental forces which are acting upon the individuals. He took the case of barley as an example. When we sow barely and hope to reap in the future, we have to have these three elements in mind: the soil and its degree of fertility, the quantity of the rains, and the labor man devotes to

---

[12] *The Works of Mencius*, Book II, Part I, Chapter I, Section 16.
[13] *Chinese Encyclopedia*, Volume 85, *General Discussions on Learning*, Book III, Page 34.
[14] " In good years the children of the people are most of them good, while in bad years the most of them abandon themselves to evils. It is

it. The same kind of seeds may produce different quantities of crops on account of the differences in the quality of the soil, in the quantity of the rains, and in the amount of labor that the farmer devotes to it.[14] In the same way, men vary greatly on account of the difference of the environment. Mencius correlated the change of the moral conditions of the people with the change of the economic conditions. He said that in good years the people as a general thing are morally good, while in bad years many of them abandon themselves to evils.[14] This shows that Mencius saw clearly how greatly the influence of environment acts upon the nature of man.

Instincts and Acquired Characteristics. In discussing the nature of man, Ching-tse (程子) emphasized the power of nurture by pointing out the importance of the acquired characteristics of man. He said that the difference between animal and man lies in the fact that the latter possesses the capacity of forming acquired characteristics. Most of the abilities of the animal are natural and unlearned, such as the building of the nests by birds and the nursing of the young by all animals. In the case of man, all his abilities are acquired excepting the sucking of the child, which is natural and unlearned. And therefore, man is different from the animal because of his ability to learn.[15]

---

not owing to their natural powers conferred by Heaven that they are thus different. The abandonment is owing to the circumstances through which they allow their minds to be ensnared and drowned in evil.

"There now is barley. Let it be sown and covered up; the ground being the same, and the time of sowing being likewise the same, it grows rapidly up, and when the full time has come, it is all found to be ripe. Although there may be inequalities in production, that is owing to the difference of the soil, as rich or poor, to the unequal nourishment afforded by the rains and dews, and to the different ways in which man has performed his business in reference to it.

"Thus all things which are the same in kind are like one another. Then, why should we doubt in regard to man as if he were a solitary exception to this? The sages and we are the same in kind."—*The Works of Mencius*, Book VI, Part I, Chapter VII, Sections 1–3.

[15] "The animal and the man are nearly alike if we do not consider the former's little or no capacity of modifications upon its natural ability. The actions of the animal are mostly natural and unlearned, such as building nests in the case of birds and nursing the young in the case of all the animals. Man is the most intelligent being in the animal kingdom. But his native tendencies are in many cases checked or remain undeveloped. With the exception of the sucking of the infant, which is natural and unlearned, all the actions of man are acquired and developed through stimulations."— *Chinese Encyclopedia*, Volume 48, *General Discussions on Human Nature* Book II, Page 5.

PART II

PRINCIPLES OF LEARNING

Learning without thinking is blind; thinking without learning is vain.—*Confucius*.

To hold that you know, when you really know; to allow that you do not know, when you do not know—this is the way to true knowledge.—*Confucius*.

PART II
PRINCIPLES OF LEARNING
CHAPTER V
THE PROBLEM OF KNOWLEDGE

General Discussions on Methodology. There is an outstanding difference in the method of knowledge followed by the European and the Chinese. In general the Chinese method, as represented by the Confucian school, is mainly aphorical. On the other hand, the European method is mainly systematic. In its later development, the tendency is more and more towards the systematic, as we have found, for example, in the writings of Tsu-tse and Wong Yang-min. No Chinese scholar, however, would fail to be impressed with the clear-cut and systematic presentation of a problem such as he finds in reading the great works of Plato and Aristotle, and no Chinese scholar, who has even a general acquaintance of both the Western and Chinese philosophy and is impartially seeking truth, but would admit that China has a good deal to learn from the West in the method of knowledge.

On the other hand, we need not underestimate the serious attempts made by the Chinese philosophers in solving the problem of knowledge. Human thought, whether East or West, seems to travel in one direction. Epistomological controversies have caused no little trouble in history of both Chinese and European philosophy.

The method of knowledge developed by the later Confucian schools is based upon Confucius and the earlier Confucian schools. That of Confucius himself is (1) the aphorical statement, " Learning without thinking is blind; thinking without learning is vain," which is found in *The Confucian Analects*. Those from the earlier Confucian schools are (2) " to investigate things in order to attain understanding," which is found in *The Great Learning ;* (3) " extensive study, accurate inquiry, careful thinking, clear discrimination, and firm action"; and (4) "Honor thy virtue [to develop virtue of man] through inquiry and study," both of which are found in *The Doctrine of the Mean*. As all the above statements are more or less aphorical, we are able to understand their meanings only through the light of later development. In this chapter and the chapter following, The Problem of Science, we are to discuss the development of the four ideas mentioned above. In addition to these, another factor has a bearing upon the problem of knowledge, namely, (5) Confucius's synthetic method of teaching as opposed to Mencius's analytic method.[1]

The problem of knowledge may be threefold: (1) *How is knowledge possible?* (2) method of knowledge; (3) the relation between theory and practice. A detailed discussion of the epistomological problem is not our purpose here; we shall limit ourselves to a presentation of those aspects of the problem which have a direct or indirect bearing upon the problem of education.

1. How Is Knowledge Possible? What is it that makes knowledge possible? Is it inborn and is all knowledge therefore innate? Is it passively received by the mind from outside through the senses and is all knowledge therefore empirical? In the history of European philosophy, we find that there are two opposite schools, one of which holds that our knowledge comes through the senses, the mind being but *tabula rasa*, which is to receive knowledge from the outside, and the other holds that the origin of knowledge is innate. The former may be represented by the English school, notably Lockian; the latter by the Continental school, notably Cartesian. To which does the Chinese school belong?

Confucius said, "Learning without thinking is blind; thinking without learning is vain."[2] In his *Critique of Pure Reason*, Kant made the same remark that "thoughts without content are empty, perceptions without conceptions are blind." Wu Lin-chuen (吳 臨 川) in discussing knowledge said that the outer experience and the

---
[1] This will be discussed when we come to *The Logical Problem of Teaching*, Chapter X.
[2] *The Confucian Analects*, Book II, Chapter XV.

inner understanding are but one. "We get our material [of knowledge] from the outer world through our senses, such as hearing and seeing; but the *reason* of what we see and hear is inborn in the mind. From the outer world we get our materials, and from the inner we derive our understanding. The theory of knowledge of the Confucian school is the unity of the two."[3] Tsu-tse (朱子) held that "the reason is not from the outside but is innate."[4] But at the same time he stated that "the sages did not get their knowledge by sitting alone with the doors closed."[5] In some other place he said that "there is no instance of a man whose hearing and seeing are narrow and yet whose mind is broad."[6] Hu Chu-jen (胡居仁) held that true knowledge must be gained through the inner process of careful examination and discrimination (of outer things).[7] Therefore true knowledge comes from the unification of the inner and outer. Empirical knowledge is possible only because we possess the inner knowledge. Without the latter, we can neither hear nor see anything. The ability to obtain knowledge through the senses is inborn. He called this inner knowledge the "natural knowledge," a term he borrowed from Mencius who defined it as the knowledge which is unlearned.[8] According to Hu Chu-jen, all knowledge is acquired through the operation of this natural knowledge. Therefore it is the source of all knowledge.

---

[3] *Chinese Encyclopedia*, Volume 89, *Tsze Tsze Pu Tson Lun*, Page 30.
[4] *Id.*, Page 13.
[5] *Id.*, Volume 85, *Hsieh Wen Pu Tson Lun*, Book III, Page 51.
[6] *Id.*, Page 18.
[7] The knowledge that is gained through senses is only secondary. The fundamental knowledge is the natural knowledge. The empirical knowledge has its origin in the natural knowledge. How can we gain an empirical knowledge if without this natural knowledge? The former is sometimes apparent and in the other times real. We have to discriminate carefully what is apparent and what is real. If we succeed in getting what is real, we have combined the inner and the outer.—*Id.*, Volume 89, *Tsze Tsze Pu Tson Lun*, Page 31.
[8] The ability possessed by men without having acquired by learning is natural ability, and the knowledge possessed by them without exercise of thought is the natural knowledge.—*The Works of Mencius*, Book VII, *Tsin Sin*, Part I, Chapter XV.

He divided knowledge into four classes.[9] First, the knowledge that is gained through reading. Secondly, the knowledge that is gained through discussion. Thirdly, the knowledge that is gained through thinking. Fourthly and lastly, the knowledge that is gained through action. For the sake of convenience, we may designate the first a *book-knowledge*, the second *dialectic-knowledge*, the third *thinking-knowledge*, and the last *action-knowledge* or practical knowledge. According to Hu Chu-jen, although we get most of our knowledge from our reading, the quickest way to get it is through discussion. The knowledge acquired through thinking is the deepest, and that which is acquired through action is the most practical.

These divisions of knowledge are of course not absolute. All other knowledge would be well-nigh impossible without thinking. We must think when we read, discuss, or act. It is merely a matter of emphasis. What Hu Chu-jen meant by *thinking-knowledge* is that which is gained chiefly through independent thinking. Dewey has well said that " *thinking cannot go on in a vacuum*, and suggestions and inferences can occur only upon a basis of information as to matters of fact."[10] "But there is all the difference in the world," says Dewey, " whether the acquisition of information is treated as an end in itself, or is made an integral portion of the training of thought. . . . The only information which, otherwise than accident, can be put to logical use is that acquired in the course of thinking. Because their knowledge has been achieved in connection with the needs of specific situations, men of little learning are often able to put to effective use every ounce of knowledge they possess; while men of vast erudition are often swamped by the mere bulk of their learning, because memory, rather than thinking, has been operative in obtaining it."

These words of Dewey illustrate well what Hu Chu-jen called thinking-knowledge. Men who possess this kind of knowledge cannot escape seeing the subtle elements of the process of logical reasoning. It is quite different from that kind of knowledge

---

[9]*Chinese Encyclopedia*, Volume 89, *Tsze Tsze Pu Tson Lun*, Page 31.
[10]Dewey, *How We Think*, Page 52.

which is superficial. This is what Hu Chu-jen meant by the deepest.

Most of our knowledge, of course, is acquired from the information furnished by books. The danger of this process lies in the fact that men generally rely too much upon the ready materials, often without *going to the trouble of thinking* by themselves. *Dialectic-knowledge* is safer because of the fact that during the course of discussion, if properly carried on, both the inquirer and the respondent cannot fail to see the logical reasoning of the subject matter, or the discussion cannot possibly go on. Therefore, a dialectic-knowledge is much nearer to thinking-knowledge.

Action-knowledge belongs to that which has to do with art, for Jevons said, " A science teaches us to know and an art to do." [11] A knowledge of art cannot possibly be acquired without doing. The art of playing the piano is acquired only by playing, and not by thinking how to play. The art of medicine is gained only by the practice of medicine, and not by thinking how to practice. It is in the same way with all other branches of art. When we want to put anything into practice, the only road to success is to practice it. After all, any branch of knowledge which had direct significance for life is the knowledge of art, the knowledge of doing. Hu Chen-Jen was right when he said that *action-knowledge* is the most practical.

Without going further into the discussion of the divisions of knowledge, it will be sufficient to state here that according to the Confucian schools, knowledge is possible only when a unity between the inner and outer is recognized. " Reason has no distinction between the inner and outer," said Wong Yang-min, " and, therefore, when we observe or dicuss something, we do not neglect the inner ; when we reflect and introspect, we do not forget the outer." [12]

2. METHOD OF KNOWLEDGE. Since knowledge is possible only when the inner and outer are recognized as an organic unity, or thoughts and sense perceptions as two integral parts of the same mental process, the method to get knowledge is the combination

---

[11] Jevons, *Lessons in Logic*, Page 7.
[12] *The Works of Wong Yang-min*, Volume 4. Book III.

of the two. According to *The Doctrine of the Mean*, the complete process of acquiring knowledge comprises five steps; namely, extensive study, accurate inquiry, careful thinking, clear discrimination, and firm action.[13]

The first step in getting knowledge is to gather data. The more data we have, the wider will be our range of vision. One will be narrow-minded if he is familiar only with a limited number of facts. An extensive study, therefore, is the primary stage of getting knowledge. After we have gathered the data, through an extensive study, the next step to do is to examine them carefully. This is what is meant by accurate inquiry. Our next step is to interpret the meaning, requiring, as *The Doctrine of the Mean* says, careful thinking. It is only through thinking that we can understand the significance of the facts. After this is done, we come to the step of distinguishing the right from the wrong, the true from the false. This fourth step is the clear discrimination. Finally, our knowledge is to be transformed into the motor activities. The final aim of knowledge is to put into effect what we know. Therefore, the fifth or final step of complete knowledge is the firm action.

To interpret psychologically, the process of knowledge begins with the sense-perception, which includes study and inquiry. The middle term is the thought, which includes thinking and discrimination; the former is the reasoning and the latter judgment. And finally, the knowledge must pass into the motor action, the doing.

To interpret objectively, the first step corresponds to the gathering of data; the second, the examination of the data; the third, the grouping and classifications; the fourth, the formulation of the uniform laws and their exception; and the final step is the application of the laws.

The two prominent later-Confucian schools interpreted these five steps of mental process according to the two different viewpoints as above mentioned. The Ch'ing-Tsu (程朱) school[14]

---

[13] *The Doctrine of the Mean*, Chapter XX, Section 19.
[14] After Ch'ing-tse (eleventh century) and Tsu-tse (1130–1200).

represents the objective; the Loh-Wong (陸王) school,[15] the psychological. These different interpretations were due to the fact that these two schools had different centers of interest in knowledge. The former sets the Truth as the center; the latter, the Mind. According to the one, any knowledge that is of worth must bear upon the development of the mind. The other maintains a different attitude. If we only seek the truth, the development of the mind will be its natural result. We cannot get truth by seeking it in our mind. Everything and every affair has its reason. Therefore, we must search for truth in the world of things and affairs. [16]

In opposition to this, the Loh-Wong school says that if we seek the truth only in the world of things and affairs, we shall be entirely at a loss. It is the mind that knows truth. The truth is in our mind. If we know what our mind is we will know what is truth.[17]

---

[15] After Loh Shang-san (1139–1193) and Wong Yang-min (1472–1528).

[16]a. This school sets the Truth as the center of interests in knowledge. Its main aim is to " exhaust the Truth " in affairs and things. According to Ch'ing-tse, there are several places where we can seek the Truth. The first is to get the truth from books, or to understand the truth discovered by the wise men of the past. The second is to study, interpret, and exercise judgment upon the historical facts or the deeds of the historical personages. The third is to seek the truth from the present world of affairs and things by studying their relations. The fourth method is to get the truth from one thing after another by careful study. By accumulation of the truths thus gained, we will some day understand the whole truth.—*Chinese Encyclopedia*, Volume 89, *Tsze Pu Tson Lun*, Page 6; also Volume 68, *Hsieh Wen Tson Pu Lun*, Book III, Page 57.

b. Tsu-tse says that " everything and every affair has its reason; we have to seek from the one and another; the more we have done this, the more our knowledge will be widened." — *Id.*, Volume 89, *Tsze Tsze Pu Tson Lun*, Page 8.

c. Also he says, " There is nothing exists in the world which has no reason, no matter large or small; the method of getting knowledge is to understand the many reasons found in the present world."— *Id.*, Volume 85, *Hsieh Wen Pu Tson Lun*, Book III, Page 20.

[17]a. Somewhere in his works, Loh Shang-san says, " If my mind knows that it is right, I will say so, no matter that it is from the mouth of an educated man or woman; on the other hand, if my mind knows that it is wrong, I will say so, no matter that it is an utterance of a wise man."

b. Wong Yang-min says, " If we try to seek the supreme good in affairs and things, we are to seek the truth outside of the self of ours; the supreme good is the nature of Mind."—*The Dialogue of Wong Yang-min*, Section 2.

c. Wong Yang-min identifies mind with reason. He says, " The mind is the reason; are there in the world such affairs or such reasons beyond our mind ? "—*Id.*, Section 3.

The best criticism of these two opposite schools may be found in the words of Huang Tson-hi (黃宗羲). I can do no better than to quote him :

"The system of Loh Shang-san (陸象山) is centered upon 'the value of virtue' [to develop the virtue of man]. He says that if we recognize the big essential [virtue], our natural endowment will not be hindered [in its development] by the small details [of outer things]. On the other hand, if we do not see clearly the 'self' in us and seek the truth outside of the 'self,' it may be likened to finding water without knowing its source.

"The system of Tsu-tse (朱子) is centered upon 'study and inquiry' [the search for truth in affairs and things]. He says that to 'exhaust the truth' by examining the things is the ladder leading up to the Great Wisdom. If we trust our mind, pass our judgments according to our own opinions and devote ourselves to the empty thoughts, we will take something which our own mind has invented as the standard of truth.

"The followers of Tsu-tse denounced Loh Shang-san as one who indulged in Buddhistic meditations [which do not lead one anywhere]; while those of the latter denounced Tsu-tse as a believer of traditions [who lost himself in worthless details]. . . . Is it not a great misfortune for the *tao* [true teachings] that these meaningless quarrels should prevail even at the present time [middle of the seventeenth century]? . . . If we inquire into the life and works of these two philosophers, we find that Loh Shang-san never neglected the study of ancient learning, although he emphasized the 'value of virtue.' We also find that Tsu-tse, while he emphasized 'study and inquiry,' never forgot his attention to reflection and the development of virtue. The difference lies only in the point of departure. But at the later age, each of the philosophers realized that he had overemphasized one of the two phases of the same problem." [18]

---

[18] Huang Tson-hi, *The History of Philosophy of the Sun and Yuan Dynasties* (960–1307), Volume 58, Pages 3–5, Third Edition, 1879. He lived in the seventeenth century. *The History of Philosophy* was written during the middle of that century. The posthumous publication first appeared in 1831, almost two centuries after his death.

Huang Tson-hi then went on giving many citations of the facts to support his arguments, which it is not necessary for us to repeat here.

As we have seen, the difference between these two opposite schools was only a matter of emphasis. Neither of the two, as Huang Tson-hi has pointed out, neglected entirely the side emphasized by the other. Yet this very difference in point of emphasis caused a great divergence in the course of development. As the Ch'ing-Tsu school puts its center of interests in the search for truth in the world of affairs and things, it was quite natural that the major portion of the energy had to be devoted to objective truth; while, as the Loh-Wong school puts its center of interests in the development of the mind, it was also natural that the major portion of its energy had to be devoted to subjective truth. Of course the founders of the schools had a clear idea in their minds as to what they were driving. Either to seek the objective truth or to develop the mind was but the means to an end. Each aimed at the same thing, the culture of the person. But as time went on, men lost sight of the original purpose. The means was regarded as the end itself. Thus we have what Huang Tson-hi called " these meaningless quarrels."

The original question at issue was the method of cultivating the person. Tsu-tse said that it was to seek the truth; Loh-Shangsan, to seek the mind. Afterward the issue of the question shifted its ground. With one school it was how to seek the mind; with the other, how to seek the truth.

In order to understand it better, let us examine what the Ch'ing-Tsu school meant by Truth. The Chinese term for Truth here discussed is *tse li* (至 理), meaning supreme Reason. It was defined by Tsu-tse as composed of two elements. On the one hand, it deals with " why is it so "; and on the other hand, with " it is as such." [18] And therefore, according to the modern sense, Truth is on one hand logical reason and on the other natural law. To seek the Truth is to know logical reason or natural law. In this respect, the attitude of the Ch'ing-Tsu system closely resembles that of modern scientific method.

---

[19] *Chinese Encyclopedia*, Volume 89, *Tsze Tsze Pu Tson Lun*, Page 22.

And what did the Loh-Wong school mean by Mind? According to Wong Yang-min, Mind is Reason, and there is no Reason beyond the Mind.[20] "To know is the inborn nature of the mind. Therefore, the mind has its natural ability to know."[21] Loh Shang-san held that the mind is superior to everything else. Only through our mind, we can pass judgment upon the validities of truths.[22] But Loh Shang-san was no Protagoras whose famous utterance was that "man is the measure of all things." This statement Plato interprets in the sense that each individual is the measure of all things, that that is true for each man which seems to him to be true, and that for the opinions of different men there is no common measure.[23] Certainly, Loh Shang-san did not mean that. With him, the mind is universal reason. He said that "the wise men of the Eastern Sea and those of the Western Sea have the same mind and, therefore, the same reason; the wise men of centuries to come will have the same mind, and, therefore, the same reason as the wise men of centuries ago."[24] In some other place, Loh Shang-san said: "We must honor what Heaven has conferred upon us. Let us ask ourselves, 'Do we want to be a man?'[25] If so, we must be independent and honor the 'self' of ours, and not follow the footsteps of others, or follow others' opinions.[26] The superior man enslaves things; the inferior man is enslaved by them. The power (of conquering things), belongs to 'me.' If 'I' let the things possess the power, 'I' will be enslaved by them.[27] If only we know the foundation of learning, the Sacred Classics are but the commentaries to the 'self' of 'ours.'"[28] Of course, what Loh Shang-san meant by the foundation of learning is the mind. The mind is reason. It is universal. It is the self and sole judge of Truth.

---

[20] See Note 17c anterior.
[21] *The Dialogue of Wang Yang-min*, Section 3.
[22] See Note 17a anterior.
[23] Rogers, *Students' History of Philosophy*, N. Y., 1913, Page 87.
[24] Huang Tson-hi, *The History of Philosophy of the Sun and Yuan Dynasties*, Volume 58, Page 2.
[25] *Id.*, Page 7.
[26] *Id.*, Volume 58, Page 2.
[27] *Id.*, Page 11.
[28] *Id.*, Page 9.

Now let us point out the merits and defects of the two different systems we have just discussed. The merits of the Ch'ing-Tsu system seem to lie in the fact that, by devoting life for the Truth, the spirit of scholarship is emphasized; while those of the Loh-Wong system, that by taking the mind as supreme and independent, the spirit of the Freedom of Thought is upheld.

The defects of the one seem to lie in the fact that by taking the mind as reason, it would create a tendency to think in a vacuum; while those of the other, that by taking Truth as an end in itself, man would become the slave of the " truth " he professed to have discovered, and the narrow view of seeking it mainly in the ancient writings would set a limit to progress.

For centuries since the time of Mencius, the Chinese mind has lost itself in seeking the masses of time-worn truths. Loh Shang-san, champion of the freedom of thought, wanted to set it free once and for all; while Tsu-tse, lamenting that the Truth had been lost on account of man's ignorance of the ancient teachings, devoted his whole life to writing commentaries on the Confucian classics.

The genius and scholarship of the latter were admired by his followers. His schools flourished and gained a great influence in China. Tsu-tse devoted his life to the Truth; but his followers were caught by the machinery he invented for the discovery of the Truth. Man's mind was drowned in the scholastic discussions of the ancient writings. " Silkworms weave their cocoons to imprison themselves." While the Loh-Wang school did not gain a strong foothold in its native land, it went across the sea and exerted a strong influence over the leaders of Japan.[29]

3. THE RELATION OF THEORY AND PRACTICE. *Conduct, the Criterion of Knowledge.* Confucius takes conduct as the standard for judging the final value of knowledge. According to him, the

---

[29] The Wong Yang-min school was introduced to Japan towards the end of the sixteenth century. It soon gained influence among the scholars and began to be at war with the Ch'ing-Tsu School, which had been introduced three centuries before. This led to the eventual suppression of the new school during the latter part of the seventeenth century. Later on, it gradually gained ascendancy and reached its culmination when the new era of Japan began.

men who possess vast erudition receive no practical benefit if they do not know how to use it. He says, " Though a man may be able to recite three hundred odes, yet if, when intrusted with a governmental charge, he knows not how to act, or if when sent to any quarter on any mission, he cannot give his replies unassisted, notwithstanding the extent of his learning, of what practical use is it ? " [30] On the other hand, the extent of one's knowledge can be judged by his conduct. Tse Hsia says : " If a man withdraws his mind from the love of pleasure, and applies it as sincerely to the love of virtue ; if, in serving his parents, he can exert his utmost strength ; if, in his intercourse with his friends, his words are sincere; although men say that he has not learned, I will certainly say that he has." [31]

Knowledge is not for knowledge's sake, but for conduct's sake. [32] Lu Tun-lai says, " The possession of a vast amount of knowledge is not for ornament, but for practical use." [33] With Ch'ing-tse, " the possession of an ' inch ' of conduct is better than a ' foot ' of knowledge." [34] With Tsu-tse, the " possession of knowledge without putting it into action is the same as not possessing it." [35]

Interrelation of Knowing and Doing. There seems to be no better illustration for this than these words of Tsu-tse. " Knowing and doing," says he, " may be likened to the two wheels of a carriage, of the two wings of a bird ; it is impossible for one to fulfill

---

[30] *The Confucian Analects*, Book XIII, *Tsze Loo*, Chapter V.

[31] *Id.*, Book I, *Heo Urh*, Chapter VII.

[32] " This is not necessarily contrary to the saying, ' Truth for Truth's sake,' which may mean either to seek the Truth without reference to its practical value or to do so without reference to the personal honor or fame. Confucius stands for ' Truth for Truth's sake' in the latter sense. With reference to one who is fond of learning, he says, ' Is he not a man of complete virtue, who feels no discomposure though men may take no note of him ? ' "—*Confucian Analects*, Book I, Chapter I, Section 3.

" In emphasizing the spirit of scholarship, Confucius says, ' If a man in the morning learns the Truth, he may die in the evening without regret.' "—*Id.*, Book IV, *Lee Jin*, Chapter VIII.

[33] *Chinese Encyclopedia*, Volume 83, *Hsieh Wen Pu Tson Lun*, Book I, Page 4.

[34] *Id.*, Volume 94, *Tuh Su Pu Tson Lun*, Book III, Page 33.

[35] *Id.*, Volume 85, *Hsieh Wen Pu Tson Lun*, Book III, Page 47.

its functions without the other." [36] In another place he says, "In view of the process, knowing is prior to doing; but in view of the emphasis, doing is more important than knowing." [37] In a letter to his friend he says : " It is a great symptom of the present time that those who devoted themselves to the pursuit of knowledge do not pay much attention to practical life, and men of practical life think that knowledge is of no value to them. But they do not realize the fact that to secure knowledge through practical life would make knowledge more certain and conduct more forcible." [38]

Knowing Is Doing. It is Wong Yang-min who firmly held to the principle that knowing is doing and doing is knowing. In a letter to his [39] friend, he says : " To do with clear sight and conscious effort is knowing and to know with true insight and definite idea is doing. On the contrary, to do without clear sight and conscious effort is doing haphazardly. It is what Confucius said, ' Learning without thinking is blind,' therefore, we must say ' to know.' And to know without true insight and definite idea is but an illusion. It is what Confucius said, ' Thinking without learning is vain.' " [40] In a letter to another friend, he says: " No knowledge in the world can be called so without putting it into action. When we start to know, we have already started to do."[41] In some other place, Wong Yang-min says: " Knowing is the beginning of doing; doing is the accomplishment of knowing. It is but one continuous process, and cannot be divided into two." [42] Again he said in an earnest manner to a disciple: " And now you want to separate knowledge and action into two parts. What is the purpose ? When I say that they are but one, what is the purpose ? If you do not know the purpose, of what use is it to discuss whether knowledge and action are two or but one ?

---

[36] *Chinese Encyclopedia*, Volume 91, *Tsze Hsin Pu Tson Lun*, Page 19.
[37] *Ibid.*
[38] *Id.*, Page 12.
[39] *Id.*, Volume 83, *Hsieh Wen Pu Tson Lun*, Book I, Page 5.
[40] *Chinese Encyclopedia*, Volume 91, *Tsze Hsin Pu Tson Lun*, Page 36.
[41] *Id.*, Volume 86, *Hsieh Wen Pu Tson Lun*, Book IV, Page 25.
[42] *The Dialogue of Wong Yang-min*, Section 26.

As I have said before, knowing is for the purpose of doing and doing is to put into effect what you know. Also, I have said that knowing is the beginning of doing, and doing is the accomplishment of knowing. If you understand its meaning, as soon as you say knowing, doing is implied; and vice versa. When the ancient philosophers say 'to do,' there is a reason for it. It is because there was a certain class of people who acted blindly without any thinking or reflection; therefore, they felt compelled to tell them to know in order to enable them to do. Again, there was another class of people who dreamed all day long without any action. Those people were simply chasing after a shadow. Therefore the ancient philosophers must tell them to do in order to enable them to know actually. . . . Nowadays, men divided knowledge and action into two courses to be separately pursued. They say that they want to know first and then they can do accordingly. They say, 'Let us pursue knowledge first; after we know well, then we may start to do.' Those people will never do anything throughout their whole life, and consequently they will never know anything. . . . When I say that knowing and doing are but one, . . . it is not something like castles in the air invented by my mind; but it is the truth and is actually so. If you understand the meaning, it would not do you any harm to say that they are two; because what you really mean is that they are but one. On the contrary, if you do not understand the meaning, no matter how many times you may say that they are but one, what good have you done? They are merely empty words!" [43]

Complete and Partial Knowledge. What Wong Yang-min meant by "knowledge and action are but one" is that complete knowledge includes both knowledge and action. For he says, " If we speak of knowledge analytically, we have five steps; namely, extensive study, accurate inquiry, careful thinking, clear discrimination, and firm action, but if we speak of it synthetically, we have only one kind of true knowledge [which includes action]." [44]

---

[43] *The Dialogue of Wong Yang-min*, Section 5.
[44] *Chinese Encyclopedia*, Volume 86, *Hsieh Wen Pu Tson Lun*, Book IV, Page 25.

Generally, when we use the word "knowledge," we mean a partial knowledge, a knowledge that is on its way to action. When one says that "knowledge is for knowledge's sake," he cannot mean that in the sense of complete knowledge. Because complete knowledge necessarily includes action. If he says that "knowledge is for action's sake," he means knowledge that is in its process towards action. Therefore to advocate "knowledge for knowledge's sake" is to advocate partial knowledge.

A theory is but partial knowledge before it is successfully applied. It occupies an organic part in the domain of human knowledge, not because as an end in itself, but as the beginning of an action. Knowledge would remain incomplete if it stops at the theory. On the other hand, if one begins to do without knowing what to do, he starts from a wrong end. Such seems to be the meaning of the philosophy of Wong Yang-min, that here I have attempted to interpret.

4. THE SIGNIFICANCE OF THE PROBLEM OF KNOWLEDGE IN EDUCATION. When education is to be dealt in relation with their mind, the problem of knowledge has direct concern with education. The intellectual training of the people has to be guided by the intellectual accomplishment of the human race. What is knowledge? How is it to be imparted to the people? What should individuals do to assimilate knowledge when it has been imparted to them? What is the final value of the knowledge which people are to receive? These can be answered by the conclusions reached from the inquiry into the problem of knowledge.

First, let me sum up what we have discussed in this chapter. Then, let us see what can be deducted from it with a view of application to the intellectual training of the people.

We already have seen before that knowledge is possible only when conception and perception work together; that in order to get knowledge, five steps of mental process are necessary; that to know is the beginning of to do, and to do is the accomplishment of to know; and that complete knowledge includes action.

When we apply these principles to the education of the mind, we see that in order to have any real knowledge, both the senses and the mind should work together; that in order to assimilate knowledge, the five steps of the mental process should be applied; that to know is the starting point of the whole series of mental process leading to the final end to do; and that in acquiring knowledge, action should be taken as the final aim.

CHAPTER VI

THE PROBLEM OF SCIENCE

Why Has China Not Developed Modern Science? After reading the previous chapter on The Problem of Knowledge, the reader, impressed with the objective view of truth as expounded by the Ch'ing-Tsu school, would naturally raise the question in his mind, Why has China not developed modern science? In view of the paramount influence exercised by modern science upon Western thought, it is one of the most important questions that the Chinese scholar has to answer.

The Western observers of China have often pointed out the fact that the Chinese people lack knowledge of modern science.[1] But we are not satisfied with simply knowing that it is lacking. We want to know the reasons for it.

Some of the Chinese Views of the Physical World. The Chinese are not uninterested in natural phenomena. They have their world scheme. According to the *Tsing Su* (晉書), records of the Tsing dynasty (A.D. 265-419), the Heaven is likened to the shape of an egg, and the Earth, the yolk which floats in the Heaven. The circumference of the Heaven is $365\frac{1}{4}°$. One half of the Heaven is above the Earth and the other half below. The Heaven is in constant motion, whirling around the Earth.[2] According to the *Tsai Su* (隋書), records of the Tsai dynasty (A.D. 589-617), the Moon has no light by itself. Its light is due to the reflection of the Sunlight. When the Sun and the Moon are facing each other, the observer standing in the middle of the two, we have the full moon. When the Sun shines upon one part of the Moon, the observer looking at the side, we have the crescent.[3] *Pen Tsao*

---

[1] Eliot, Charles W., *Some Roads to Peace*, a report to the Trustees of the Carnegie Endowment for International Peace on observations made in China and Japan, 1912, Pages 26-29.
[2] Chan Yuan-lun (陳元龍), *History of Physical Sciences*, published in 1723, Book I.
[3] *Id.*, Volume 2.

Kan Mu (本草綱目) tells us that the animal's hair looks like grass because it is living in the mountains and the bird's feathers look like leaves because it habitates the trees.[4] The *Seh Yuan* (釋源) tells us that man is erect and therefore he knows perfectly; animal is horizontal and therefore it knows partially; the plant is upside down and therefore it has no sense of knowing.[5]

Chan Yuan-lun (陳元龍), in his *History of Physical Sciences* (格物鑑源),[6] besides dealing with topics on practical arts such as Carriages and Ships, Buildings, Musical Instruments, and so on, includes Astronomy, which is subdivided into The Heaven, Sun, Moon, Stars, Wind, Thunder and Lightning, Clouds, Dew, Frost, Snow, Hail, Rainbow, and Fog and Mist; Geography, which is subdivided into The Earth, Mountains, Ocean, Water, Well, Bridges, City, Graves, and so on; The Human Body, subdivided into The Head, and Brains, Hair, Heart, Liver, Lungs, etc., Hands, Feet, Bones, Blood, etc.; The Grains, subdivided into Rice, Oats, Wheat, etc.; The Vegetables, subdivided into Sunflowers, Onions, Ginger, Eggplant, etc.; Trees subdivided into Fir, Palm, Camphor, Mulberry, Willow, etc.; Grass, which contains some fifty varieties; Flowers, some sixty varieties; Fruit, some forty; Birds, some sixty; Animals, some thirty; Fish; and Insects.

The contents of the different topics are gathered from various books from the writings of the earliest period of Chinese history down to the beginning of the Ming dynasty (A.D. 1368). It is therefore physical science as revealed through books. The divisions and classifications are unscientific in the modern sense—as, for example, cats are placed in the same group with dogs and pigs, because they are all domestic animals, and tigers with the other wild animals such as wolves and foxes. They are not grouped according to their inherent nature as in modern zoölogy, but according to their uses and modes of living.

---

[4]Chan Yuan-lun (陳元龍), *History of Physical Sciences*, Volume 9.
[5]*Id.*, Volumes 77 and 82.
[6]Published in 1723.

In the preface, Chan Yuan-lun says: "The physical bodies are everywhere. The Heaven and Earth are physical bodies. Human knowledge has no boundaries. Whatever is in our mind is knowledge. The true scholar is ashamed if he leaves one thing unknown. For this reason we must investigate things. The functions of the physical bodies are called 'affairs.' Those by which they are called are names. The groups into which they are gathered are called classifications. . . . They take form according to the various combinations of the five elements: Metal Wood, Water, Fire, and Earth, and are in active life and motion according to *tao* [truth, natural law]. When examined by the human agencies, such as hands, eyes, mouth, and ears, the *reasons* for their existence are inexhaustible through time eternal."

The author of the *History of Physical Sciences* views, as it was traditionally so, the Universe as a material world. The five elements are the mother of all physical bodies. By the various combinations of these five elements, the physical world, whether animate or inanimate, is produced. There is the natural law, *tao*, which controls the various combinations.

Speculations on the Physical World. Tsu-tse, whose chief interest was to study the teachings of Confucius, discussed the geological formations of the Earth in the following manner:

"Before the birth of the world, it is presumed that there are only two elements, namely, Water and Fire. The substance of the water solidifies and becomes the Earth. When we view the other mountains on the top of a mountain, we see that they take the form of waves. These are formed by water. It is unknown why it coagulates. At first it must be very soft, and gradually it becomes solid."

In discussing the geological changes of the Earth, Tsu-tse said: "We often find the shells [fossils] of clams and other shellfish upon the top of the mountains, even in the rocks. These rocks were once earth and the shells contained in the rocks were once sea shells transferred from the bottom of the ocean to the top of the mountains as are the shells, and changed from soft form into the solid body as the rocks. If we think deeply, we may discover the reasons why these shells have been transferred from the bottom of the ocean to the top of the mountains, and why rocks have taken their solid form from soft matter."[7]

Wong Yang-min's Turning Back to the Inner Truth. Wong Yang-min, who had learned from earlier philosophers that everything contains truth and that a single stalk of grass or a single tree contains *tse li*, or Supreme Reason, took a piece of bamboo that grew near his study windows and investigated it with deep thinking until he became ill as the result of continuous effort.[8] In his later years, he related this to his disciples as an illustration of the principle that only in the mind men can find truth. He said : " People have said that to search for truth one should follow Tsu-tse's method of investigating things [material]. But they never did practice it. It was I myself who did use his method in all seriousness. Years ago Mr. Chien and I myself decided that to be a sage, one must investigate the physical bodies in the world. Then I told him to take a piece of bamboo and investigate it. Mr. Chien worked continuously attempting to find out what truth there is in the bamboo, until the third day when he became ill on account of mental fatigue. I told him that he was not physically fit for that work, so I began to do it by myself. I too spent days and nights, but failed to discover any truth in the bamboo, and became ill on the seventh day. We both sighed and said, ' It is hardly possible to be a sage, because we are not equal to the sages both mentally and physically to investigate the things.' Afterwards, when I was in exile, I thought about the matter and realized that no physical bodies in the world are worth investigation. To investigate things means to investigate our own mind. Then I was fully confident that everybody could be a sage."[9]

What the Chinese Philosophers Are After. The aim of Tsu-tse and Wong Yang-min is to prove that Reason, *tse li*, or truth exists everywhere. Their main interest is not in finding out the reasons for the existence of particular physical bodies, such as the fossils in the rocks or the formations of the bamboo ; but by proving that

---

[7] Huang Tson-hi, *The History of Philosophy During the Sun and Yuan Dynasties*, Volume 48, Pages 20, 21.

[8] *The Works of Wong Yang-min*, Volume I, *Biographical Notes.*

[9] *Id., Dialogues*, Section 196.

their existence has a cause, and that it is to support the existence of the Unitary Ideal called Reason, *tse li, tao*, or Truth. While Tsu-tse was apparently satisfied with his naïve way of observing the geological formations of the Earth or the formations of the fossils in the rocks, by means of *unaided senses* and *thinking*, Wong Yang-min closed his door to the physical world and contented himself in searching for inner truth in the mind.

Unitary Ideal as Compared with Division of Knowledge. So far as our investigations are concerned, we can here dismiss Wong Yang-min who turned back to the mind in which he searched for Reason. On the other hand, Tsu-tse was seeking for truth in the physical world. But his main interest did not lay there. He was seeking for the Unitary Ideal through the partial light revealed by the investigation of physical bodies. Therefore his aim and method were fundamentally different from Aristotle. The latter, " instead of the deeply poetic temperament [that of Greek philosophy prior to Aristotle], which sees all things in relation to a unitary ideal, fuses them to form a single picture, and endeavors, by all sorts of partial lights, to adnumberate the definite and unspeakable," possesses " what is more closely allied to the scientific type of mind, parceling out the universe into several spheres, untiring in its search for facts, fertile in its explanations which are marked by practical good sense, and which are based on historical and scientific considerations."[10]

The parceling out of the universe into several spheres and searching for facts therein, the essential process in the scientific method of searching for truth, are wanting in the Confucian philosophy.

Aristotle divides knowledge into several spheres as follows: Logic, the method to his philosophical investigations;[11] Metaphysics, the task for the investigation of the causes of reality; Physics, for the investigation of the causes of natural existence;[12] Practical philosophy, which consists of Ethics and Politics, dealing " with an activity to which knowledge serves only as a means."[13]

---

[10] Rogers, *Students' History of Philosophy*, N. Y., 1913, Page 102.
[11] Zeller, *Aristotle*, Chapter V.
[12] *Id.*, Chapters on *Metaphysics and Physics*.
[13] *Id.*, Chapter XII.

Chinese philosophy, as represented by the Confucian school, is mainly interested in practical philosophy, namely, Ethics and Politics. All other interests are subordinated to the main one. Later we shall see why it leads from an interest in Ethics and Politics to an interest in searching for the Universal Reason.

The effort of the Confucian school to search for the Universal Reason in the investigation of particular things, as long as the aim remains unchanged, will not likely lead to the study of the parceled-out spheres of the universe and the causes and relations therein. The investigations conducted by the Chinese philosophers in the physical world are not primarily for an interest in Nature for its own sake, but for seeking through the partial light a better understanding of the Universal Reason, to which the existence of all things in the universe is due.

Beginning of Modern Science in Europe. As long as there is no great interest taken in Nature, there can be no natural science. This can be made plain by inquiring into the causes for the birth of modern scientific thought in Europe during the Renaissance. In the philosophy of the Renaissance, according to Höffding, there is " a great enthusiasm for, and confidence in Nature." It begins with " the assertion of the rights of human nature " and " afterwards leads to the development of a new conception of Nature, and to a new method of investigation."[14] But it is " through the beliefs and methods of the Greeks, that the Renaissance students were led to direct observation and experimentation with natural phenomena."[15]

It was in Italy first that the Renaissance became an accomplished fact. Here, in philosophy, "nearly every system of ancient times was revived. Plato, the artistic among philosophers, attracted a large following, and a Platonic Academy was founded in Florence. In opposition to him, other schools set up Aristotle, interpreted not as he had been by the church, but freely and naturalistically." [16]

---

[14] Höffding, *History of Modern Philosophy*, Volume I, Page 9.
[15] Monroe, *Textbook on the History of Education*, Page 356.
[16] Rogers, *Students' History of Philosophy*, Page 224.

THE PROBLEM OF SCIENCE 73

Great impetus to the birth of modern science was given by the increased commercial and industrial activity among the Italian towns. A great industrial rivalry sprang up among the towns. Each sought to surpass the other in technical skill, and jealously guarded new inventions and machines. "This practical turning to account of the forces of Nature," says Höffding, "increased the knowledge of their mode of working and could not fail to arouse interest in the discovery of their laws." "The appearance of a Leonardo or a Galileo is only comprehensible when taken in connection with Italian industry, just as Pomponazzi and Machiavelli are only comprehensible in connection with the intellectual development and the politics of Italy."[17]

In quick succession came a series of inventions of world-wide significance. The telescope laid open the structure of the Heavens; the compass enlarged the boundaries of the earth. "To realize the new possibilities in the way of knowledge, a brilliant group of scientists of the first magnitude—Tycho Brahe, Copernicus, Galileo, Kepler, and others—whose investigations gave a firm foundation to those scientific methods and conceptions which were destined to enter so vitally into all future thought."[18]

Chief Reasons Summarized. After a study in the birth of natural science during the Renaissance, we find the chief reasons are: (1) Revival of Greek learning, (2) great enthusiasm for Nature, (3) new methods of investigation, (4) impetus given by industrial and commercial activity of the Italian towns.

Chinese Thought as Compared with European. The great revival of learning during the Sun dynasty (A.D. 960-1277), during which period the great philosophers Ch'ing-tse and Tsu-tse and their opponent Loh Shang-san lived, is comparable with the revival of Greek learning during the Renaissance. The teachings of Confucius were then seriously studied and invigorated. The methods to knowledge, namely, investigation of things in order to attain understanding, and the five steps—extensive study, accurate inquiry, careful thinking, clear discrimination, and firm action—

---

[17] Höffding, *History of Modern Philosophy*, Volume I, Page 161.
[18] Rogers, *Students' History of Philosophy*, Page 226.

found their origin in the two Confucian classics: namely, *The Great Learning* and *The Doctrine of the Mean*. Upon these the philosophers of the Sun dynasty built their edifice of methodology which we have discussed in the previous chapter.

Aphorical as Against Systematic Presentation. But two important elements of the Greek methods to knowledge are lacking in Confucius. The one is the systematic presentation of a problem like Plato and Aristotle, for Confucius never was a systematic philosopher in the Greek sense. His statements of truth are essentially aphorical. Besides the methods as mentioned above, Confucius as well as Mencius has not left to the Chinese thinkers any comprehensive system comparable with that of the Greek philosophers. The aphorical statements of Confucius give room to various interpretations, while the systematic presentation of knowledge by Plato and Aristotle gives the Western world a comprehensive method of systematizing, and thereby controlling, knowledge.

The other element, which is lacking, as we have pointed out before, is the parceling out of the universe into several spheres and the search for facts therein.

This lack of system and division of human knowledge creates unfavorable conditions for studying natural phenomena. What the Renaissance students got from the Greeks, the philosophers of the Sun dynasty failed to obtain from the ancient Chinese.

No Great Enthusiasm for Nature. The philosophers of the Sun dynasty never felt great enthusiasm for Nature. As we have seen before, the incidental and isolated study of Nature by these philosophers was for the purpose of searching for the Universal Reason through the investigation of particular physical bodies. Consequently there was devised no new method of investigation.

The sole aim of the investigation of things, as we have seen before, is to prove that the Unitary ideal called Reason exists everywhere and in everything. Ch'ing-tse said that " nothing exists without *li* or Reason. Only by the investigation of things you will understand the existence of Reason." " To know the names of birds, animals, herbs, and trees is for the understanding of Reason."[19] Then why is it that these Chinese philosophers of the Sun dynasty were so much interested in seeking Reason?

The Central Problem of the Confucian School is what may be termed the politico-ethical problem. As we have discussed it in Chapter I, *Background of Education*, suffice it to state here the meaning of politico-ethical: that it is for the interest of the state, that the individuals must devote themselves to their personal culture, and that upon the basis of morals the state must conduct its affairs.

The Great Learning tells us that the method for the cultivation of the person is to secure understanding. The method to secure understanding is to investigate the things. What is understanding? The philosophers of the Sun dynasty answered that it is to understand Reason.[20] Hence, the whole problem is to search for Reason for the purpose of the cultivation of the person leading to the final aim—governing the state.

Why Search for Reason. Stimulated by Hindu philosophy which had taken root in China, and the philosophy of Lao-tse, commonly known as Taoism, both of which are something more than the practical trends of thought of the Chinese, and vexed with the chaotic social and political conditions, and with the continuous threatenings of the Tartars, the philosophers of the Sun dynasty attempted satisfactorily to solve the problem. Hindu philosophy and the philosophy of Lao-tse they denounced as impracticable for governing the state. They sought for enlightenment in Confucian philosophy. The teachings of Confucius and his school had never been so systematically studied as they were then. It was the first time that the Confucian methodology was so seriously applied in searching for truth. As before, their main interest was centered in the politico-ethical problem. They attempted to show by means of Reason that there is a natural order

---

[19] *Chinese Encyclopedia, Tsze Tsze Pu Tson Lun*, Volume 89, Page 27.

[20] Tsu-tse said: "To govern the State, to attain peace in the world, to be sincere in thought, to cultivate the person or to govern a family is but one Reason. What *The Great Learning* means by 'to secure understanding by means of the investigation of things' is but to seek for Reason. This is the fundamental idea of that great book."—Huang Tson-hi, *The History of Philosophy of the Sun and Yuan Dynasties*, Volume 49, Page 1.

in which all politico-ethical affairs exist. Every happening or occurrence in political and moral affairs is not haphazard. Therefore, in order to have the proper administration of the state and proper conduct of men, the law of this natural order must be found to serve as a proper guidance. This is what the philosophers called Reason, which they endeavored to discover. It may in a way be called positive politico-ethical science.

Reason as a Panacea. Had they used this conception as the basis and studied the cause and effect of the politico-ethical phenomena without generalizing in the unitary ideal, Reason, they might have achieved certain results. But they went too far. They took Reason as some kind of panacea by means of which all politico-ethical diseases could be cured.[21]

By going one step further, they endeavored to support the existence of Reason by showing that even in the physical world, Reason also reigns supreme.

SUMMARIZED ANSWER TO OUR QUESTION. The main problem is politico-ethical. Reason is the universal weapon by means of which the problem is to be solved. Unlike Plato and Aristotle, Confucius's method of presenting truth is aphorical instead of systematic. Unlike Aristotle, Tsu-tse seeks for the unitary ideal, Reason, instead of parceling out the universe into several spheres. Unlike Kepler and Galileo, Tsu-tse's interest in Nature is only secondary. Philosophically speaking, these are the main reasons why China has not developed Modern Science.

SCIENCE and MODERN CHINESE EDUCATION. Science has Nature as its subject matter with a systematic method of investigation. We must no longer allow politico-ethical problems to occupy all the spheres of knowledge. An intense enthusiasm

---

[21] In his two memorials to Emperor Hsiao-Tsong, Tsu-tse said : " A sovereign should secure his learning by investigation of things in order to attain understanding. The changes in affairs and things must be observed. Then wherever the truth is, your Majesty will be able to see it clearly. Thus your Majesty will be naturally sincere in thought and rectified in mind. This is the way to manage the affairs in the world."—Huang Tson-hi, *The History of Philosophy of the Sun and Yuan Dynasties,* Volume 48, Page 1.

" The method explained in *The Great Learning* teaches one to investigate things in order to attain understanding. Your Majesty has not tried to see Reason in the affairs and use Reason to manage them. This is why that peace and prosperity have not been attained."—*Ibid.*

THE PROBLEM OF SCIENCE 77

for Nature must be aroused and a systematic method of investigation must be introduced. We must enter into the spirit of Science.

The mere introduction, into the schools, of physics, chemistry, or other sciences taught in a formal way, would not have much result in cultivating scientific interest unless we understand the spirit of Science. In order to balance the overemphasis of politico-ethical problems, the students in the Chinese schools must be directed to make friends with Nature and must be led to systematic experimentation and observation.

CHAPTER VII

RELATIVE VALUES IN KNOWLEDGE

In the previous chapter, we have shown how politico-ethical problems occupied the main attention of the scholars of the Confucian school and therefore, knowledge concerning the solution of these problems is of most worth. The sphere of these problems, however, is so wide that no individual could ever grasp the whole field. The Chinese philosophers were conscious of this fact. Tsu-tse, therefore, in his *Aims of Study* (學 的), said, " The search for truth should aim at what is in close relation to the self." " If we try to seek the truth of everything in the world without regard to close relation to the self," said he, " it may be likened to riding on a wandering horse without a destination."[1] Su Tun-pu (蘇 東 坡), famous essay writer of the Sun dynasty, told us that to get what the individual wants should be the guiding principle of study. To quote him : " To study may be likened to setting sail to seek goods. When you find so many things that you cannot possibly take them all, you choose just what you want."[2]

These views on relative values of knowledge as expressed by the Chinese scholars are similar to those of a modern Western scientist and scholar, David Starr Jordan, who, in answering Spencer's question, " What knowledge is of most worth ? " said, " That which is of most worth to me."[3]

While Spencer, in his Education, held that since Science is most valuable to the service of men, knowledge that is most

---

[1]*Chinese Encyclopedia*, Volume 85, *Hsieh Wen Pu Tson Lun*, Book III, Page 38. While Tsu-tse was consciously seeking for the Universal Reason which he regarded as a kind of panacea by means of which all political and ethical diseases could be cured, yet here he contradicts himself by recognizing relative values in reasons or that reasons have different values to different individuals or to the different purposes of the individuals.

[2]*Id.*, Volume 92, *Tuh Su Pu Tson Lun*, Book I, Page 37.

[3]Jordan, *The Voice of the Scholar*, Chapter IV, *Relative Values in Knowledge*, San Francisco, 1903.

worth is Science; Jordan, by going one step further, held that since the field of Science is so wide that no one can ever master all sciences, a different sort of answer should be given. He advocated that in a real Republic of the University all men and all studies must be put on one footing. "The student of the human body, the investigator of matter and force, the lover of Greek art, all meet on equal ground on the university's hospitable campus" (page 91). "This once done," said Jordan, "the question of 'what knowledge is of most worth?' is one for each man to answer for himself. What knowledge is of most worth to me?"

But how is this to be answered? Jordan went on to say this: "Let the young man or young woman of to-day ask, 'What knowledge is of most worth to me?' In the course of study of our American universities will be found the unhampered answer, the answer of Herbert Spencer, if you like, the answer of Agassiz, or Emerson or Eliot or White, the materials for your own answer, whatever it be. And whatever you may require, you will not turn away empty-handed" (page 94).

With Spencer, there is an order in which the different branches of knowledge are to be arranged according to their intrinsic values; that education which prepares for direct self-preservation, that which prepares for indirect self-preservation, that which prepares for parenthood, that which prepares for citizenship, that which prepares for the miscellaneous refinements of life. Thus Spencer measured relative values in knowledge from the standpoint of education for the human race: while Jordan tackled the problem from the standpoint of education for the individual.

Tsu-tse and Su Tun-pu viewed the problem from the same angle as Jordan. For "to get what you want," with Su Tun-pu, or "to seek truths shall be guided by what is of close relation to the self," with Tsu-tse, is a problem for the individual to solve for himself.

With Jordan there are two conditions that are necessary before each individual is able to answer for himself the question "What knowledge is of most worth to me?" These are (1) a proper curriculum from which the individual is given opportunity to select, and (2) the personal influence of the teacher from whom the individual can look for guidance.

The conditions Tsu-tse had in mind, we have no means of proving. Presumably they are the teachings of Confucius and his school from which the individual is to select what is of close relation to himself. Su Tun-pu set up a purpose according to which the individual is to select what he wants. To quote him: " The learner should have only one purpose at a time in his study. For example, if he wants to learn the causes of the rise or downfall of dynasties, or prosperity or declining of a country, he keeps this alone in view and seeks only for that which is related to his purpose." Thus Su Tun-pu did not discuss relative values in knowledge *per se*, as to compare the one body of knowledge to the other as Spencer did : but they were to be determined by the purpose of the learner. Tsu-tse, likewise, did not view the problem from the angle of relative values in knowledge *per se*, but set up " what is of close relation to the self " as the criterion for determining relative values in knowledge. However, this comparison of the one body of knowledge to another seemed to these Chinese scholars to be unnecessary, since their main attention had been occupied by the politico-ethical problems and implicitly that knowledge concerning the solution of these problems was regarded of most worth.

In the old time when China was by herself and life was simple, the political and ethical teachings of the Confucian school might be sufficient for attaining personal culture and national solidarity ; but in modern times, on the other hand, when she is no longer an isolated nation and life is becoming more and more complex on account of modern industrial and commercial activities, to limit the sphere of knowledge in the Confucian school, or even to extend to all the knowledge possessed by the old China, and to determine relative values therein, is nothing short of a suicidal policy.

As we have seen repeatedly in the previous chapters, the chief interest of the Chinese philosophers of the Confucian school is politico-ethical. Any interest beyond that is more or less subsidiary. How are we to secure the well-ordered state? they asked. The answer was to have a well-ordered family first. To have a well-ordered family required first of all the cultivation of the individual. "From the sovereign down to the mass of people, the cultivation of the person is the root of everything."[4]

And naturally what has most directly to do with the cultivation of the individual with a view of securing the well-ordered state is rather politico-ethical knowledge than the knowledge of Nature. Hence, social philosophy is inevitably held superior to natural philosophy.

It is undeniable that to govern a nation well we must have the cultivation of the person as the foundation. Uncontrolled natural forces just as much as uncontrolled human forces, however, will do violence to a nation. The frequent overflow of the Hui River, carrying with it through many centuries innumerable numbers of houses, crops, and human life, and frequent visits of plagues sweeping away a larger number of life, have done just as much harm to the people as a poor statesman who held the reins of government.

The above illustration is only a negative factor. When we take the positive side into consideration, who can deny that the development of national resources just as much as the development of the personal character of that people, is essential to the welfare of the people? To the knowledge of the conduct of man, therefore, must be added the knowledge of the conduct of Nature. Who will be the Chinese Spencer who is to expound the value of science in China?

Two scholars of the old time, Tsu-tse and Su Tun-pu, and a scholar of modern time, Jordan, took *selection by the individual* as the criterion for judging relative values in knowledge. But Jordan, being a modern man and profiting by modern experience, pointed out the conditions under which the individual is at liberty to answer by himself " what knowledge is of most worth to me? " a proper curriculum from which the individual is to select what is of most worth to him, and a proper teacher from whom he is to seek for advice.

Tsu-tse and Su Tun-pu, being men of the twelfth century whose mental horizon was limited to the ancient knowledge, contented themselves with selecting what the individual wants in

---

[4] *The Great Learning, Text of Confucius*, Section 6.

the narorw field. Of course it was undreamed of by them that any knowledge beyond the scope of ethics and politics would have equal value.

I am not criticizing the scholars of the old time, rather is it my purpose here to tell the modern Chinese that those old sayings which are of value must be adjusted to modern conditions.

Before following the advice of these two scholars as to relative values in knowledge, we must consider first under what conditions their suggestions are valuable. The conditions are this— Let the varieties of different fields of knowledge as essential to the many-sided activities of modern life be put before the learner, and opportunities be given every one to select what will adequately suit his purpose or needs. Once this is done, these views of the Chinese scholars will be a valuable guidance to the learner.

China needs well-organized modern institutions of learning, where the admirer of the teachings of Confucian schools, The advocator of Greek art, the investigator of microörganisms, the student of plants or of animals, the builder of railways and bridges, the student of modern Western philosophy, all meet on equal ground. Once this is done, the question of relative values in knowledge may be determined either by Tsu-tse's doctrines that the search for truths must be guided by what is of close relation to the self, or Su Tunpu's idea to get what one wants according to the purpose of the learner.

CHAPTER VIII

THE FUNDAMENTAL ELEMENTS OF LEARNING

The process of learning is indeed a complicated one. What we attempt to discuss here are some of the fundamental elements which are, according to the various Chinese philosophers, essential to successful learning. As the materials were scattered in the voluminous writings of the various thinkers, I have here endeavored to systematize them under the following headings: (1) General Attitude of the Mind Towards Learning, (2) Factors in Learning, and (3) The Use of Knowledge.

1. GENERAL ATTITUDE OF THE MIND TOWARDS LEARNING

Definite Purpose. It is of paramount importance to set up a definite purpose or aim in learning. " To study," remarked a Chinese scholar in the old time, " was just like learning how to shoot. When you had a bow and arrow in your hands, you must know first the target and then you could practice shooting at it. If the shooter did not care to locate the target, what was the use for him to hold the arrow and bow and practice shooting? "[1]

Practically all the Chinese philosophers put special emphasis upon having a definite purpose in learning. Such leading thinkers as Ch'ing-tse, Tsu-tse, Loh Shang-san, and Wong Yang-min discussed its paramount importance. To quote Wong Yang-min: " There is nothing more important in learning than to set up a definite purpose. If there were none, it might be likened to a tree without roots. It was simply useless to water and manure it."[2] Once he said to one of his disciples: " When one did not succeed in learning what the sages had taught him, the reason was to be found in having no definite purpose. When one aimed

---

[1] *Chinese Encyclopedia*, Volume 85, *Hsieh Wen Pu Tson Lun*, Book III, Page 7.
[2] *The Works of Wong Yang-min*, Volume V, *Essays*, Book IV.

at making chariots, he would become a chariot maker, and when he aimed at making clothes, he would become a tailor. . . . I have not yet seen any one who did not succeed in doing certain things if he had aimed at them. . . . I have not yet seen any person who did succeed in doing certain things if he had not aimed at them. Have a definite purpose first and then you can begin to learn. For instance, you are a native of Min and are naturally interested in that place. If I were to talk to you about Hsieh, my native place, you would not pay much attention to me. I am a native of Hsieh and interested in that place. If you were to talk to me about Min, your native place, I would not pay much attention to you."[3] On one occasion in giving advice to his disciples, Wong Yang-min said : " If one had no definite purpose, he might be likened to a boat without a helm and a horse without a rein. He was simply wandering about without any definite destination."[4]

These words of Wong Yang-min illustrate very well the importance of a definite purpose or aim. In modern educational theory, McMurry's insistence on a definite aim for the pupil, and in modern psychology, Thorndike's general law of behavior on attitudes, dispositions, preadjustment or " sets " as a condition of learning are notable illustrations.[5] It will suffice us to say here that in study or learning, we must have a definite purpose or aim around which all our interests shall cluster and towards which all our energy shall be directed.

Concentration or " Seeking for the Lost Mind." After we have a definite purpose, we must work whole-heartedly towards it. To quote Ch'ing-tse : " If one has a definite purpose and did not make advancement in his knowledge, it was because he was lacking in energy [on account of dissipation]."[6] Mencius's doctrine of "Seeking for the Lost Mind" was taken by the later Chinese philosophers as the guiding principle for the necessity of concentration

---

[3] *The Works of Wong Yang-min*, Volume V, *Essays*, Book IV.
[4] *Id.*, Volume XII, *Supplements*, Book I.
[5] McMurry, *How to Study*, Boston, 1909, Chapter II. Thorndike, *Educational Psychology*, N. Y., 1913, Volume II, Chapter II.
[6] *Chinese Encyclopedia*, Volume 85, *Hsieh Wen Pu Tson Lun*, Book III, Page 10.

in learning. "When men's fowls and dogs were lost, they knew how to seek for them," said mencius, "but they lost their mind and did not know how to seek for it. There is nothing more important than to seek for the lost mind." [7] What Mencius meant by the "lost mind" is dissipation of the mind; by "seeking for the lost mind," concentration of the mind.

Mencius took the case of chess playing as an illustration of the value of concentration. There were two men who were studying chess playing under the best chess player in the country. The one gave his whole attention to the subject and did nothing but listen to the teacher. The other, although he seemed to be listening to him, directed his mind to a swan which he thought was approaching, and wished to bend his bow, adjust the string to the arrow, and shoot it. Thus his attention was divided, and therefore, although he was studying along with the other man under the same famous teacher, he did not make as much progress in the art of chess playing.[8] Of course, there were other factors to be considered in the case of learning chess playing that Mencius told us, such as unequal intelligence, previous training, and the like. Other things being equal, concentration of the mind to the activities of the work engaged in is one of the most important factors in learning.

Open-mindedness. In order to receive anything, the mind must be in a receptive mood. Any prejudice on the part of the learner would undoubtedly impair his growth in knowledge. "The improvement in one's self," says the book of *Shu Kin*, "is derived from studying with open-mindedness and continuous activity."[9] "At the beginning of learning," said Lu Tun-lai, "one must be open-minded in order to receive good things in the world. Arrogance is contrary to the proper way of learning."[10] "The learner should not hold fast to his old views," said Tsu-tse; "in order to see the new meaning he must first get rid of his old views.

---

[7] *The Works of Mencius*, Book VI, *Kao Tsze*, Part I, Chapter XI.
[8] *Id.*, Chapter IX, Section 3.
[9] *Chinese Encyclopedia*, Volume 83, *Hsieh Wen Pu Tson Lun*, Book I, Page 5.
[10] *Ibid.*

We must empty the dirty water in order to give way to the pure water." [11]

8. FACTORS IN LEARNING

Memory and Thinking. In practice, especially in recent times, Chinese education puts too much emphasis upon memory. Professor Paul Monroe, in the discussion of Chinese education in his *Text-Book on the History of Education* has pointed out the fact that, especially in the lower types of schooling, education is almost exclusively a memory training.[12] But this type of training is a degenerated form of Chinese education instead of a conscious effort of the leading educators. As early as the middle of the sixteenth century, Wong Yang-min attacked the existing elementary schools by saying that " since the bad practice of memory training and training in the formal essay writing began, the true teachings of the ancient sages were lost."[13] If we go back to the earlier times, we find the facts that the Chinese educators stood for thinking in preference to memory.

Ch'ing-tse (A.D. 1032–1107), in discussing the method of studying history, said, " In studying history, it is not sufficient merely to memorize the facts; it is more important to understand the causes of the rise or downfall of a country."[14] Lu Tung-lai said, " The youth who is bright and memorizes a large amount of information is not to be admired; but he who thinks carefully and searches for [truth] diligently is to be admired."[15]

Tsu-tse held a somewhat different view. "When you read," said he, " first, you should memorize it well so that the words contained in the book would be as familiar to you as if they were uttered by your own mouth; and then you should think carefully so that the ideas would be as clear to you as if they sprang from your own mind."[16] Thus he stated the order, first memorizing and then thinking, but not the point of emphasis.

---

[11] *Chinese Encyclopedia*, Volume 92, *Tuh Su Pu Tson Lun*, Book I, Page 26.
[12] *Id.*, Page 39.
[13] *The Works of Wong Yang-min*, Volume 4, *Essays*, Book III.
[14] Tsu-tse, *Chien Sze Lo*, Volume 3.
[15] *Chinese Encyclopedia*, Volume 94, *Tuh Su Pu Tson Lun*, Book II, Page 5.
[16] *Chinese Encyclopedia*, Volume 92, *Tuh Su Pu Tson Lun*, Book I, Page 31.

THE FUNDAMENTAL ELEMENTS OF LEARNING

When we come to Wong Yang-min, we find an entirely different attitude in reference to memory and thinking. One of his students asked him one day what could be done, for he could not memorize what he had studied. To this, Wong Yang-min replied, " What you want is to understand and not to memorize [what you have studied]." He went on further saying that " to understand [what you have studied] is only of secondary importance ; what you want is to know the sources [of truth] in yourself through study. If you simply want to memorize, you will not be able to understand ; and if you simply want to understand [what you have studied], you will not be able to know the sources [of truth] in yourself." [17]

Here we see that Wong Yang-min pointed out three points in getting knowledge. The first is memory, the second is to understand what is in books, and the last is to incorporate what one gets from books into his own experience. To regard memory as an end in itself is to be discouraged. To understand what is in books without reference to personal needs or experience is of secondary importance. The most important point is to digest thoroughly what one gets from books so that it becomes an integral part of his own experience.

Memory has its place in learning. As thinking cannot possibly go on in a vacuum, a certain amount of facts are required to furnish the materials for thought. Therefore the learner has to possess the essential facts in any given field of knowledge. But memory is often misused. It is misused when it is taken as an end in itself ; or to memorize isolated or nonessential facts ; or to memorize a given amount of undigested information.

Memory must be economized. It is too wasteful to follow the dictum of Tsu-tse that " you should memorize it well so that the words contained in the book would be as familiar to you as if they were uttered by your own mouth." Ch'ing-tse and Lu Tunglai told us that thinking is more important than memory, while Wong Yang-min stated that to take memory as an end in itself would prevent us from the proper understanding of a subject. These statements are in themselves pedagogically sound. But

---

[17] *The Works of Wong Yang-min, Dialogues,* Section 175.

we want to know more. We want to know what is the appropriate place for memory in learning and what is the proper method of using it, problems which these philosophers have not solved for us, and for which we must seek enlightenment from modern experimental psychology.

Thinking. " Learning without thinking is blind," said Confucius.[18] " Learning has its foundation in thinking," said Ch'ing-tse.[19] To quote him at further length : " The mind will be beclouded without thinking."[20] " Wisdom is from thinking. If one thinks long enough, wisdom will be the result."[21] To quote Ch'ing-tse : " In learning there is nothing more precious than thinking." " We must stand in awe before one who thinks searchingly, for truth is deep and only through exhaustive thinking, can one obtain it."[22]

There is abundance of evidence that the Chinese philosophers held thinking to be one of the most important factors in learning. But what seems to be wanting is a working method of thinking. The Chinese philosophers did not teach us how to think except in a fragmentary way. Here are a few of the specimens :

" If you cannot think out a certain thing, change to another thing to think with. Do not think on one thing all the time. For when one's thinking is choked in a certain direction, one cannot think it out no matter how hard he tries."—*Ch'ing-tse.*

" When you see something in reading, do not take for granted that what you see is right. Suspend your judgment for the time being. Then read more in order to get a new view. If you hold fast to one particular view, your mind will be colored by that particular view."—*Tsu-tse, Method of Study.*[23]

---

[18] *The Confucian Analects*, Book II, Chapter XV.
[19] *Chinese Encyclopedia*, Volume 89, *Tsze Tsze Pu Tson Lun*, Book V.
[20] *Id.*, Volume 85, *Hsieh Wen Pu Tson Lun*, Book III, Page 11.
[21] *Id.*, Volume 89, *Tsze Tsze Pu Tson Lun*, Book VI.
[22] *Id.*, Volume 105, *Tsze Tsze Pu Tson Lun*, Page 9.
[23] *Id.*, Volume 92, *Tuh Su Pu Tson Lun*, Book I, Page 36.

THE FUNDAMENTAL ELEMENTS OF LEARNING 89

However, it has been advocated by some of the philosophers that there should be a method of thinking if one desires to get a good result. To quote Wu Lin Chuen : " Any ordinary man thinks. Why does he not get any result ? Because he does not know the right method. Thinking without method is called haphazard thinking. How can one get results by engaging in such kind of thinking ? Thinking must be in accordance with a proper method." [24]

Assimilation. Knowledge is valuable to a learner only when it is incorporated into his own experience. It may be likened to food which is useful to the body only when it is properly digested. To quote Wong Yang-min : " Food is used to nourish the body. After eating, it must be digested. If it is merely deposited in the stomach without being digested, it decays. How can you expect it to aid the growth of your muscles ? Nowadays, learners obtain a vast amount of knowledge and deposit it in their minds (without being assimilated). This is a symptom of indigestion." [25]

Independent Spirit. True knowledge must be obtained for and by the learner himself. " To gain knowledge may be likened to taking food," said Tsu-tse; "when one is hungry, he will eat. . . . It concerns himself only. If one studies in that way, he will obtain a good result." [26] To learn is to satisfy one's mental hunger. It is for himself, rather than for others. " To learn diligently must be in accordance with one's own will," again said Tsu-tse. " He studies not because his parents or teachers want him to, but because he is so eager to learn. If, on the other hand, he does so because his parents and teachers want him to, he does it for them and not for the cultivation of his own person. There will be no good result." [27] One must learn by himself.

---

[24] " As he went on, he shifted his discussions to the moral ground saying that to think morally is the right thinking."—*Chinese Encyclopedia*, Volume 105, *Tsze Tsze Pu Tson Lun*, Page 14.

[25] *The Works of Wong Yang-min, Dialogues*, Section 161.

[26] *Chinese Encyclopedia*, Volume 85, *Hsieh Wen Pu Tson Lun*, Book III, Page 51.

[27] *Id.*, Volume 86, *Hsieh Wen Pu Tson Lun*, Book IV, Page 7.

In short, one must not be dependent upon others in learning. To quote Tsu-tse again: "If you are in doubt, think it out by yourself. Do not depend upon others for explanations. Suppose there was no one you could ask, should you stop learning? If you can get rid of the habit of being dependent upon others, you will make advancement in your study." [28]

Organic Growth. There was no occasion that the Chinese philosophers ever conceived the mind as *tabula rasa* on which knowledge could be inscribed. They always conceived that the growth of the mind was just like the growth of a grain of seed or a tree. The mind has its natural power to grow. Learning is simply to act in such a way that you will let your mind grow. "You cannot add a particle to your mind by learning," states the essay *Honoring Thy Teacher.* "You learn because you want to develop your natural ability. To learn properly is to nourish what is given by nature without hurting it [by artificial method]." [29] Men must seek knowledge just like a grain of seed does fertilizer. "The work of nourishing the mind is just like that of nourishing a grain of cabbage seed," said Tsu-tse. "A grain of seed contains potential life elements. In order to grow it needs to be watered and given fertilizers. If you say that the seed is there and it will send out its sprouts and roots by itself without necessary nourishment, it will never grow. So it is with your mind. When you see the truth, and say it is there and therefore that is enough, it will remain the same day after day, and year after year without any growth. This is just like the case of a grain of seed which will never grow without watering and manuring." [30]

It is the work of men to give nourishment; it is the work of nature to grow. What men can do is to provide the nourishment, and nature will take care of the growth. In discussing the relations between the work of nourishment and growth, Wong Yang-min said: "What you can see, hear, talk about and think is the work of nourishment; what you cannot, growth. Like planting a tree,

---

[28] *Chinese Encyclopedia*, Volume 85, *Hsieh Wen Pu Tson Lun*, Book III, Page 42.
[29] *Id.*, Volume 45, *Miscellany*, Book III.
[30] *Id.*, Volume 85, *Hsieh Wen Pu Tson Lun*, Book III, Page 46.

watering and manuring is the work of nourishment. What goes on day and night without interruption from sprouting till foliage is growth. Men cannot render any help to it. What can be done through the senses and mind is the work of nourishment, with growth is the natural result. What the sages taught us, no matter how deep it is, is but the work of nourishment. The learner is required only to do this tangible work; the intangible growth will take care of itself. He does not need to work for it." [31]

3. The Use of Knowlege

In the chapter on The Problem of Knowledge, we have discussed the relation between theory and practice or conduct as the criterion of knowledge. We now come to the discussions of the use of knowledge.

Knowledge as Instruments. Knowledge is the instrument by means of which men accomplish their work. " The mechanics make tools for the purpose of using them [to accomplish their work]," said Ch'ing-tse. " They will not make the tools that will be useless. So it is with knowledge. If knowledge is not for the sake of using it, for what purpose does one learn ? " [32]

Knowledge Not to Be Detached from the Actual Life. An under-officer, after listening to Wong Yang-min, said to him : " I am very much interested in what you said about learning. But I am fully occupied with my official duties, and therefore have no time to devote to learning." To this Wong Yang-min replied : " I have never taught you to detach yourself from your official duties and devote yourself to learning in a speculative way. Since you have official duties to perform, verily, true learning lies in your official duties. Suppose there is a lawsuit brought before you, do not be angry because of the rudeness of the defendant and thus let your judgment be affected by it. Do not be pleased because of the flattering words of the defendant and thus let your judgment be affected by it. . . . Do not render careless judgment because you are busy with other official affairs and have no

---

[31] *The Works of Wong Yang-min, Dialogues,* Section 24.
[32] *Chinese Encyclopedia,* Volume 85, Hsieh Wen Pu Tson Lun, Bock III, Page 9.

time to study the cases thoroughly. Do not let your judgment be influenced by the persuasion of others. . . . In your official duties lies proper learning. If you detach yourself from actual affairs, your learning will be up in the air." [22]

This teaching of Wong Yang-min explains explicitly and clearly that real knowledge is that which deals directly with one's actual life. As soon as one detaches himself from it, the so-called learning is superfluous and unreal.

The idea of this great teacher with regard to learning is twofold: for personal efficiency and for social good. The under-officer must handle his cases well—in other words, must be personally efficient. He must handle them with utmost justice, for social good. Then, if one is a doctor, his true learning lies in perfecting the art of medicine with a view to render services to his fellow men. If one is a teacher, his true learning lies in mastering the art of teaching with a view to render services for the young generation.

Knowledge, if it is properly acquired, is a means or way to right living. There are methods by means of which men acquire knowledge properly. We have discussed in this chapter some of the essential elements which the Chinese educators believed to be fundamental in acquiring true learning. There must be methods to knowledge and in turn knowledge itself is but a method to life.

---

[22] *The Works of Wong Yang-min, Dialogues*, Section 106.

PART III

PRINCIPLES OF TEACHING

When there is right way of teaching, there will be men of true wisdom. Teaching is to start from the common people. The training of wisdom is to start from children.—*Chen Hun-mao.*

There is no person in the world who is unfit to be taught; there is also no person in the world who should be neglected to be taught.—*Chen Hun-mao.*

To teach not by means of utmost sincerity is self-deception; to instruct not in an orderly way is but a stupidity.—*Wong Yang-min.*

PART III
PRINCIPLES OF TEACHING
CHAPTER IX
METHOD OF ELEMENTARY EDUCATION

Elementary Education as Differing from Higher Education. According to the Chinese principles of education, there is a fundamental difference, both in contents and method, between elementary education and higher education. The distinction between the two was clearly marked in the earliest time of the history of Chinese education. According to *The Book of Rites* (禮 記), during the Chow dynasty (周) (1122-255 B.C.), the period for elementary education was between the age of eight and fifteen. Higher education began at the age of fifteen and continued for nine years. In the primary or elementary school, the boy was taught sprinkling and sweeping the ground (洒 掃), answering and replying questions put to them by the teacher and elder (應 對), and advancing or receding properly before an elder (進 退). He was also taught the six arts (六 藝 : rituals, music, archery, charioteering, writing, and arithmetic. In the higher institutions the student was taught the method of seeking truth (窮 理), personal culture (修 身), and governing the state (治 國).[1]

The contents and method of higher education have already been discussed in the second chapter. Here it will suffice us to say that it takes the cultivation of the person as the foundation and then is followed by governing the family, the state, and finally the world. To attain *summum bonum* is the final aim of the cultivation of the person. To investigate things in order to attain proper understanding is the starting point. Therefore, the method of higher education is to develop the individual by means of *knowledge*, the method of elementary education, by means of *conduct*.

---

[1] Tsu-tse (朱 子), *The History of Elementary Education* (小 學).

Method of Elementary Education[2]

The Aim. To form a right habit for the youth to serve as the foundation to higher learning is the aim of elementary education. In the introduction to *The History of Elementary Education*, Tsu-tse says that the elementary education for forming right habits must precede higher learning. " The learner must be taught to practice while a youth in order that the growth of wisdom may be correlated with that of habit, and the development of the mind with that of character, thus eliminating the conflicting tendencies between the two."

The Ancient Curriculum. During the Chow dynasty (1122-255 B.C.) the Ministry of Education established a curriculum for teaching the youth throughout the country. How far and how extensively it was carried out we have no means of knowing. So far as we can find from the ancient documents, the curriculum consists of three headings (大司徒以三物教萬民). The first is for the training of virtue ; the second, conduct ; the third, arts. There are six virtues (六德) which are to be trained. The first is wisdom (智), to teach the virtue of knowing ; the second, benevolence (仁), to teach the virtue of being benevolent ; the third, sagacity (聖) ; the fourth, righteousness (義) ; the fifth, truthfulness (忠) ; the sixth and last, harmony (和), to teach the virtue of the harmonious adjustment of feelings.

Under the second heading, for the training of conduct, there are again six kinds of conduct (行六). The first is filial piety (孝) ; the second, brotherly love (友) ; the third, *meh* (睦), to teach the conduct of love for the relatives in the same clan ; the fourth, *yin* (婣), to teach the conduct of love for the relatives by marriage ; the fifth, responsibility (任), to teach the conduct of willingness of taking responsibility ; the sixth, and the last, charity (恤), to teach the conduct of helping the poor and sick.

Under the third and last heading, for the training of arts, there are again six divisions. The first is rituals (禮) ; the second,

---

[2] This section is based upon Tsu-tse's *The History of Elementary Education* unless otherwise noted. It was first published March 1 (Chinese), fourteenth year of the reign of Hsiao Tsong of the Sun dynasty, A.D. 1170.

music (樂); the third, archery (射); the fourth, charioteering (御); the fifth, writing (書); the sixth and last, mathematics (數). There are five kinds of rituals, six kinds of music, five kinds of archery, five kinds of charioteering, six kinds of writing, and nine kinds of mathematics.

The training for virtue, conduct, and arts is commonly called the teaching of the three things (三 物 之 教). It has been taken as a model in a modified form by the Chinese educators during the subsequent ages. It consists mainly of moral training with some of the elements for intellectual and physical education. However, as time went on, the emphasis gradually shifted its ground. No matter how vague may be its meaning, the ancient curriculum seems to be well balanced. During the subsequent ages, however, the training for conduct overbalanced the rest, and finally the training for the six arts was almost unheard of, except rituals and writing. The training of virtue, which consists both of intellectual, such as wisdom and sagacity, and moral such as benevolence, righteousness, truthfulness, and harmonious adjustment of feelings, was regarded the same as the training of conduct.

Tsu-tse's Idea of Elementary Education. Tsu-tse, in *The History of Elementary Education*, which he claimed to be an attempt to restore the lost teachings of the ancients, includes mainly instances of the famous men and women in history teaching the youth the proper conduct, or examples of their own conduct. In the preface, summarizing the method of primary education of the ancient time, he says: " The method of primary education is to teach sprinkling and sweeping the ground, replying and receding ; and love for parents in the home and respect for elders out of the home. If the youth is capable of doing more besides, he is to be taught poetry and reading, and singing and dancing." Wong Yang-min, whose method of teaching children contains, as we shall see later, many essential elements of modern ideas of teaching, had essentially the same program as Tsu-tse.

Wang Yang-min's Curriculum for Primary Schools.[3] As we have seen in the previous chapter, Wong Yang-min (1472-1528)

---

[3] *The Works of Wong Yang-min*, Volume IV, *Essays*, Book III; *General Idea of Teaching Children*, instruction to teachers, Liu Peh-chun and others.

belongs to the school of independent thought. To him education is of an organic growth.[4] But no matter how independent one's thought may be, no man seems to be able to free himself entirely from traditions. So he simply took the traditional curriculum with some modifications. As marked out by tradition, his chief aim of education was to teach a modified form of six conducts, or almost the same as a part of Tsu-tse's method ; that is, to teach love for parents in the home, respect for elders out of the home, and, if the youth is capable of doing more, he is to be taught poetry and reading, and singing and dancing.

While he was about to leave his official post, perhaps as imperial examiner for the civil examinations for the province of Shantung, Wong Yang-min described his method of teachings in his instructions to the teachers under his jurisdiction. An exact translation of the text is as follows :

1. CONDUCT

" Every morning when the children come to school, the teacher should ask them, one after another, whether they practiced love for the parents and respect for their elders as they ought to when at home ; whether they behaved properly on the streets while on the way to school ; whether their words, thoughts, and conduct were faithful and earnest. The children must answer truthfully. If they have deviated from the above teachings, they must be taught not to let it happen again. If not, they must be encouraged to keep on improving it. The teacher must see to it that the particular cases are studied and proper ways used to advise them. These being done, the pupils are to be seated and study their lessons.

2. SINGING

" The pupils are required to resume proper posture in singing. The breath must be regulated properly. The voice must be clear

---

[4] Attention of the reader is called to the fact that Wong Yang-min derived his naturalistic idea of education from Mencius.

and distinct. Attention should be paid to rhythms and notes. After singing properly for a while, the pupils will feel to be in good spirit and their thoughts and feelings well balanced and harmonized. In each school the pupils are to be divided into four classes. Take one class each day. While the class is singing, the other three classes are to be seated and to listen attentively. Every fifth day, all the four classes are to sing together. Every fifteenth day, on the first and fifteenth of each month, all the pupils in the different schools are to gather together and sing at the neighboring college.

3. PRACTICE OF RITUALS

" In practicing rituals, the pupils are required to be calm in mind, dignified in manner, and proper in motion. After considerable practice along these lines, they will be dexterous in performance and firm in virtue. The pupils are to be divided into four classes, as in singing, and are to take one class every other day. While the class is practicing, the rest of the three classes are to be seated and to watch attentively. These pupils are to be excused from copy writing, which is to be taken up on alternate days. On every tenth day, all the four classes are to practice together. On every fifteenth day, on the first and fifteenth of the month, all the pupils in the different schools are to gather together and to practice at the neighboring college.

4. READING

" In reading, it is not the quantity that counts but thoroughness. The individual difference should be the determining factor for the amount of work given. If a pupil is capable of reading two hundred words a day, give him just one hundred words. Always make the pupils feel easy in study. Thus he will not get tired of study, and, besides, he will enjoy studying by himself. When pronouncing the words, he should concentrate his mind. While he is uttering sounds from his mouth, he should think in his mind. Every word and sentence should be studied again and again. Regulate his voice and pacify his mind. After some time, he will see the meaning in the proper light and thus his wisdom will be developed day by day.

5. THE ORDER OF DAILY WORK

"The daily work should be carried out in the following manner: First, examine the conduct of the pupils; then hold recitation and reading; next, practice rituals or copy writing, followed by reading and explanation; lastly, singing. The practice of rituals and singing are to help the child concentrate his mind, making him enjoy his work without being tired and thus keeping him from doing evil.

"If the teacher knows the above-named suggestions well, he will have no difficulties in carrying out the proper teaching. However, this is only a general plan. It is to be left to the teacher himself to see the true spirit of teaching."

Wong Yang-min's Principles of Teaching Children.[5] There are several points which are fundamental to Wong Yang-min's idea of teaching children. As it has been commonly held by all leading Chinese educators, moral training is above everything else. He attacked the prevailing system of education in his time, which was formalism. The children of his time were taught to memorize past records for the purpose of composing formal essays. This was regarded as a stepping-stone to pass state examinations in later years; but it had no bearings upon the actual moral life of the child. Therefore, Wong Yang-min said that since the education of this formalism began, the ancient principles of giving moral training to children were lost. According to him, the child should be taught the fundamental elements of moral training, such as filial piety, brotherly love, loyalty, truthfulness, and the like. These he took to be the fundamentals of teaching. Besides, the child should be taught the cultural elements, as Wong Yang-min called them: singing, practicing rituals, and reading. According to him, singing was to be taught for the expression of emotions; the practice of rituals, for the development of manners; reading, for the development of intelligence. But all of those were taken as aids to the moral development of the child. By means of singing,

---

[5] *The Works of Wong Yang-min*, Volume IV, *Essays*, Book III; *General Idea of Teaching Children*, instruction to teachers, Liu Peh-chun and others.

practice of rituals, and reading, the child is unconsciously led to the harmonious development of its moral nature.

All these things should be taught according to the natural interest of the child. To quote him directly: " The child is naturally fond of play and afraid of being restrained. The child grows like a bud springing. If given freedom, it grows; if prevented, it withers. Therefore, the child must be guided towards natural activities. Its mind must be made happy, in order not to check its growth. Good teaching to the child may be likened to a timely rain or a spring breeze to the plant. When plants receive the beneficial effects of a timely rain or a spring breeze, they send out their buds. Day by day, and month by month, they grow! On the other hand, if a frost comes, the life of plants will fade fast away!" [6]

Wong Yang-min, therefore, regarded the growth of the child like that of the plant; he compared good teaching to the child with a timely rain or a spring breeze to the plant, and bad teaching with frost. While the growth of the child is natural, it is conditioned by good or bad teaching.

Why must singing be taught? According to Wong Yang-min, pupils, through singing, are given opportunity for free expression of their play-instinct as well as to the expression of emotions. Again, through the practice of rituals, they are given the opportunity of physical exercises and of cultivating good manners; for the various motions they go through in practicing rituals will aid the circulation of the blood and will exercise the muscles. Reading is not only for the development of intelligence, but also for keeping pupils' minds occupied.

Wong Yang-min advocated that a school should be a place where the children would feel happy to go. He criticized the existing conditions in schools, and the methods of teaching then practiced. He said that the children were treated as prisoners who were constantly under whips and in chains. To quote his own

---

[6] This naturalistic idea of education of Wong Yang-min is undoubtedly derived from Mencius. Mencius, in enumerating five ways of teaching, said that one of these is to teach like a seasonable rain.—*The Works of Mencius*, Book VII, *Tsin Sing*, Part I, Chapter XI.

words : " In recent times, a teacher knows only how to force the children to read sentences and to practice copy writing daily. He compels them to restrain themselves without the proper guidance through practicing rituals. He exacts wisdom from them without nourishing them properly. He whips and chains them as prisoners. It is no wonder that the children regard the schoolhouse as a prison and are afraid to enter, and regard the teacher as an enemy and hate to see him. Naturally they will escape from the school in order to satisfy their instincts of play, and lie and cheat to evade punishment and thus let loose their bad traits. Deceitful and stupid they go down and down, day after day. While the teacher is thus forcing pupils to a lower level, he expects them to do good. How absurd it is ! "

From the discussion given above, it may be seen that Wong Yang-min's principles of teaching children embodied the embryonic ideas of modern pedagogy as advanced by Rousseau, Pestalozzi, and Froebel. With Wong Yang-min, the child was not regarded as a small man, but as the human bud. Its growth is organic and natural. Teaching was regarded as a timely rain or a spring breeze. The right of children to play was recognized, and the instincts of play were to be guided and harnessed through singing and practicing rituals. The interest of the child was taken as the guiding principle of teaching, and the harsh treatment of the child by the teacher was denounced and discouraged. Children must be made happy and free in school. They must be made to feel that they study not because the teacher wants them to, but of their own will. If we try to read into the mental picture of Wong Yang-min of a school, do we see that the buds on the trees in a garden send out their tender tips while a timely rain is sprinkling or a spring breeze is gently blowing ? Do we see that the gardener is busy weeding, fertilizing, and clipping and trimming ? Thus may we say that Wong Yang-min anticipated the idea of the kindergarten three centuries before Froebel ?

As every one of the principles of Wong Yang-min given above is contained in his instructions to the teachers under his jurisdiction, it is reasonably sure that they were more than a mere paper document. They contain not only the principles of teaching, but also a working program. How much influence he exercised upon the schools of his time, we are at the present moment not yet able to tell.

The Place of Music and Physical Training in Elementary Education. Chinese education, whether in the elementary or higher stage, was permeated with moral atmosphere. Every activity was dominated with the moral idea. Modern educators are interested to see whether the Chinese have seen the importance of music and intellectual and physical training in elementary education. As we have seen before, the ancient curriculum contained wisdom as one of the six virtues. We have no means of knowing how this was to be taught. In the six arts, writing and mathematics may be regarded as two of the elements of intellectual training, and archery and charioteering, of physical training. Music was one of the six arts. It has been commonly interpreted that these six arts contained the elements which come under the three essential divisions of modern education; namely, moral—rituals and music; physical—archery and charioteering; intellectual—writing and mathematics. But this interpretation seems to read too much of modern ideas into old education.

The ancients did not plan out the curriculum to conform with modern views. They had their own purposes and viewpoint. Moral education was carried out in the six virtues and the six conducts. The six arts were to supply the demand of the practical life of the time.

At this point a brief review of the social life during the Chow dynasty (1122–255 B.C.) seems to be necessary. The most important phases of social life during that time were worship and war. In connection with the worship of heaven, earth, stars, and other sublime forces of nature, and also the spirits of ancestors, there were varieties of rituals, as recorded in *The Book of Rites*. The youths, in order to be admitted later to society, were naturally required to know the various rituals and ceremonials. So it is with music, which was inseparable from worship and the other activities of social life.

In ancient times, during the period of feudalism, wars were conducted by means of chariots. The contributions for war from the feudal lords were, therefore, made in the form of chariots. On each *chin* of land, about one third of a square mile, one chariot, with several tens of men, was required for the contribution. Thus, a feudal lord who owned one *tun*, or one hundred *chin*, of land had to contribute a hundred chariots with a sufficient number of men. So it was obvious that the youths on the land were required to practice charioteering. So it was with archery, also a necessary art of warfare.

Writing and mathematics, it may be presumed, were taught as a rudimentary knowledge for the practical life, and not for the purpose of intellectual training.

As time went on, the conditions of social life were gradually changed. Youths were not required to prepare for their practical life by learning archery and charioteering, so these two arts disappeared. The case was the same with rituals. The chief aim of elementary education was to cultivate the moral conduct of the youths. The six arts were only for the practical purposes. The physical development resulting from parcticing archery and charioteering was only a by-product. The later philosophers interpreted the spirit of old elementary education only from their own viewpoint. Tsu-tse included, in his ideas of teaching children, reading, singing, and dancing, besides the moral training which was never lost sight of by any later philosophers. Singing, as his predecessor, Ch'ing-tse, declared, was to "nourish the feelings" and dancing to "help the circulation of blood."[7] Wong Yang-min, as did Tsu-tse, held that moral training was fundamental to education. He added to it the cultural elements which he called "the method of cultivation and nourishment." The cultural elements consist of singing, practicing rituals with dancing, and reading. As we have seen before, with Wong Yang-min, singing was for the expression of emotions as well as of the instincts of play; the practice of rituals, for the cultivation of good manners as well as for physical exercise; reading, for the development of intelligence as well as for keeping the mind occupied. Therefore, both Tsu-tse and Wong Yang-min saw the value of physical

---

[7] Tsu-tse, *Chin Sze Lu* (近思錄); *Collections on Philosophical Thoughts*, Book XI—A.D. 1176.

erexcises and intellectual training besides moral training, although the first two were regarded only as supplementary to the last one.

Let us briefly consider music. The ancient Chinese regarded music as a part of life. Ancient records tell us that music was then heard everywhere. Confucius was very fond of music. *The Confucian Analects* tell us that the Master did not appreciate the taste of good meals for three months after he had heard the music of Siao, in the kingdom of Hsi, which he liked so much. In *The Book of Filial Piety*, Confucius said that to reform a society, no influence was greater than music. " Hu An-tin (胡 安 定), after completion of the regular work, gathered all the students in the Ken-Zen Hall to sing and play on diverse kinds of musical instruments until the approach of darkness. And the students also sang and played when they went back to their dormitories. The whole school was filled with melodious airs." [8]

Furthermore, there was music connected with singing and dancing in Tsu-tse's program of teaching children; for a commentator told us that " singing was to match the tones and dancing, the air of music." Wong Yang-min did not tell us whether he required music in singing and practicing rituals. That, however, is immaterial, for not a philosopher in the Confucian school ever slighted music.

Will the Chinese Method of Teaching Children Help Solve Some of the Problems of Modern Education? The final aim of Chinese education is moral, but the Chinese do not regard morality as an isolated and abstract science, but as daily conduct. It is more obvious in the training of children. As Tsu-tse has well said: " The learner must be taught to practice when in youth in order that the growth of wisdom may be correlated with that of habit, and the development of the mind, with that of character, thus eliminating the conflicting tendencies between the two." If the art of life is living, the art of moral life is living morally. As to know is only the beginning of to do, mere knowing will not

---

[8] Wong Tson-hi, *The History of Philosophy of the Sun and Yuan Dynasties*, Volume I.

necessarily be carried into action. Then can we assure ourselves that the moral teaching we give abstractly and isolatedly to the children will be the guiding principles for moral life when they grow up? If so, moral teaching will be, indeed, very easy. Just give the children rules of conduct and ideas of right action and they will consult them when they grow up, just like engineers will consult their mathematics tables. If not, what is the use of giving them this so-called moral training?

Morality is an art. It is the art of action. Like piano playing, it cannot be taught *theoretically*, yet piano playing is comparatively more simple than moral conduct. The teacher of the piano knows only too well, that to teach piano playing is a continuous process of daily practice. On the other hand, the teacher of morals thinks that a few *theoretical* lessons in each week or on Sundays will impart to the children the complex art of moral conduct. What a miracle!

What shall we do then? We must know that to teach morals means to teach the intricated art of conduct. It can be acquired only through the continuous exercise of the conduct of daily life. Final success depends upon the daily accumulation and repetitions of every single proper conduct of daily life. Children must be made to realize that a single proper conduct contributes towards a large whole as " a small stream of water towards a river." Why did Wong Yang-min insist upon the teacher's questioning the children every morning when they come to school about their conduct at home and on the streets? It was exactly this idea of daily accumulations and repetitions of proper conduct. It is immaterial to define the standards for judging good conduct, for different social ideals in different times and places create different standards. The fundamental idea is that once it is considered a good conduct, the surest and most effective way of teaching it to the children is to put it into practice. After all, aside from its limitations and shortcomings, does it seem to us a wise plan that the method of elementary education as theorized and practiced by the Chinese is by emphasizing conduct in order to work out the correlation between the development of the mind and character?

The Danger of the One-sided View on Conduct. As to know is only the beginning of to do, over-intellectualizing would hinder action. On the other hand, practice without seeing the purpose or reason of it may tend to form undesirable habit. The reason for this seems to lie in the fact that modern society is dynamic, and therefore the individual is not only required to build up his character, but also to be able to adapt himself to the ever-changing condition of modern society. At the present time, China is actually experiencing two opposite extremes. The Chinese of the older generation, although of good character, seems to be unable to adjust himself to the novel situation that confronts his country. On the other hand, the young Chinese, although possessing new ideals of life and knowledge of new ethics, seems as yet unable to carry them into action. Consequently, the one is criticized for his stubbornness; the other, despised for his sophistication. During a transitional period of a nation's history, such a condition as this seems to be unavoidable. Education, however, will be considered a failure if it is unable to meet the demand of the time.

The effective side of the method of Chinese elementary education is its emphasizing of conduct. Its defect seems to lie in the fact that very little room has been left to the child to exercise his initiative or selective power. The logic of the moral training seems to be that moral laws are inviolable and unchangeable and the child must put them into practice. This logic is not based on the educational principle itself, but on the static view of social philosophy. The old Chinese society was chiefly agrarian, and consequently the moral laws were based on family ethics. As there is little change in an agrarian society, so long as the social strata remain unchanged, the old moral laws seem to need very little modification. But at the present time, industrialism has forced its way into China. A new set of social conditions has presented itself visibly in the life of the nation. As the old agrarian society is being rapidly transformed into the new industrial or economic society, family ethics have to be transformed into social ethics in order to meet the social demand.

Another defect seems to be that there is too little room given to the child for understanding the meaning of conduct. The idea that the child is incapable of understanding the meaning and therefore he must be taught to practice blindly what the adult thinks right, has to be banished from modern pedagogy. Under modern social conditions, blind conduct without the implication of the child's own purpose has little if any moral value.

The old idea of emphasizing practical conduct is not intrinsically mistaken. It has fulfilled the demand of static society by maintaining social stability. But as the new situation arises, the old idea has either to be modified or reconstructed. Therefore, in order to meet the new social demand, conduct, if a right one, has to be measured by its social value and must be a purposive action of the child.

CHAPTER X

THE FUNDAMENTAL ELEMENTS OF TEACHING

1. General Discussions

Why We Teach. Teaching is a direction or method the teacher gives to the learner to help him to discover by himself what and how to learn. Teaching as an end in itself does not exist. It is only a means to an end, that is, learning. "Nature that produces human kind has its inviolable ways," said Mencius, in quoting Yi Yin, "that those who know *the truth* prior to others shall, by virtue of the heavenly duty, guide them to know the same. . . . Since I see *the truth* first, I shall impart it to the people."[1] Mencius has thus expressed the true spirit of teaching.

A true teacher is the one who knows the true spirit of teaching. "The function of the teacher," said Han Yu, "is to impart truth, transmit learning, and clear away doubts." To quote him further: "Men were not born with knowledge, and therefore they have doubts. Those who are in doubt and do not know enough to seek for a teacher will be always in doubt. He who was born before us, and knew the truth earlier than we did, is our teacher. He who was born after us, in the case of his knowing the truth earlier than we, is also our teacher. We are but to learn the truth from teachers irrespective of whether they are older or younger than we, or whether they are of a higher station in life or a lower station of life than we are. Where the truth is, there is the teacher."[2]

Learning and Teaching but One Continuous Process. One cannot teach well unless he can learn well. A good teacher must be at the same time a good student. For if one does not know how to learn, how can he teach others how to learn? On the other hand, the ability to learn well does not necessarily imply

---

[1]*The Works of Mencius*, Book V, Part I, Chapter VII, Section 5.
[2] Han Yu, essay on *The Teacher*.

the ability to teach well. Learning is the foundation upon which teaching is to rest. Can we say that we have a house if in fact we have only a foundation? Learning is the beginning of teaching and teaching is the accomplishment of learning. "Teaching occupies a half of learning," says *The Book of History;* " we start from learning and end in teaching; learning and teaching are but one." [3]

Confucius is one of the greatest teachers of mankind and at the same time one of the greatest learners. Mencius told us that when Tsze Kung asked Cônfucius whether he was a sage, the Master replied that he did not dare to assume the title of a sage. But he said this to the disciple, " I learn without satiety and teach without being tired." Then Tsze Kung said to the Master: " To learn without satiety is wisdom and to teach without being tired is benevolence—wise and benevolent Master, you are a sage." [4] Thus Confucius was recognized by his disciple as a sage because he learns and teaches well at the same time.

Wong Yang-min also told us that learning and teaching are but one thing. When Wong Sin-fu, who was teaching at Yin Tien, asked him how to teach, Wong Yang-min replied: " To learn is the way to know how to teach. If you learn with your utmost energy, you will know how to teach." Again Wong Sin-fu asked, " How do we learn? " He replied: " To teach is the way to know how to learn. If you teach with your utmost energy, you will accomplish your learning. The wise man expects from the others only what he himself can do." [5] Then Wong Yang-min went on discussing the individual differences, which we shall see later.

2. THE PSYCHOLOGICAL PROBLEM IN TEACHING

Individual Differences. One of the most important elements in the method of teaching and probably the one most emphasized by all the philosophers of the Confucian school is the doctrine of Individual Differences. Confucius, both in theory and practice,

---

[3] *The Book of History*, quoted in *Chinese Encyclopedia*, Vol. 83, *Hsieh Wen Pu Tson Lun*, Book I, Page 6.
[4] *The Works of Mencius*, Book II, Part I, Chapter II, Section 19.
[5] *The Works of Wong Yang-min*, Volume V, *Essays*, Chapter IV.

THE FUNDAMENTAL ELEMENTS OF TEACHING

recognized that since the intelligence of the individuals is so much at variance, teaching cannot be extended uniformly to every one. As we have seen in the chapter on Nature and Nurture, Confucius told us that the highest class of men are born with knowledge; the next acquire knowledge readily through learning; the next, although slow, yet acquire it through a persevering application to learning; the last and the lowest are slow and stupid, yet do not learn.[6] Since there is the hierarchy of intelligence, we cannot do otherwise but to recognize the facts as they are when we come to the method of teaching. Therefore, Confucius told us that the highest branches of learning can be taught to those who are above mediocrity; but to those who are below it, the highest branches of learning cannot be taught.[7] The facts are further supported by this saying of Confucius: "Without giving teaching to the men who are fit to receive, we mistreat the men; if, on the other hand, by giving teaching to the men disregarding its fitness, we misapply teaching. A wise man neither mistreats the individual nor misapplies teaching."[8]

By recognizing generally that the intelligence of individuals is not equal, Confucius actually and specifically applied his doctrines. Thus he gave to the different disciples different ways of carrying out the principles of benevolence and filial piety. Here are a few of the examples taken at random. When Fan Che asked Confucius how to act according to the principles of benevolence, the Master said, "It is to love all men."[9] When Yen Yuen asked the same question, the Master said: "To control one's self and return to propriety is to act according to the principles of benevolence. Once you control yourself and return to propriety, the world will follow the principles of benevolence. It is you yourself to start the practice of benevolence and not the others.[10] Replying to the question asked by Tsze Kung, the Master said, "Do not do unto others as you would not wish others to do

---

[6] *The Confucian Analects*, Book XVI, *Ke She*, Chapter IX.
[7] *Id.*, Book VI, *Yung Yay*, Chapter XVIII.
[8] *l.*, Book XV, Chapter VII.
[9] *Id.*, Book XII, Chapter XXII, Section 1.
[10] *Id.*, Book XII, Chapter I, Section 1.

unto you."[11] To the question asked by Sze-ma New, he replied: "The benevolent man is cautious and slow in his speech; when a man feels the difficulty of doing, can he be other than cautious and slow in speaking?"[12] When Tsze Chang asked Confucius about the conduct of a benevolent man, the Master said: "If you are able to practice the five things, namely, respectfulness, generosity, truthfulness, earnestness, and kindness, you will be acting in accordance with the principles of benevolence."[13]

Confucius did the same thing when he taught filial piety to his disciples.[14] When Mang-Woo-Tse asked how to act according to filial piety, Confucius replied, "Parents are constantly worrying lest their children should be sick." To Tsze Yew, he said: "Filial duty nowadays means the support of one's parents. But dogs and horses likewise are able to do something in the way of support. Without reverence, what is there to distinguish the one support given from the other?" Confucius also gave different replies to different disciples when they asked about the conduct of government and the conduct of a superior man.

As to the meanings of the sayings of Confucius given above, some of them are quite obscure to us, especially to a Western reader. However, we are not concerned here to explain them. What we are interested in is that Confucius, as shown by the quotation given above, applied the doctrines of individual differences in his teaching.

The facts are further supported by Confucius's own explanation that he gave different instructions on the same subject to different disciples owing to the fact that there exist individual differences. *The Confucian Analects* tell us that when Tsze Lu asked whether he should immediately carry into practice what he learned, the Master said to him: "Since there are your father and elder brothers to be consulted, why should you act on that principle of immediately carrying into practice what you have learned?" But when Yen Yew asked the same question, the Master, on the contrary, said to him, "Immediately carry into practice what you

---

[11] *The Confucian Analects*, Book XII, Chapter II.
[12] *Id.*, Book XII, Chapter II.
[13] *Id.*, Book XVII, Chapter VI.
[14] *Id.*, Book II, Chapters VI, VII.

have learned." Being puzzled with these apparent contradictory words of Confucius, Kung-se Hwa asked the Master the reason why. The latter replied, " Kew [Yen Yew] is retiring and slow ; therefore I urged him forward. Yew [Tsze Su] is aggressive and forward ; therefore I kept him back." [15]

Commenting on Confucius giving different answers to the same question asked him by the different disciples, Tsin Teh Shu said : " The Master was acting on the principle that the different capacities or different intelligence of the individuals shall be developed in different ways. The sage teaches the people just like a carpenter makes his articles—in making different articles, various kinds of materials are used to suit the particular purpose." [16]

Now let us go back to Wong Yang-min.[17] To Wong Sin-fu, whom we have mentioned elsewhere in this chapter, Wong Yang-min told the reason why a teacher must know the principle of individual differences. After being told the unity of learning and teaching, Wong Sin-fu asked, " Since, as a matter of fact, there exist differences in such individual qualities as sternness or tenderness, or refinement or rudeness, can we apply one principle of teaching to all individuals ? " To this Wong Yang-min answered : " Since we act according to the principle of unity, we must recognize the principle of variance. When Nature produces things, there are differences in size : some are large and others are small ; some long and others short. But there exists a unity. It is the same with practical arts. Archmakers possess a different art than the metallurgists. But both are useful members in society. The carpenters make the frames of a house, the bricklayers build the walls, the painters paint them ; but there is only one aim, that is, all aim at building a house. Therefore, to acquire a particular method of doing things is an art. There are different kinds of skill, but for one sole purpose : to be useful.

" So it is with teaching. To give instruction according to individual differences is teaching. Each man is taught to develop

---

[15] *The Confucian Analects*, Book XI, Chapter XXI.
[16] *Chinese Encyclopedia*, Volume 107, *Tson Lun*, Book II, Page 6.
[17] See Note 5, anterior.

his particular abilities. But there is only one goal : good. From the method that Confucius used to teach benevolence and filial piety . . . we can learn the true meaning of teaching."

Then Wong Yang-min went on saying that " if every one be made an archmaker, there would be no metallurgist, and if every one be made a carpenter, there would be no bricklayer or painter. Different individuals are to be taught the different arts according to their fitness. Their usefulness is but one."

" The sages wish every one else to become a sage ; but the qualities of one individual are so much at a variance with those of another that various methods must be devised to suit each case. In variance, however, there lies a unity, and in changeability, there lies a universal method. To give instruction according to the individual differences in order to attain the same good is a universal method. Intelligence is different in each individual, but nature is common to all. Since human nature is good, teaching is only a return to the original nature of man."

Here we see that Wong Yang-min has three points in view. The first is that individuals are different in intelligence. The second is that human nature is universally good in spite of the varying degree of intelligence. The third is that teaching must be carried out in accordance with the above principles. Every man must be directed to the same goal—the good. But the same can be attained only through that teaching which is particularly fit to each individual.

A further study of this topic seems to lie in two directions. The first is to have an intensive study of individual differences in intelligence, capacity, or ability. Such study as this belongs to the field of experimental psychology. The attention of the reader is called to Thorndike's *Educational Psychology* on Individual Differences.[18] As it is beyond the scope of this treatise, we shall not attempt to discuss it here. The second is to have a particular study of the different social needs of pupils. As the modern school attempts to educate all the pupils of varying degrees of intelligence from different social environments and of different habits or

---

[18] Thorndike, *Educational Psychology*, Volume III, New York, 1913.

purposes of life, it is futile to attempt to give all the same course of study. Aside from underlying studies common to all, each pupil should be studied with regard to the habits and purpose of his life, and individual instruction should be given, so far as it is practicable, to each person.

Interest. By common experience alone, we know that the pupils learn better if they are willing to learn. How to make the pupils willing to learn is therefore an ever-present problem in teaching. Confucius never tried to force the pupils to learn, but led them to do so in an orderly way. In admiration of the Master's teaching method, Yen Yuen, the most promising disciple of Confucius, sighed and said : " When I looked up to my Master's teaching, it seemed to become higher ; when I tried to penetrate it, it seemed to become firmer ; and when I looked at it before me, suddenly it seemed to be behind. The Master gives me, step by step in an orderly way, the proper stimuli in such a manner that he leads me on and on." [19]

Mencius always made a point, in teaching people, to first arouse their interest. In this respect he was the most skillful of all teachers. His method was to start with what the person would likely be most interested in, and then to lead him to the desired topic. We can do no better than let Mencius speak for himself through his own writings.[20]

"Mencius, one day, called on King Huai of Liang. The king went and stood with him by a pond, and looking round at the large geese and deer, said, " Do wise and good princes also find pleasure in these things ? " Mencius replied : " Being wise and good, they have pleasure in these things. If not, though they have them, they find no pleasure in them. It is said in *The Book of Poetry* :

> " ' He measured out and commenced his Spirit-Tower;
> He measured it and planned it.
> The people addressed themselves to it.
> And in less than a day completed it.

---

[19] *The Confucian Analects*, Book IX, Chapter X.
[20] *The Works of Mencius*, which contain seven essays.

When he measured and began it, he said to them—
Be not so earnest :
But the multitudes came as if they had been his children.
The king was in his Spirit-Park ;
The doves reposed about,
The doves so sleek and fat :
And the white bird shone glistening.
The king was by his Spirit-Pond.
How full was it of fishes leaping about ! '

"King Wen used the time and energy of the people to build his tower and his pond, and yet they rejoiced to do the work, calling the tower ' The Spirit-Tower,' the pond ' The Spirit-Pond,' and rejoicing that he had his large deer, his fish and turtles. Because the ancient wise men had pleasure together with the people, they could enjoy it.

"In *The Declaration of T'ang*, it is said, ' O sun, when wilt thou expire ? We will die together with thee.' The people wished for Kee's death, even though they should die with him. Although he had towers, ponds, birds, and animals, how could he have pleasure in them alone ? " [21]

From these words of Mencius, we come to see clearly how skillfully Mencius led King Huai from his interest in geese and deer in his royal park to an interest in his people. He led him by quoting *The Book of Poetry* and *The Declaration of T'ang* to see that in order to enjoy these things, he must enjoy them together with his people, or they would rebel against him.

Mencius's teaching to the princes of his time was to love their people. They must administer their governments according to the principles of benevolence and righteousness. Moreover, instead of teaching them by dry-cut method, he always aroused their interest first. Mencius told us how he led King Huai of Liang from his love for war to love for his people,[22] how he led him from his love for music to love for his people ; [23] how he led King Shen of Tse from his sympathy for a trembling ox, which

---

[21] *The Works of Mencius*, Book I, Part I, Chapter II.
[22] *Id.*, Book I, Part I, Chapter II.
[23] *Id.*, Part II, Chapter I.

was about to be killed to consecrate a bell with its blood, to sympathy for his people;[24] how he led him on several occasions from his love for valor, for wealth, and for women, to the love for people.[25]

Mencius told the princes that their love for music, for wealth, and even for women was a good thing. But step by step he led them to see that their people, as themselves, were also fond of the same. So if they would enjoy together with their people, their love for them would bring happiness and prosperity to their kingdoms. Their fondness for war and valor also was good if, by means of these, they might attain a benevolent and righteous end.

What we have discussed above about Mencius's method of arousing interest may not be called teaching in the sense of school education. But this method of Mencius has exercised a profound influence upon Chinese educational thought. We may safely take this, therefore, as a method of teaching in the history of Chinese education.

The Chinese philosophers in teaching their pupils invariably held that willingness to learn is the starting point to successful learning; and the way to bring about willingness is to arouse the interest of the pupils. "If the pupils do not receive your teaching," said Chang Huang-chu, "it is of no use to force it upon them."[26] But the pupils would not be willing to learn unless they have sufficient interest in learning. "If you could not arouse the interest of the pupils," said Chen Min-tao, "they would not be willing to learn. Teaching them to sing and dance is a method of arousing their interest."[27] Tsu-tse told us that the interest of the students is more important towards maintaining discipline in the school than rules and regulations. In his instructions to teachers concerning the administration of schools, he said: "We do not have to be afraid of lack of rules and regulations in administering schools. What we should be afraid of is that the truth we try to impart to the students is not sufficient to arouse their

---

[24] *The Works of Mencius*, Part I, Chapter VII.
[25] *Id.*, Part II, Chapter III, Sections 4-8, Chapter V, Sections 4, 5.
[26] *Chinese Encyclopedia*, Volume 107, *Chiao Jen Pu Tson Lun*, Book II, Page 2.
[27] Tsu-tse, *Chin Sze Lu, Collections on Philosophical Thought*, Book XI.

interests. If they have not sufficient interest in what they study, the rules and regulations are inadequate for maintaining discipline in schools. If you try to carry out discipline by means of rules and regulations, it may be likened to checking the rapids, which run to a thousand feet below, with straws and weeds. There will be no effect whatever." [28] As we have seen in the previous chapter, Wong Yang-min maintained very strongly that the pupils must be made happy in schools and all the studies must be taught according to the natural interest of the child.

3. THE LOGICAL PROBLEM IN TEACHING

While the problems of interest and individual difference are psychological and taken as important elements of the method of teaching by practically all the Chinese philosophers, including Confucius, Mencius, Ch'ing-tse, Tsu-tse, Wong Yang-min, and others, there remains the logical problem whose issues caused a good deal of philosophical controversy in the later Confucian schools since the Sun dynasty (A.D. 952–1276).

Confucian and Mencian Types of Teaching. Although Mencius was the chief exponent of the teachings of Confucius a century after the death of the Master, and honored by the later Confucians as the sage second only to Confucius himself, there is a fundamental difference between the two in the logic of teaching. The teaching method of Confucius is to start from the actual conduct in particular cases to the generalization of the fundamental principles; while the method of Mencius, conversely, is to start from the fundamental principles which are, later on, substantiated by conduct in particular cases. Tsu-tse pointed out the difference by saying that "Mencius taught the people with emphasis on the big principles; Confucius, on the other hand, based his teaching on the practical application of conduct." [29]

As we have seen in the section on Individual Differences in this chapter, Confucius, in teaching the principles of benevolence

---

[28] Tsu-tse, *Instructions to Teachers. Chinese Encyclopedia,* Volume 106, *Chiao Jen Pu Tson Lun,* Book I, Page 31.
[29] *Chinese Encyclopedia,* Volume 106, *Chiao Jen Pu Tson Lun,* Book I, Page 27.

THE FUNDAMENTAL ELEMENTS OF TEACHING 117

and filial piety, always gave one phase of the big principles to various disciples. He told each of them the different things under one principle and, of course, expected the recipients to put them into practice. He even gave the different things under one principle to the same disciple at different times. We find in *The Confucian Analects* that Fan Che asked thrice about the conduct according to the principles of benevolence. Each time, Confucius gave a different answer. As we have seen before, the Master told Fan Che that to love all men is to act according to the principles of benevolence. Yet once he told him that "the benevolent man makes the overcoming of difficulty his first business, and success only a secondary consideration." And another time, he said to him that to act according to the principles of benevolence is "in retirement, to be sedately grave; in the management of business, to be reverently attentive; in intercourse with others, to be strictly sincere. Though a man may go among rude, uncultivated tribes, these qualities may not be neglected." [30]

Confucius's logic in teaching is to teach the individual conduct in particular cases and by the accumulation of particular cases, the learner will sometime see the whole truth spontaneously. "I accumulate truths by constant study," said Confucius, "and my growth is spontaneous." [31] When Confucius said this, he meant that in his daily work, he gathered his particular experiences, and from his experiences he spontaneously discovered the fundamental principles. One day he said to Chuen-tse, "Chuen, my way of discovering truth is but one—a unity all-pervading." [32] On another day he asked Tsze Kung, "Tsze, you think that I understand the truth because I learned many things?" Tsze Kung replied, "Yes; perhaps it is not?" "No," said Confucius, "by a unity all-pervading, I see the truth." [33] Thus Confucius held that the truth is only one—a unity all-pervading. By accumulating many a particular experience, one will see this all-pervading unity. On

---

[30] *The Confucian Analects*, Book VI, Chapter XXXI, Book XIII, Chapter XIX.
[31] *Id.*, Book XIV, Chapter XXXVII, Section 2.
[32] *Id.*, Book IV, Chapter XV, Section 1.
[33] *Id.*, Book XV, Chapter II.

the other hand, one must be conscious of this unity in order to understand the meaning of a particular experience. For example, benevolence is a unity which pervades all particular benevolent actions. To love all men is a benevolent act. To refrain from doing unto others what one would not wish others to do unto him, is a benevolent act. To act according to the five qualities—respectfulness, generosity, truthfulness, earnestness, and kindness—is also a benevolent act. These are particular actions, but pervading all these particular cases, there is a unity—benevolence.

Therefore, Confucius's logic in teaching is from the particular to the universal. On the other hand, the logic of Mencius is just the reverse. He always tackled the fundamental principles first. He taught others at the very outset to hold to the big principles and then showed them the methods by means of which they could attain the goal. Mencius told us in his own writings:

"Mencius called on King Huai of Liang. The king said: 'Venerable Sir, since you have not counted it far to come here a distance of a thousand *li*, may I presume that you are likewise provided with counsels to profit my kingdom?'

"Mencius replied: 'Why must your Majesty use that word *profit*? What I am provided with are counsels to benevolence and righteousness, and these are my only topics.

"'If your Majesty say, What is to be done to profit my kingdom? the great officers will say, What is to be done to profit our families? and the inferior officers and the common people will say, What is to be done to profit our persons? Superiors and inferiors will try to snatch this profit one from another and the kingdom will be endangered. . . .

"'There never has been a man trained to benevolence who neglected his parents. There never has been a man trained to righteousness who made his sovereign an after consideration.

"'Let your Majesty just say, Benevolence and righteousness, and these shall be the only themes. Why must you use that word *profit*?'"[34]

---

[34] *The Works of Mencius*, Book I, Part I, Chapter I.

During the first visit to King Huai of Liang, Mencius at the very beginning told him to hold the principles of benevolence and righteousness. During subsequent visits, Mencius explained to the king how he could make his kingdom prosperous by carrying out these fundamental principles in the administration of his government.

Here is one of the ways Mencius told the king for carrying out the principles of benevolence:

"If the seasons of husbandry be not interfered with, the grain will be more than can be eaten. If close nets are not allowed to enter the pools and ponds, the fishes and turtles will be more than can be consumed. If the axes and bills enter the hills and forests only at the proper time, the wood will be more than can be used. When the grain and fish and turtles are more than can be eaten, and there is more wood than can be used, this enables the people to nourish their living and bury their dead without any feeling against any one. This condition, in which the people nourish their living and bury their dead without any feeling against any one, is the first step of a benevolent government." [35]

In discussing the moral courage of man, Mencius told his disciple that his moral courage can never be affected by the outer forces, since he was forty years of age. The disciple asked him how he did it. Mencius said, "I am skillful in nourishing my vast, courageous morale." "What do you mean by your vast, courageous morale?" asked the disciple. Mencius replied: "This is the courageous morale—it is exceedingly great and exceedingly strong. Being nourished by rectitude, and sustaining no injury, it fills up all between heaven and earth—it is the mate and assistant of righteousness and truth. Without it, man is in a state of starvation."

Then Mencius told the disciple the method of attaining it by saying that "this courageous morale is produced by the accumulation of righteous deeds; it is not to be obtained by incidental acts of righteousness. If the mind does not feel complacency in the conduct, this courageous morale becomes starved." [36]

---

[35] *The Works of Mencius*, Book I, Part I, Chapter III, Section 3.
[36] *Id.*, Book II, Part I, Chapter II.

Thus Mencius first told his disciple the fundamental principle of maintaining moral courage—the vast, courageous morale—and then told him the method of attaining it by the accumulation of righteous deeds.

Therefore, Mencius's logic in teaching is from the universal to the particular.

Confucian Types of Teaching in the Later Confucian School. The representatives of this school are Ch'ing-tse and Tsu-tse.[37] Both of them believed in Confucius's synthetic method of teaching. Ch'ing-tse said: " If people want to understand the truth [universal], they must investigate things [particulars]. . . . And if they continue on doing this way many times [accumulation of particulars], some day they will spontaneously understand the truth [universal].[38] In another place, he said: "To exhaust the truth [universal] neither means to examine all the truths [particulars] in the world, nor means to examine just one truth [one particular case]; but it means the accumulation of many a truth [accumulation of many particulars]; and if many a truth has been accumulated, the understanding of the truth will come spontaneously." [39]

We find that Tsu-tse held the same principle as Ch'ing-tse. To quote him : " Everything and every affair [particular, objective] has its reason [universal, objective]. If we find one part of reason

---

[37] In advocating Confucius's logic of teaching, Tsu-tse said: "The desire of a learner for knowledge should be the same as that of a hungry man for food or a thirsty man for water. He should look upon knowledge as a matter of daily life. On the other hand, if he loves to talk about something extraordinary and uncommon, he speculates on something empty and unreal and deviates from the truth. Nowadays, the learner discusses the principles of benevolence with a view of understanding the meaning of it. Even should he see the true meaning of benevolence, he is not in the possession of it with reference to actual conduct. In *The Confucian Analects* you will find that the Sage taught his disciples to do just the practical work—starting from the lower plane and gradually ascending upward, from what is near to that farther away step by step. By the accumulation of daily practice in an orderly way, you will land somewhere."—Huang Tson-hi, *The Philosophy of the Sun and Yuan Dynasties*, Volume 48.

[38] *Chinese Encyclopedia*, Volume 89, *Tsze Tsze Pu Tson Lun*, Book III.
[39] *Id.*, Volume 85, *Hsieh Wen Pu Tson Lun*, Book III, Page 57.

in things and affairs [particular, objective], we will understand one part of the truth [particular, subjective]. The more you examine the truths [particulars, objective], the more you will understand them [particulars, subjective]. By piecemeal, we investigate things, and, as a whole, we understand the truth. Understanding and 'investigating things' are but one process. Speaking objectively, it is to investigate things; speaking psychologically, it is to understand them." [40]

Since Ch'ing-tse's logic is that of the accumulation of particulars, the universal principle is so deduced; while Tsu-tse, who held the same logic, went a step further by recognizing the existence of objective and subjective or psychological truth. The subjective truth is the result of the understanding of objective truth through the investigation of things. The subjective truth is conditioned by the objective truth. The truth exists in things (physical matter) independent of the mind. The mind understands the truth only through the investigation of things.

Directly opposed to the doctrines of Ch'ing-tse and Tsu-tse are those of Loh Shang-san and Wong Yang-min.

Mencian Types of Teaching in the Later Confucian School. The two last named are the representatives of this school.[41] As we have seen before in the chapter on The Problem of Knowledge, Loh Shang-san and Wong Yang-min held that truth exists only in the mind, and there is no truth outside of the mind. Take the principles of benevolence for example; benevolence is based upon the instinct of commiseration. Through the development of this instinct, it grows into maturity. It is the mind that recognizes benevolent deeds; and by accumulation of these deeds, the sphere of benevolence is gradually extended. Now, if we do not establish this fundamental principle as the controlling idea, the benevolent deeds one may do are but incidental.

---

[40] *Tsu-tse, Aims of Study*, quoted in *Chinese Encyclopedia*, Volume 89, *Tsze Tsze Pu Tson Lun*, Page 8.

[41] Commenting on Loh Shang-san, Chien Tsu-fong (全 祖 望) said: " Loh Shang-san's principle of learning is based on holding the essentials and is based on Mencius. This is a good remedy for those who have been drowned in the unworthy details."—Huang Tson-hi, *The History of Philosophy of the Sun and Yuan Dynasties*, Volume 58, Page 1.

There are two fundamental issues in these two types of the later Confucian schools. The one is subjective truth versus objective truth, which we have discussed in the chapter on The Problem of Knowledge. The other is analytic versus synthetic method of teaching, which is here under discussion. [42]

Loh Shang-san, as Mencius, in his logic of teaching, always started with the fundamental principles. "We must first pick out the big principle," said he, " and then we go to the details. If we do that way, we would feel free like a fish swimming in the sea." [43] In criticizing *The Confucian Analects*, he pointed out that " many a saying in *The Confucian Analects* is lack of the principal points." "For example," said he, "Confucius said, 'when a man's knowledge is sufficient to attain and his virtue is not sufficient to enable him to hold whatever he may have gained, he will lose again." [44] It does not tell us what it is to attain and to hold. Again Confucius said, ' Is it not pleasant to learn with constant perseverance and application ? ' [45] It does not tell us what it is to learn with constant perseverance and application. Therefore, if one does not possess the fundamental principles, these sayings are not easy to understand. On the other hand, if one does possess the fundamental principles, he will know that it is these principles that are to be attained with knowledge and to be held with virtue, and to be learned with constant perseverance and application. " [46]

It is the same with human experience. Unless there is a controlling idea, the fragmentary experience does not give us any meaning. It is the underlying principle that gives import to our experience.

---

[42] In the chapter on The Problem of Knowledge, we have discussed the controversies of the Ch'ing-Tsu and Loh-Wong schools. We have seen that the fundamental issue is epistemological—objective truth versus subjective truth. Here we are discussing the other issue in the controversy, i. e., logical—synthetic versus analytic method. These two issues are fundamental in the development of the later Confucian schools.

[43] Huang Tson-hi, *The History of Philosophy of the Sun and Yuan Dynasties*, Volume 58.

[44] *The Confucian Analects*, Book XV, Chapter XXXII.

[45] *Id.*, Book I, Chapter I.

[46] Huang Tson-hi, *The History of Philosophy of the Sun and Yuan Dynasties*, Volume 58.

THE FUNDAMENTAL ELEMENTS OF TEACHING

Wong Yang-min pointed out that " only with a controlling principle will our experience have a foundation." " Although the discrepancy between a principal idea and a particular experience may not be thus avoided, yet we will be able to control the general direction. To learn with a controlling principle may be likened to sailing with a helm. By turning the helm, the ship goes in the desired direction. Otherwise, although we are diligent in learning, we are simply gathering the incidental experiences which will have no bearing upon right conduct. This is neither a solid foundation nor a straight path [for seeking for truth]." [47]

Criticism. We cannot settle the question in the scholastic controversy by getting into the controversy ourselves. We must attack the problem from a different angle. Only from our own experience are we safe to seek for a new light in the old problem. So let us ask these two questions: How far do our particular experiences become universal? How far do our universal ideas control our particular experiences?

How Far Do Our Particular Experiences Become Universal? An isolated experience has no meaning. One way or another it must be connected with some other past experience, in order to understand the meaning of a new experience. For illustration, take the case of malaria. The primitive man believes that malaria is caused by the work of evil spirits, because he insinuated from the tradition that evil spirits are capable of making a person sick. The modern man discovered that malaria is caused by a certain kind of mosquito which carries malaria germs into the system of the infected person; because by virtue of his past experience he knows that germs are capable of causing diseases. The primitive man's idea of malaria is a certain kind of symptom caused by the work of evil spirits. To the modern man, it is a certain kind of symptom caused by the germs carried into the blood of the infected person by a particular kind of mosquito. A particular experience which has meaning must invariably be connected with some other experience.

---

[47] *The Works of Wong Yang-min, Dialogues,* Section 107.

But there is a world of difference between a right connection and a wrong one. In order to form a right connection, the connecting links must be consciously controlled. In the case of discovering the causes of malaria,—there are general principles used to control the connecting links. All the important factors of the controlling principle must first be laid out and then a definite scheme must be devised to carry out the experiment. In the case of malaria, two factors of the general principle must first be taken into consideration : (1) That germs are capable of causing disease. (2) That there must be some medium which carries the germs into the human body. Based on these two factors of the general principle, the questions are : (1) What are the particular germs that cause malaria in the human system ? (2) What is the medium that may possibly be found where the disease occurs ? All the precautions of modern scientific method and the aid of microscopes and other medical apparatus, lead to the discovery of the malaria germ and its carrier, a certain kind of mosquito.

Perhaps the primitive man, too, discovered the causes of malaria by particular experience. When the disease occurred, there might appear in the night some kind of objects which the primitive man believed to be evil spirits ; or the infected person, before being infected, might have visited some " haunted " place which the primitive man believed to be the den of evil spirits. If these incidents happened several times, he came to the conclusion that malaria was caused by a certain kind of evil spirits.

A certain kind of particular experience repeated for a number of times, would naturally lead to a certain general principle ; as Ch'ing-tse said, if we accumulated many a particular experience, we would some day understand the truth spontaneously.

However, there are particular cases which a person may have experienced, yet which will not lead to a general principle, no matter whether good or bad, right or erroneous. When a number of particular experiences leads to a general principle, whether good or bad, it necessarily implies the conscious effort of the person who is experiencing. It implies the " whyness " of the particular experience. When the primitive man discovered in the work of evil spirits the cause of malaria, it was most likely that he first inquired into the "whyness" of the disease. If he did not, he would not even be able to identify one case of malaria with another, not to speak of the cause of the disease.

Therefore, the consciousness of "whyness" of a particular experience links it with some other experience and thus gives it meaning, whether right or wrong. If we are to get the right meaning, we must start from a general controlling idea which in itself has been proved right.

When Ch'ing-tse and Tsu-tse said to investigate things, of course there is implied the question of "whyness" of the things. By the accumulation of many particular investigations, it is but natural that the understanding of the general principle will come to one's mind spontaneously. But it does not insure that this understanding is a right one if there is no right principle upon which the understanding is based.

Although providing from the particular to the universal. Ch'ing-tse and Tsu-tse's method cannot be called an inductive method in the modern scientific sense, because the general principle is worked out by the psychological aspect of the mind rather than by its logical aspect. The control of the particular experience by adequate means in modern inductive method for insuring the right meaning of that particular experience and right conclusion drawn therefrom is found wanting in the method of Ch'ing-tse and Tsu-tse.

How Far Our Universal Ideas Control Our Particular Experiences. From the general principle that evil spirits are capable of causing disease, the primitive man believed that malaria is the work of a certain kind of evil spirits. From the general principle that germs are capable of causing disease, the modern man discovered that malaria is caused by malaria germs carried into the human system by a certain kind of mosquito. Therefore, if the general principle is traditional, irrational, or unverified, its application to a particular case only leads to a wrong conclusion. On the other hand, the application of a rational or verified general principle to a particular case does not necessarily lead us to a right conclusion. It is conditioned by a good or a bad method. The malaria germs could not have been discovered by simply applying the general principle that germs are capable of causing disease, without taking various factors into consideration, and without adequate means to control the experiment.

There are particular situations and various factors which have to be taken into consideration to apply a general principle to a particular case. Acting according to the principles of benevolence, not a few have resorted to an inadequate means of extending indiscriminating charities. An indiscriminating charity will tend to create the habit of dependence and laziness among the people; it does harm to the society in general. Acting according to the principles of democracy, the form of long ballots was introduced with the idea that a direct control of the government, either state or municipal, by the people is a method to democracy. But the result was quite to the contrary, because many names of the nominees entered into the long ballots are unfamiliar to the voters, not to speak of the qualifications and abilities of the nominees. Thus it gives room for malpractice in politics. While the aim is democracy, the result is antidemocracy.

A general principle is but a working hypothesis. It only serves as a starting point or a general direction. To apply it successfully, it needs adequate means to control the various factors of a particular experience or experiment. Wong Yang-min was right when he pointed out that although the discrepancies between a general principle and a particular experience sometimes do exist, a general principle gives us opportunity to exercise a control over the general direction. But a general direction does not necessarily imply the " go " of our action.

A particular experience has no meaning unless there is a controlling principle; a general principle has no value unless it can be successfully applied to particular cases and solve specific problems. Perhaps both the Ch'ing-Tsu and Loh-Wong schools would agree to that. Both, however, seem to have neglected the problem of how to control the connecting links between the general principle and the particular experience.

PART IV

PRINCIPLES OF MORAL EDUCATION

The feeling of commiseration is the starting point of benevolence.—*Mencius.*

What Heaven has bestowed upon us is exceedingly great, strong, and just. What is the use of being a man if he is so petty and selfish?—*Loh Shang-san.*

In teaching children, they should be awakened to see the importance of self-reliance.—*Loh Shang-san.*

Even if I could not read and write a single word, I want to be a man—upright, free, and unhampered with worthless details. — *Loh Shang-san.*

Sincerity is the path of heaven; to be sincere is the path of man.—*Confucius.*

PART IV
PRINCIPLES OF MORAL EDUCATION

CHAPTER XI
TYPES OF MORAL THEORY

1. CONFUCIAN SCHOOLS

The central problem of the Confucian school, as we have mentioned in the preceding chapters, is the politico-ethical problem. As Confucius inherited the aristocracy of learning of ancient China it is inevitable that he views everything from the standpoint of the state. His moral heroes are the seven ancient wise rulers, Yao (堯), Sing (舜), Yu (禹), Tang (湯), Wen (文), Wu (武), and the prince regent, Chow Kung (周 公).[1] A well-ordered state must be based upon good morals. " To administer the state on the basis of virtue," said Confucius, " may be likened to the Northern Star to which all the other stars pay their tributes."[2] " The ancient wise rulers had a commiserating mind, and they, as a matter of course, had likewise a commiserating government. When with a commiserating mind was practiced a commiserating government, the governing of the empire was as easy a matter as making anything go round in the palm."[3]

On the other hand, good morals are but the means to attain the ideal state. *The Great Learning* tells us that to develop the illustrious virtue is the means to attain the well-ordered state. Therefore, every person in the state from the sovereign down to the lowest of the proletariat must take the cultivation of the person as the foundation of everything.[4] This interweaving of politics

---

[1] The later Confucians ranked Confucius together with the seven ancient wise rulers, making a total of eight sages.
[2] *The Confucian Analects*, Book II, *Wei Ching*, Chapter I.
[3] *The Works of Mencius*, Book II, Chapter VI.
[4] *The Great Learning*, Text of Confucius, Part I, Section 6.

and morals as one and indivisible is what we call the politico-ethical problem of the Confucian school.

All the types of moral theory in the Confucian schools are politico-ethical, because they aim at the solution of the same central problem. But they reach different points of departure in solving the problem. Hence they may be divided into several types.

1. *Naturalistic.* This type of moral theory holds the view that morality is an inner growth. The great exponent of this theory is Mencius. To him, all the moral ideas of man are but the natural growth of his moral instincts. The principle of benevolence has its source in the instinct of commiseration; the principle of righteousness, in the instinctive feeling of shame and dislike; the principle of propriety, in the instinctive feeling of modesty and complaisance; the principle of wisdom, in the instinctive feeling of right and wrong.

To prove his theory, Mencius said that "all men have a mind which cannot bear to see the sufferings of others." For example, " If men suddenly see a child about to fall into a well, they will without exception experience a feeling of alarm and commiseration. They will feel so, not as a ground on which they may gain the favor of the child's parents, nor to seek the praise of their neighbors and friends," but because it is their instinctive feeling. The principle of benevolence is this instinctive feeling of commiseration fully nourished and developed to its maturity.[5] " He who is a great man does not lose a child's heart." [6]

2. *Corrective.* This type of moral theory holds the view that morality is nothing more than a set of social codes by which the selfish (anti-social) tendencies of man are harnessed and directed into the right channels. Morality is created by the sages, or leaders of men, to suppress evil instincts of the individual, and to maintain social order and peace.[7] The expounder of this type of moral theory is Sin-tse (荀 子).[8]

---

[5] *The Works of Mencius*, Book II, *Kun Sun Chow*, Part I, Chapter VI.
[6] *Id.,* Book V, *Le Low*, Part II, Chapter XII.
[7] *The Works of Sin-tse*, Chapter II, *On Personal Culture*, and Chapter XXIII.
[8] See Chapter I, Section II, *Development of Chinese Thought*, Politico-ethical school, Sin-tse.

3. *Practical Conduct.* This type of moral theory claims that moral laws have no practical value unless they are actually put into practice. Morality means actual conduct. " Put what we know into practice with great effort and keep on patiently extending the sphere of our conduct. Extending step by step, gradually and orderly from what is easy and near at hand to what is hard and far, we will see the good result day by day." [9] The representative of this view of morals is Tsu-tse (朱 子).

4. *Fundamental Human Rights.* The assertion of the fundamental moral right of man is, to this type of moral theory, the fundamental principle of morals. Man derives his existence from Heaven (Nature). What Heaven has bestowed upon him is exceedingly great, strong, and just.[10] Therefore he must be left free to develop his natural moral endowment, and no traditional moral laws should hamper his development. The exponent of this theory is Loh Shang-san (陸象山).

5. *Intuitive.* This type of moral theory claims that morality has its foundation on the intuitive knowledge of right and wrong. According to Wong Yang-min (王陽明), " It is intuitive knowledge that knows what is right and what is wrong." [11] What is intuitive knowledge ? According to him, it is the " cosmic reason lodged in the mind ever-bright, ever-alert, and ever-conscious [in and by itself]." [12] It is the knowledge that is instinctive and unlearned. And without thinking it knows what is right and what is wrong.[13] It is the only true knowledge that man possesses ; and beyond that there is no knowledge.[14]

The true moral conviction, then, is that which is formed by this intuitive knowledge. It is the sole judge of right and wrong.

---

[9] *Complete Works of Tsu-tse*, Volume III, *On Learning,* Chapter III.
[10] *The Abbreviated Works of Loh Shang-san*, Volume III.
[11] " The intuitive knowledge knows right and wrong."—*The Works of Wong Yang-min, Dialogues*, Section 195.
[12] *The Works of Wong Yang-min*, Volume II, *Essays,* Chapter I, *Letter to Shu Ko Hsun.*
[13] *Id., Dialogues*, Section 261.
[14] *Id.*, Volume II, *Essays*, Chapter II, *Letters to Ma Tsze Sin.*

2. Non-Confucian Schools

Generally speaking, the moral theories of non-Confucian schools exercised an influence upon Chinese life, only when they had been borrowed, either consciously or unconsciously, by the Confucian schools. For this reason, we have separated, in this chapter, the moral theories of non-Confucian from Confucian schools.

1. *Materialistic.* The type of moral theory which claims that the good morals of men depend upon the economic welfare is materialistic. This theory is advanced by Kwan-tse (管子). " If the barns are full, people will observe the principle of propriety ; if clothing and food are plenty, they will differentiate honor from disgrace.[15]

2. *Radical-Individualistic.* This type of moral theory claims that the social institutions are fundamentally evil because they interfere with the freedom of man. " Abandon so-called benevolence and righteousness," said Lao-tse (老子), " people will return to parental kindness and filial piety ; when laws and regulations multiply, the world will be full of robbers and thieves."[16] " What is stuck together in reality is so by nature, and not by means of glue," said Tsong-tse (莊子) ; " and what is restrained in reality is so by nature, and not by means of ropes and bandages. . . . Why shall we stick and bind the world together by means of glue and ropes and bandages, such as benevolence and righteousness ? "[17]

3. *Humanitarian.* Me-tse (墨子), the founder of the Humanitarian school, claimed that only by means of universal love—love for all men—can the real peace of society and of the world be maintained. The disturbances in society and wars among the nations are fundamentally caused by the lack of men's love for one another.

4. *Penal.* This type of moral theory closely resembles the corrective theory. The only difference lies in the fact that the

---
[15] *The Works of Kwan-tse,* Chapter I.
[16] *Tao Teh King,* Chapter LVII.
[17] *The Works of Tsong-tse,* Chapter VIII.

penal theory demands severe punishment and heavy rewards as the sole means to maintain social order. Moral laws are denounced as impracticable for maintaining peace and order in society. " If we count the number of people who will do good from their own will," said Han-Hui-Tse (韓非子), " we will not find more than ten out of a hundred persons. But if the people are restrained from doing evil by penal laws, peace and order will reign in the whole country." [18]

5. *Hedonistic.* To indulge in sensual pleasures in order to enjoy life and to escape from the miserable world is here called the hedonistic theory of morals. This type of moral theory was born during the Wei (魏) and Tsin dynasties (晉) (A.D. 220-419), when the country was torn to pieces by continuous wars. The following quotation is the representative view of hedonism :

" If we could live to a hundred years, we would be considered to have lived to the limit of human life. Yet less than one person out of a thousand would live so long. Suppose there is a person who lives a hundred years. Childhood and old age occupy a half of it. Sleep again takes away half of the remainder. Then how many days are there to be left ? Moreover, sickness, sorrows, sufferings, and distresses will perhaps take away half of the rest. How many days are there in a life of a hundred years that may be considered care free and happy ? What is the purpose of living ? How little can we enjoy living ! To die at ten years of age is death ; to die at a hundred years of age is no less than death ! " [19]

---

[18] *The Works of Han-Hui-Tse*, quoted by Tsai Tsin, *History of China Ethics*, Page 81.

[19] Quoted in Tsai Tsin's *History of Chinese Ethics*, Chapter VI, Page 28.

CHAPTER XII

THE FUNDAMENTAL ELEMENTS OF MORAL TRAINING

1. THE PROPER SPHERE OF MORAL CONDUCT IN EDUCATION AND ITS SUBJECT MATTER AND PROBLEMS

The problem of intellectual training starts from the method of knowledge and ends in the relation between theory and practice or knowledge and conduct. The problem of moral training begins where the problem of intellectual training ends, and its proper sphere is the method of conduct. The central problem of intellectual training is " how we know " and the central problem of moral training is " how we do." Of course there are no distinct lines that can be drawn between knowledge and conduct. We mark off the one from the other more or less arbitrarily only for convenience in discussion.

The Subject Matter of Moral Training. The ethical ideal of the race is the subject matter of moral training. For the sake of furnishing the subject matter, we have discussed in the previous chapter types of moral theory. But I wish to point out here that although there are a number of types of moral theory, the one which exercises a continuous influence upon the Chinese people is the politico-ethical type of the Confucian schools. The other types as represented by the non-Confucian schools, which had flourished for a time and then died down, never enjoyed such continuous prosperity as the Confucian schools. As the politico-ethical ideal is fundamentally Chinese and the Confucian scholars were so much interested in politics and education, they naturally controlled the government and culture. They were always prepared for serving the state and spreading culture. In the government, the best types of statesmen were teacher-statesmen, and in the schools, the best types of teachers were statesmen-teachers. To govern the state well is their aim; to cultivate good morals is the means to the end; and education is the instrument to cultivate good morals.

THE FUNDAMENTAL ELEMENTS OF MORAL TRAINING 133

The Problem. How to govern the state is the ever-present problem of the Confucian school. The answer lies in the cultivation of good morals through the instrumentality of education. How to cultivate good morals is the ever-present and central problem in education. It is this latter question that we try to answer in this chapter.

2. Two Fundamental Factors that Presuppose Moral Conduct

1. *Moral Knowledge Is the Starting Point to Conduct.* All the Chinese philosophers would agree to this idea. In the chapter on The Problem of Knowledge, we have discussed the relation between theory and practice. What we are going to say here, therefore, is more or less a review. In that chapter, however, we emphasized conduct as the final aim of knowledge. Here, we are to emphasize knowledge as the starting point or torchlight to conduct. To quote Ch'ing-tse : " Knowledge should be placed before conduct as a guidance. For example, if we want to travel, we have to get a torchlight to lead us."¹ Again he said : "Conduct should be presupposed by knowledge. Not only is it hard to do, but it is also hard to know." ²

" In view of the general process of doing a certain thing," said Tsu-tse, "it is no doubt that knowledge is prior to conduct."³ " Doing without clear sight and conscious effort," said Wong Yang-min, " is doing haphazardly." ⁴

2. *The Will Is Fundamental to Moral Conduct.* The will ⁵ is the directing force to moral conduct. Without will, there can be no forcible conduct. It is will power that enables man to conquer obstacles and move forward. " The will is the commander

---

¹ Hun Kving, *Collections on Philosophical Thoughts*, Volume 48.
² *Id.*, Volume 48.
³ *The Complete Works of Tsu-tse*, Volume III, *Learning*, Section on *The Relation of Knowledge and Conduct*.
⁴ See Note 38, Chapter V, The Problem of Knowledge.
⁵ The word "will" is translated from the Chinese word "*tsi*" which has a double meaning. In one sense it means " definite purpose " and in the other, " will." For its use in the sense of " definite purpose," see Chapter VIII, Section 1.

of emotions," said Mencius, " and emotions pervade and animate the body. The will reigns supreme in the mind, and emotions are but the subordinates of the will. Therefore, hold firm the will and do no violence to emotions."[6] " If the learner is able to hold firm his will," said Tsin Teh-sher, " emotions will follow its command. Then he will not dissipate himself in idleness. The will may be likened to a general and emotions to the soldiers. When the soldiers are under the command of a general with a military system and martial orders, they cannot indulge in loose habits even though they would otherwise wish to."[7] Again he said, " Wherever may go the will, it will pierce through everything; nothing is hard enough to prevent it. No army, however efficient, is strong enough to resist an invincible will."[8]

Method of Training the Will Power. Then how is this will power, which to the Chinese philosophers seems so important, to be trained? According to Loh Shang-san, it is by means of knowledge that men are to secure will power. " Man must have strong will power," said he, " but the common man indulges in sensual pleasure and material comforts; his natural tendency to good is therefore checked. Then it is hardly possible for the common man to understand the importance of will power unless they have secured knowledge first."[9] According to Tsu-tse, it is by earnest desire and hard work. To quote him : " Encourage yourself and go on working straightforward. Put your whole heart to work. As when you go to war, and drums are beating, do not ask what is in front of you, but just sweep forward and march on and on. This is the only way that you can do real work. On the other hand, if you fight in a half-hearted way, as weeds floating to and fro in the waves, what could you accomplish ! "[10]

---

[6] *The Works of Mencius,* Book II, *Kung Sun Chow,* Part I, Chapter II, Section 9.
[7] *Chinese Encyclopedia,* Volume 62, *Tse Chi Pu Tson Lun,* Page 11.
[8] *Id.,* Page 13.
[9] Huang Tson-hi, *The History of Philosophy of the Sun and Yuan Dynasties,* Volume 58.
[10] *Chinese Encyclopedia,* Volume 85, *Hsieh Wen Pu Tson Lun,* Book III, Page 2.

THE FUNDAMENTAL ELEMENTS OF MORAL TRAINING   135

According to Wong Yang-min, it is by concentration of the mind. He took Mencius's metaphor of chess playing for illustration.[11] He said: "To hold firm the will means to set your mind to learning and learning is the way to develop the will. Let us take chess playing as an example. Chess playing is learning. To give one's whole mind and bend one's will to it is concentration of the mind. To direct his mind to a swan which he thinks approaching is divided attention. To do nothing but listen to the teacher of chess playing is to occupy himself whole-heartedly with learning. To think of bending his bow and shooting the swan is to let himself be occupied with something else while he is doing one thing."[12] Thus, with Wong Yang-min, will power means the ability to direct one's whole attention to the work he is engaged in. Hence, by working wholeheartedly in a well-defined field one is able to develop his will power.

3. TYPES OF METHOD OF MORAL CONDUCT

Moral conduct does not necessarily mean the conduct which conforms to moral standards alone, but it means any human conduct that is consciously directed by human effort; for any conduct which has any social value is, broadly speaking, moral conduct.

Why Method Is Necessary. Since there is method to knowledge, there is also method to conduct. Any being is capable of securing knowledge; but a good or bad knowledge is conditioned by a good or bad method. The mere possession of knowledge will not necessarily be carried into action. For putting knowledge into action, besides the will, requires a kind of skill. So it is with moral knowledge and moral action. It is true that if one knows definitely and clearly he would likely put into action what he knows. But the degree of its effectiveness depends upon the method of action. Tsu-tse argued that every one knows that if he jumps into the water, he would be drowned and if he plunges

---

[11] See paragraph to Note 8, Chapter VIII, The Fundamental Elements of Learning.

[12] *The Works of Wong Yang-min*, Volume IV, *Essays*, Chapter 3, *Instructions to Tsu Sir-chia.*

into the fire, he would be burned and therefore he will not go into either the water or fire, because he knows the result definitely and clearly.[13] This argument seems to be true so far. But it is also true that it requires a method to save one's self if he happens to find himself in the water or in a burning house.

Moreover, there is a vast difference in the degrees of complexity in knowledge and conduct. This "water-and-fire-not-to-plunge-in" theory is too simple to cover the relations of the more complex knowledge and conduct.

In Chapter X, The Fundamental Elements of Teaching, Section 3, The Logical Problem in Teaching, we have discussed the difference between Confucian and Mencian types of teaching; and we have come to the conclusion that Confucius's logic in teaching is from the particular to the universal and, on the other hand, Mencius's logic in teaching is from the universal to the particular. These two systems of logic hold true in moral training. In speaking of the training of conduct, Tsu-tse said: " Confucius, in teaching conduct, starts from the middle of the whole process and asks the pupil to practice from there. After practicing for a while, he will gradually ascend to a higher plane of truth. This is what is meant by ' to study in the lower plane and the natural growth will bring one to the higher plane.' On the other hand, Mencius, from the beginning to the end, always wants people to understand first the ultimate truth of the mind and nature [human][14] and then practice according to the fundamental principles."[15]

1. *Accumulative or Applicative Method.* This may be called the Confucian type of moral training. The advocator of this method was Tsu-tse. He said: " According to the method practiced by the Sage, when the pupil asks one question, the Sage gives him just one practical answer to that question. The pupil, after

---

[13] *The Complete Works of Tsu-tse*, Volume II, *On Learning*, Chapter III.

[14] Mencius invariably held that a proper nourishment of the mind and the development of the good nature of man are the foundations for moral training.

[15] *The Complete Works of Tsu-tse*, Volume V, *On Learning*, Chapter V, *On Teaching*.

receiving the instruction, puts it into actual practice. Nowadays, the teacher talks a good deal at one time, and the learner never looks at the instruction from the viewpoint of putting it into practice. When I am trying to teach here, the learner is expected to apply it to conduct, for if he takes my teaching as mere talk, it would not have any effect." Again Tsu-tse said : " If mere talk without application to actual conduct would be the whole thing in learning, it would be enough for the seventy famous disciples to finish their study after two days' talk with Confucius. Why did these disciples study under Confucius for so many years ? Would any one think that those famous disciples of Confucius were all idiots ? "[16]

The surest way to moral conduct is, according to Tsu-tse, the accumulation of daily practice. To quote him : " In forming good conduct, the learner should practice daily in his relation with his parents, and elder brothers, or in contact with his fellow men, or in doing certain work. He should try harder if he finds that he cannot carry out what he intends to do. If he keeps on doing that way for some time he will unconsciously make improvement in himself ; and pretty soon he will form a habit and then find this work of forming right conduct as easy as common daily work."[17]

This method of accumulative daily application of moral conduct is of a predominate type in Chinese education, especially in primary education. The notable illustrations are to be found in Tsu-tse's doctrine that " the learner must be taught to practice in his youth in order that the growth of wisdom may be correlated with that of habit and the development of the mind, with that of character," and Wong Yang-min's insistence upon the teacher's questioning the children every morning when they come to school about their conduct at home and on the streets. As the effectiveness and the defects of this method have been fully discussed in Chapter IX, Method of Elementary Education, we shall not attempt to repeat them here.

---

[16] *The Complete Works of Tsu-tse*, Volume IV, *On Learning*, Chapter IV, *On Conduct*.
[17] *Id.*, Chapter V, *On Human Relations*.

2. *Method of "Holding the Fundamentals."* This may be called the Mencian type of moral training. We have just stated that Tsu-tse pointed out the fact that Mencius wants people first to understand the ultimate truth of the mind and nature and then practice according to the fundamental principles. As we have seen in Chapter X, Mencius first told his disciple the fundamental principles of maintaining moral courage—the vast, courageous morale—and then told him the method of attaining it by the accumulation of righteous deeds.[18]

Tsu-tse himself did not believe in this method of "holding the fundamentals" although he did not make any direct attack upon Mencius. He said: "In teaching conduct, the teacher should show the learner a practical method according to his individual needs. Thus, without resorting to much talking, the learner is led to a plain and easy path. On the other hand, if the teacher indulges in making generalizations, and the learner is left by himself to find out the practical method, it is to be feared that the teacher is merely helping him to go astray." [19]

However, when we come to Loh Shang-san, we find an entirely different view. He held that it is the fundamental principles that the learner should know first and then he would be able to practice according to the fundamental elements of moral life. On the other hand, if the learner were not taught in holding the fundamentals, he would be drowned in worthless details. To quote Loh Shang-san: "If a man does not discriminate the detail from the fundamental, and the insignificant from the weighty, he will be drowned in the insignificant details and unable to see the big things." [20]

Loh Shang-san himself told us that in his method of teaching he generally emphasized the fundamental principles, so that the fundamental issues would not be beclouded by the details. He said: "In all things, there is a difference between the root and branches. Only a big root can bear long and prosperous branches.

---

[18] See Chapter X, paragraphs to Note 36.
[19] Hu Kwang, *Collections on Philosophical Thoughts*, Volume 51, *On Learning*.
[20] *Abbreviated Works of Loh Shang-san*, Volume III.

In my method of teaching, I generally emphasize the importance of the root, so that the tree will not be borne down by the overgrown branches." [21]

The following quotations from the sayings of Loh Shang-san would enable us to see clearer his method of teaching:
" To concentrate the mind and to nourish the nature of man are the work of the master [of first importance]; to locate the faults in one's self and avoid their repetition and to find good points and strengthen them by practice are but the work of the slave [of secondary importance]. In teaching children, they should be awakened to see the importance of self-reliance."
" What heaven has bestowed upon us is exceedingly great, strong, and just. What is the use of being a man, if he is so petty and selfish ? Therefore, our mind should be kept in the condition of justice and righteousness." One day Loh Shang-san told a friend of his: "A man without will power is to be pitied. If one possesses a will, he can accomplish whatever he wants to do. However, if one has already possessed will power, he should discriminate righteousness from selfishness. . . . My friend, if you can see that what is bestowed upon us by Heaven is so good and so precious, you would not fail to be a man." His friend asked, "If so, where shall we start to practice in our daily conduct ? " He replied:
" If you can see that what is bestowed upon us by Heaven is so good and so precious and to seek truth afar not in the sense of eccentricity,[22] but for seeking what is right, and moreover know that what is true and right is to be found in ourselves ; [you will not fail in practice]." [23]

Criticism. The best criticism of these two methods is to be found in the mutual attacks made by two opponents, Tsu-tse and Loh Shang-san. As we have seen before, one attacked the other's method of accumulative application of daily conduct on the ground

---

[21] *Abbreviated Works of Loh Shang-san*, Volume III.

[22] It is commonly accepted in the Confucian school that truth is to be sought near at hand (in common daily life) and not to be sought afar (away from common daily life). In breaking off this tradition, therefore, Loh Shang-san said that to seek truth afar was not in the sense of eccentricity, but to seek what is right.

[23] *Abbreviated Works of Loh Shang-san*, Volume III.

that it would cause the learner to be drowned in the insignificant details; the other attacked the one's method of "holding the fundamentals" on the ground that it would lead the learner into empty talks.

The main difference, however, seems to lie in the point of emphasis. Each seems to have emphasized the different stages of the same process of moral conduct. It is undeniable that a mere possession of the fundamental ideas could not very well be carried into effect without a practical method. On the other hand, it is also true that to put into practice nonessential ideas would not have much more, if any, moral value. The method of selecting fundamental ideas should be employed before the method of carrying them into action, in order to save one from being drowned in the insignificant details, and the latter should follow the former in order to form right conduct.

The Stages of Moral Conduct. The whole process of forming right conduct seems to be in the following order: The first stage is to have an intellectual background in order to determine the import of ethical values. The second is to determine the relative importance of ethical values in order to determine the relative values of moral conduct. The third is to form right conduct through constant daily practice. The first stage seems to be generally agreed upon by the two schools. The method of "holding the fundamentals" seems to be an emphasis on the second stage. This is what Loh Shang-san called the root of moral conduct. The accumulative or applicative method seems to emphasize the third or last stage. For Tsu-tse himself has pointed out that Confucius, in teaching conduct, starts from the middle of the whole process—that is to say, from the point where the second stage ends and the third stage begins. Of course the one who sees the second stage is the teacher who gives direction to the learner and the latter under his directions starts to practice. The accumulative result in conduct will lead him later on to see the fundamental principles that are behind the practice.

3. *Reflective Method.* With Loh Shang-san, the Chinese thought began to assert the right of man. To hold the fundamentals are to uphold the rights of man. "Even if I could not

THE FUNDAMENTAL ELEMENTS OF MORAL TRAINING   141

read and write a single word, I want to be a man—upright, free, and unhampered with worthless details." [24] This assertion of human right culminated in the teaching of Wong Yang-min. With him, the mind is the sole judge of right and wrong.[25] He identified mind with cosmic reason which is ever-bright, ever-alert, and ever-conscious. This he called intuitive knowledge, which knows right and wrong. No standard of right and wrong can be set unless it is examined by the mind.[26]

Intuitive Knowledge and Idea.[27] If intuitive knowledge knows right and wrong, then why does man sometimes do wrong? It is the uncertain idea that leads to wrong. What is idea? Intuitive knowledge lies latent. But it becomes kinetic when it is in response to the outer stimuli. The idea is intuitive knowledge in the kinetic state.

Cosmic Reason and Human Passion. Intuitive knowledge is cosmic reason and *the idea not directed and controlled and scrutinized by cosmic reason is human passion.* When the uncontrolled idea, which is called passion, runs wild, cosmic reason will be beclouded by it, just as the sun is covered up by the cloud. Nevertheless, cosmic reason is there, just as the sun is there even when it is covered up with cloud and fog.

Emotions and Passions. Pleasure, anger, sorrow, fear, love, hate, and desire are seven emotions. They are naturally active and are but the functions of intuitive knowledge. Intrinsically,

---

[24] *Abbreviated Works of Loh Shang-san,* Volume III.
[25] See Chapter XI, Types of Moral Theory, Intuitive.
[26] " If all the people said it is right, I dare not say it is right if my mind does not see it ; if all the people say it is wrong, I dare not say it is wrong, if my mind does not agree with it."—*The Works of Wong Yang-min,* Volume IX, *Miscellaneous Collections, Letter to Hsu Chin Tse.*
[27] The materials for the discussions on Wong Yang-min were drawn from the following sources, unless otherwise noted: *The Works of Wong Yang-min,* Volume I, *Dialogues,* particularly, sections 186, 192, 195, 213, 233, 250, 251, and 261; Volume II, *Essay,* Chapter I, *Letter to Hsu Ko Hsiun; Reply to Wei Sze Sai, Letter to Ma Tse-hsin, Reply to Tun Hsun and Lo Seh;* Volume IV, *Essays,* Chapter III, *Reply to Ku Tun-chiao,* Section 8, *Reply to Lo Tsun-an, Reply to Euyang Tson-yeh ;* Volume V, *Essays,* Chapter IV, *On the Importance of the Will, Chun Wu Tao Ren Chi,* and preface to the original text of *The Great Learning.*

they are neither good nor bad. They are bad only when they are in response to outer stimuli without being controlled and directed by cosmic reason. When they are thus uncontrolled and not well directed they become passions.

Idea and Emotion. All the emotions conceived by man are in terms of ideas. When things or affairs that appeal to us as a pleasure or give us the feeling of pleasure, we recognize it in terms of ideas. Therefore what are called pleasure, anger, sorrow, fear, love, hate, and desire are really the ideas of pleasure, anger, sorrow, etc. Therefore ideas are emotions recognized by the mind. There will be no emotions if the mind does not recognize them in terms of ideas.

The Relations of Cosmic Reason, Mind, Intuitive Knowledge, Ideas, Emotions, and Passion. Cosmic reason and intuitive knowledge are one and the same thing with different manifestations. Cosmic reason is the source of mind. Mind is cosmic reason in man. Intuitive knowledge is cosmic reason lodged in mind: ever-bright, ever-alert, and ever-conscious. Emotion is the natural function of intuitive knowledge, cosmic reason, or mind. Idea is intuitive knowledge, cosmic reason, or mind in kinetic condition, and is formed in the recognition of emotions in response to outer stimuli. Passion is emotion misdirected. Therefore, the object of moral training is to attain intuitive knowledge. The way to attain it is to get rid of human passions. The way to get rid of human passions is to form clear, sincere, and true ideas.

The True and the False Self.[28] Intuitive knowledge is our true self, because it knows the real sense of right and wrong. The passions are our false self, because what they crave is not what intuitive knowledge wants. Intuitive knowledge loves what is right and the whole world loves what is right. Therefore the true self loves what the world does. Thus our mind will always feel complacent, no matter where we may go and whatever conditions of life we may be in. On the other hand, if we love what the false self does, we love what the whole world hates. Conse-

---

[28] *The Works of Wong Yang-min,* Volume V, *Essays,* Chapter IV, *Chun Wu Tao Ren Chi.*

quently we will be hated by the whole world. Thus our mind will always feel troubled and become the slave of outer things.

Formation of Clear, Sincere, and True Ideas. The first is to recognize the ever-presence in the mind of intuitive knowledge, which is the sole judgment of right and wrong. Yet the question of right and wrong comes only when there is the idea. And the idea is formed only in response to outer things and affairs. When the idea is in conformation to the true and actual conditions of things and affairs, it is called a clear, sincere, true idea. Therefore, the proper method is to study the things and affairs in terms of ideas that are presented before us. When an idea occurs in our mind, we must ask ourselves, " Is this idea sincere, clear, and true ? " By a close examination of the idea by our mind, intuitive knowledge will tell us whether it is right or wrong.

Knowing Is Doing. If we see clearly that an idea is right, and we love it as convincingly as we love what is beautiful, we will carry it into action. If we see clearly that an idea is wrong, and we hate it as convincingly as we hate a bad smell, we will stamp it out from our mind so that it will not be carried into action. On the other hand, if we carry into action what we know to be wrong, we take wrong for right by rebelling against our intuitive knowledge and hence our idea has not yet been clear, sincere, and true. If we do not carry into action what we know to be right, we take right for wrong by rebelling against our intuitive knowledge and hence our idea has not yet been clear, sincere, and true. Our idea is clear, sincere, and true only when we are sure of it as we are sure of our love for what is beautiful or of our hate for a bad smell.

The Central Problem of the Reflective Method. From the discussion given above we come to the conclusion that the central problem of the reflective method is how to form a right moral conviction. In doubting the values of traditional moral standards, Wong Yang-min, influenced by Loh Shang-san, takes the mind as the ultimate judgment of right and wrong. " If my mind tells me what is wrong, I dare not take it to be right even though it was taken to be right by Confucius ; . . . if my mind tells me what is right, I dare not take it to be wrong even though it was taken to be right only by an insignificant person." Intuitive knowledge knows right and wrong.[29]

A Comparative Criticism of the Three Types of Method. As a method for handling our discussions, we have formulated three successive stages of moral conduct. And we have discussed that the accumulative or applicative method as advocated by Tsu-tse belongs to the third or last stage, and the method of "holding the fundamentals" as advocated by Loh Shang-san belongs to the second stage. With Wong Yang-min we come to the first stage— to determine the import of ethical values. Tsu-tse takes traditional moral standards as the final judge of moral conduct and begins with the application of these standards. Loh Shang-san begins to inquire into the validity of traditional standards and asserts the rights of man to form a moral standard. Wong Yang-min goes one step further by formulating a method to assert the right of man. Who is to formulate the moral standard? It is man himself. What is the true self of man? It is the mind. What is mind? It is cosmic reason in man. Cosmic reason is the source of all truth. In man the cosmic reason in the form of intuitive knowledge knows what is right and what is wrong, hence intuitive knowledge is the sole judge of right or wrong.

Ethical and Moral. As we have already criticized the method of Tsu-tse and Loh Shang-san, we need not repeat here. Let us now examine Wong Yang min's doctrine of intuitive knowledge. Is it true that intuitive knowledge is the sole judge of right or wrong? Before answering that question, we have to ask what does "right" or "wrong" mean? Right or wrong, as commonly accepted, seems to have a double meaning. When applied to action, we mean that an act is wrong if it does not conform to the best social standard and it is right if it conforms to it. The modern social standard says that it is wrong to impose an "eye-for-eye" and "tooth-for-tooth" punishment. So if a people practice that punishment, we will say it is wrong for us to do. The social standard says that it is wrong to tell a lie. So if we

---

[29] *The Works of Wong Yang-min,* Volume IV, *Essays,* Chapter III, *Reply to Lo Tsun-an.*

tell a lie, we know that it is wrong. The social standard says that it is right to keep a burglar in a prison. So if we caught a burglar, we know it is right to send him to prison. The social standard says that it is right to tell the truth; so if we tell the truth, we know it is right. The conformation of conduct to social standard is commonly known as moral act. Therefore, morally speaking, right or wrong is measured by the social standards.

But when we come to ask " Is a certain social standard right or wrong ? " right or wrong has a different meaning. Different schools of thought would have a different interpretation. Suppose we say that it is right for the state to restrain individual freedom in order to maintain the social welfare. Any one who believes in the state would say, Yes, it is right. But the radical-individualistic school would say, No, it is wrong, for the state has no right to hamper individual freedom. The same action would be differently judged by different schools of thought on the ground that each school has a different theory of the individual right. Hence right or wrong is to be determined by logical reasoning. This is commonly known as ethical interpretation of right and wrong.

What does Wong Yang-min mean by " Intuitive knowledge is the sole judgment of right or wrong " ? The meaning of the statement is twofold. First, he means that the validity of moral judgment or conviction is to be determined by the logical reasoning of the mind, and not by traditional standard. The latter is to be accepted only when it has gone through the scrutiny of the mind. Thus Wong Yang-min has started a new critical ethical school as against the old traditional moral school. Secondly, he means that as soon as a moral conviction is reached, intuitive knowledge will see to it that it be carried into action.

Conscience and Moral Action. The last interpretation resembles closely the commonly accepted meaning of conscience. What do we mean when we say that A has a conscience and B has no conscience ? We mean this : A has a conscience because he acts according to his moral conviction and refrains from action if it is against his moral conviction ; B has no conscience because he acts with no regard to his moral conviction. A acts or refrains from action as his conscience dictates ; B acts with no regard to the dictation of his conscience. But why? The common answer is this: A always obeys his conscience and therefore it is strengthened; B always disobeys his conscience and therefore it is weakened or killed. Why does A obey his conscience and B disobey it? Wong Yang-min would say, Because A has true conviction—a clear, sincere, and true idea. B's conviction is only a vague, insincere, and unreal idea. It is not because the conscience is weakened or killed, but because it is beclouded by vague, insincere, and unreal ideas. Therefore, the way to attain intuitive knowledge is to have the ideas clear, sincere, and true.

Danger of Commonly Accepted View of Conscience. It is a commonly accepted belief that conscience knows right or wrong. But this commonly accepted view neglects the fact that conscience knows right or wrong only when we already have possessed the conviction as to what is right or wrong. The mere conviction of what is right or wrong may not be necessarily so. Conscience will support a traditional, habitual, or erroneous conviction just as much as an enlightened one. History has furnished us good examples. The act for the persecutions of witchcraft in Scotland, and religious persecutions and intolerance during the medieval ages were carried into effect, it can be reasonably assumed, by parties who believed that their convictions were right and acted only according to the dictation of their conscience. At the present day, we find the old fashioned moralists who stand firmly for their convictions which may actually hinder social progress. "Conscience implies a knowledge of the whole act—purpose, motive, and deed."[30] A deed carried out as a blind obedience to conscience without inquiring into the purpose and motive behind the moral standards may be in view of social progress, an unmoral act.

True Meaning of Intuitive Knowledge. Intuitive knowledge is enlightened conscience which implies a knowledge of the whole act—rational conviction with clear insight and definite purpose, absolute obedience to the dictation of the inner voice, and the will power to carry the rational conviction into action.

---

[30] Dewey and Tufts, *Ethics*, Page 183.

4. THE PRESENT-DAY MORAL PROBLEMS IN CHINA

China is no longer a world by herself. She has been dragged into world politics. She must play her part or else submit to others. I ask the leaders of China, "Are we willing to submit to the dictation of other peoples?" If not, what are we going to do to solve the thousand and one problems that confront us? Loh Shang-san has well said that "in all things there is a difference between the root and branches." And we must hold the fundamental principles so that the fundamental issues would not be beclouded by the details.

We cannot solve our problems by responding vaguely to the thousand and one things. We must hold the fundamentals. Who can deny the fact that the moral problem is one of our fundamental problems?

Change of Environmental Forces. With world intercourse, a new philosophy and science and art have forced their way into China. Modern industrialism and commercialism are to force her to change her method of production and means of transportation. The very foundations of Chinese society have been shaken. Military and naval armaments and the present and the future possible world wars with their deadly weapons have threatened the very existence of our nation.

Change of National Life. The change of environmental forces means a change of the national life. A change of the national life means a change of the purpose of life. What are the purposes of life and by what are the purposes to be carried into deeds? This is the moral problem. The old traditional standard of morals were even found inadequate by Loh Shang-san in the twelfth century and Wong Yang-min in the sixteenth century. Therefore a reconstruction of our moral ideals is necessary in order to suit present-day conditions.

Rational Morality, Wong Yang-min's Contribution. Tsutse's accumulative or applicative method of moral training is valuable only when there exist fundamental moral ideals. Loh Shang-san's method of "holding the fundamentals" is good only when the fundamental moral standards are rational. Wong Yang-min, in formulating the reflective method, has definitely entered into the stage of rational morality which is fundamental to modern progressive society.[31]

Reason and Experience. According to Loh Shang-san and Wong Yang-min, reason is universal to all men. As Loh Shang-san has well said, the Sages from the Eastern Sea have the same reason, and therefore the same mind, as the Sages from the Western Sea. But although the rationality of man is universal, his experience is not, because a different environment, physical and social as well as spiritual, will offer different opportunities for the individuals or races to gain a different set of experiences.

Comparative Ethics. Hence rational morality implies not only the rationalizing factor alone, but also the moral experience of the different races at the different stages of development. A study of comparative ethics, therefore, is the means to put rational morality upon a sound basis, for reason cannot work in a vacuum. Undoubtedly Wong Yang-min, in his construction of reflective moral ideals, has owed a good deal to his comparative study of the ethical ideals of Buddhistic and Confucian schools, and the schools of Lao-tse. Similarly, in the reconstruction of moral ideals for modern China, a comparative study of the ethics of different races is an indispensable instrument.

Psychological and Sociological. From Loh Shang-san's assertion of the right of man in the moral world, it leads to Wong Yang-min's idea of rational morals. The reflective method is the method to rational morals and is essentially a psychological method. Although Wong Yang-min does not neglect entirely the sociological aspects of morality, he has not formulated any problem sociologically. Moreover, he has gone too far in believing that reason is the panacea for all moral diseases.[32] The change

---

[31] Dewey and Tufts, *Ethics*, Chapter IX.

[32] " If any one knows the secrets of intuitive knowledge, no matter how much evil thought one may have, they will melt away by a mere reflection on reason. Truly it is a dose of Spirit-pills which will ' change iron into gold. ' "—*Dialogue*, Section 250.

This is the general intellectual atmosphere of Chinese philosophy since the Sun dynasty, see Chapter VI, The Problem of Science, paragraph to Note 21.

in moral ideas and method is generally brought about, either consciously or unconsciously, by the change of social forces. Therefore, a reconstruction of moral ideals is not only to be based upon the rational power of man, but also the social conditions in which he lives. Wong Yang-min has formulated the psychological problems of morals; we now have to continue his work started four centuries ago by the formulation of the sociological problem of morals by means of modern science and art.

5. Moral Training in Schools

The Morals of the Chinese. Honesty and patience are two recognized virtues of the Chinese. He is honest in his business dealings, and loyal to his friends and patient in his work. But he is a victim of traditions and lack of initiative. He is absolutely loyal to personal friends but unscrupulously lacking in the sense of responsibility to artificial persons, such as public institutions and corporations. As a result of loyalty to friends and a lack of the sense of responsibility to artificial persons, he is a loyal member to his family, but an indifferent citizen to the state.

The Demand of New Morals. As modern individualism demands initiative, industrialism demands coöperation, and nationalism demands individual responsibility towards the state, the old morals are inadequate to meet the new social demands. In former days, the family was the center of all activities. It was at the same time a state, a school, a bank, a machine shop, and a factory. Therefore if he was a loyal member of the family, he would be able to manage well the affairs of the family. But modern individualism is loosening his family ties, nationalism enlisting him to citizenship, and industrialism taking away a major part of family industry.

The True Meaning of New Morals. Since the conditions of life are being changed, the moral system must be reconstructed to suit the changing conditions. In order to meet the demands of modern individualism, industrialism, and nationalism, the individual must be trained in initiative to think and to do, in coöperative thinking and concerted action, and in citizenship. It must not be forgotten that morality fundamentally means the inner moral force of man. No matter what kind of environmental forces act upon man, the inner moral force is one and the same—to act according to different moral standards in different times, and different stages of social development, are but different manifestations of the same inner moral force. It is the same loyalty no matter whether the individual is loyal to his personal friends or to artificial persons. The only difference lies in the general ways of manifestation. To reconstruct morals does not mean to reconstruct the inner moral force; it means to reconstruct the moral ideals and standards according to the social demands; and new moral training means to direct the same old inner moral force to the new channels.

The Function of Schools in Moral Training. The school is the place where the young generation is trained to live a proper life in harmony with the social stage in which it lives. The school is useless if it deviates from society. Therefore, the moral training in the school means to train the young generation to live morally according to the best moral ideals and standards of the time. The school is no place to form new moral ideals and standards for society; but to train the young generation to adjust themselves to the best moral ideals and standards.

Method of Moral Training in Schools. While the best moral ideals and standards are but a part of the general intellectual and social movement and are more or less out of control of the school, the method of inculcating these ideals to the pupil is essential to moral training in the school. We have discussed, in this chapter, the different types of method of moral training. Tsu-tse emphasized practical conduct; Loh Shang-san, fundamental human rights; and Wong Yang-min, intuitive knowledge or conscience. Therefore, with Tsu-tse, the method of moral training is daily practice; with Loh Shang-san, " holding the fundamentals "; and with Wong Yang-min, reflection. As we have also mentioned, there are three stages in moral training. The first stage is to form moral conviction; the second, to select moral judgments according to their relative values; and third, to put moral ideals into action Wong Yang-min's method belongs to the first stage; Loh Shang-san's, the second; and Tsu-tse's, the third. Only by a combination of the three can the complete process of moral training be formed. Moral ideals have very little value if not transformed into conduct, and moral conduct has very little value if it is not of a purposive action. There are also higher and lower purposes. The individual must be trained in selecting the moral purposes according to their relative values. There may also be foolish or intelligent purposes. The individual must be trained to form intelligent ones. The training in forming intelligent purposes requires a general intellectual and social background. We cannot trot in the dark. We must have the torchlight to guide us.

CONCLUSION

The storm center of the world has gradually shifted to China. Whoever understands that mighty empire socially, politically, economically, and religiously, has a key to world politics for the next five hundred years.—*John Hay.*

CONCLUSION

CHAPTER XIII

SOME OF THE PROBLEMS OF CHINESE CULTURE

The Signs of the Times. Seventeen years ago from this moment of writing, in the year 1900, through the conservative and ignorant forces of the government and misdirected patriotism of a certain class of people, China resorted to her unwise means of ousting the foreigners. Then came the punitive expedition of the Allied troops with modern weapons of war to fight her ill-equipped army and " first " volunteers of the peasant class, and exacted from her an indemnity of Tls. 450,000,000. What does it all mean?

In 1875 China was defeated in the Franco-Chinese War on account of Annam; and in 1894 she was again defeated in the Sino-Japanese War on account of Korea. In 1897 Germany grabbed Kiaochow; in 1898, England leased Weihaiwei, and Russia, Port Arthur; and in 1899, France leased Kwangchow Bay. What does it all mean?

China knew too well that she was going to be swallowed up, bit by bit, by the powers, and her ultimate fate would be that of Poland and India.

What was she going to do in order to save herself? There were two answers. The enlightened leaders answered that the only way to save her was a policy of reforms. The conservative and ignorant forces answered that the way to save her was to oust the foreigners through a miracle. The former led to a radical measure of reforms in 1898. The latter led to the " Boxer War " in 1900. The reforms of 1898 collapsed, but the spirit of reforms was growing. The conservatives brought about a great national calamity in 1900, and at the same time dug their own graves.

In view of the hopeless plight the Manchu dynasty was in, the spirit of reform took the direction of a revolutionary movement.

The Russo-Japanese War with Japan's victory over Russia convinced the general public that the only hope for China was a thorough and radical reform. In 1911, the undercurrent of the new movement was suddenly brought to the surface. One of the greatest republics of the world was born.

The Spirit of the World. With the birth of the Republic, China has definitely entered into the new spirit of the world. New spirit begets new problems and adds new responsibility to the people. In the inspiration of the new era of national life, this little volume is written as a humble attempt to state China's fundamental cultural and educational problems.

Education would be a failure if by means of it life was not to be enriched. The ideal of Chinese life is mutual devotion;[1] while it is good in itself, life can be greatly enriched by incorporating:

1. THE GREEK IDEA OF LIFE. While the Chinese ideal of life is duty, the Greek ideal is quite different. It is true that no happiness can be attained without duty; yet duty alone does not mean the whole happiness.

Conception of Happiness. According to Aristotle, the end of life is happiness. It is different from a pleasure or a bundle of pleasures "in being an abiding consequence or result, which is not destroyed even by the presence of pains [while a pain ejects a pleasure]."[2]

Man must be a master of himself and all his faculties.[3] It is the higher purpose of life that counts. A pleasure or a pain is but incidental to this end. He takes either a pleasure or a pain with no other consideration but to suit his high purpose.

Happiness is intrinsic. It is the inner satisfaction of man's soul.[4] The mere seeking of a pleasure or avoiding of a pain without a higher purpose is not happiness.

Then, what is happiness? It is "the performance of function," "activity of the soul according to excellence," "the manifestation

---

[1] See Chapter I, Section I.
[2] Dewey and Tufts, *Ethics*, Page 250.
[3] Muirhead, Aristotle's *Ethics*, Page 250.
[4] *Id.*, Page 46.

of the highest virtue in energy."[5] Then what is this function of man? It is not vegetative life, which man has in common with plants; it is not the life of sense, which he has in common with animals. What remains is "the life of a being who possesses reason and manifests himself in conduct."[6] This life of man is his soul. Now his soul may be in a static or an active condition. But what concerns us most is when it is active. Therefore, man's function is "an activity of the soul determining itself rationally."[7] Hence happiness is the exercise of the rational function of man.

While it is true that both Aristotle and Confucius recognized that there is a higher purpose in man's life and he takes either a pleasure or a pain, or rejects either a pleasure or a pain, only with a view to suit his object, yet there is a great difference as to what is this higher purpose. According to Aristotle, it is man's rational power; according to Confucius, it is social duty or mutual devotion.

Aristotle differentiates man from animals in view of his rational power; on the other hand, Confucius, in view of his power of performing social duties. Perhaps this difference in the meaning of excellence, supreme good, or *summum bonum*,[8] through its later development, makes this great divergence between Western and Chinese thought.

Life and Intellect. In Chapter I, Section I, we discussed life and duty in such a way as to present the fundamental ideal of Chinese life. We are here to discuss life and intellect in such a way as to present the fundamental ideal of Greek life. No Chinese scholar who has but a general acquaintance with Greek philosophy but would be impressed with the free intellectual activities of the Greeks. The clear-cut mind of the Greeks, with the intellectual interest of "seeking knowledge for knowledge's sake" and inquiring "into nature, into man, into the natural and the supernatural,"[9]

---

[5] Muirhead, Aristotle's *Ethics*, Page 43.
[6] Nichomachean Ethics, *The Elements of Happiness*.
[7] *Ibid.*
[8] See Chapter II, Section 3.
[9] Monroe, *History of Education*, Page 55.

presents to him a mental picture that is a great contrast to his picturing of the philosophical activities of the creative period (ante-Chin period of) Chinese civilization.[10] "The application of the intellect to every phase of life was the task of the Greeks."[11] The application of the social or moral idea to every phase of life was the task of the ancient Chinese. This does not mean that the Greeks neglected man's moral nature, nor the ancient Chinese neglected his intellect. But the Greek morals are intellectualized morals and the Chinese intellect is moralized intellect. With the assertation of human rights by Loh Shang-san, and intuitive reason as sole judgment of moral act by Wong Yang-min, Chinese morals began to be rationalized. The Chinese intellect, however, has not yet been emancipated from moral restraint.

Individualistic and Socialistic. There are, perhaps, different viewpoints from which the Greeks and the Chinese looked at man. The Chinese looked at man as in relation with his social group; the Greeks, on the other hand, looked at man as his own self. Therefore, the one took the view that man is different from animals because of his rational power; the other took the view that man is different from animals because of his being able to fulfill mutual obligation in the social group. Hence, the Greek view of life is individualistic; the Chinese view of life is socialistic.

Conception of Physical Perfectness. There is another factor in Greek life which deserves the attention of the modern Chinese. It is the Greek idea of physical beauty. *Mens sana in corpore sano.* "To the Greeks a good body was the necessary correlative of a good soul." The balance and harmony of mind and body is essential to the formation of æsthetic personality. The Greeks " could scarcely believe in the beauty of the spirit, unless it were reflected in the beauty of the flesh." [12]

To the Chinese, as well as according to the modern common conception in America, the development of the body is but a means to an end. The body is regarded as a machine to " turn out goods. "

---

[10] See Chapter I, Section II.
[11] Monroe, *History of Education*, Page 56.
[12] Dickinson, *Greek View of Life*, Pages 130, 131.

SOME OF THE PROBLEMS OF CHINESE CULTURE

To the Greeks, the body was not regarded as a machine, but a work of art. In Greek athletics, the practice of contending nude is permeated with the æsthetic idea. To the combatants, as well as to the spectators, " the plastic beauty of the human form grew to be more than its prowess or its strength, and gymnastics became a training in æsthetics as much as, or more than, in physical excellence." [13] The Greek sculptor or painter, who spent a great part of his day in watching the exercise of men, drew from the physical beauty of the race an inspiration which is the basis of Greek art.[14]

Sense of Beauty. To the Greeks, art was " regarded as the central point of their scheme of life." [15] " In religion, in ethical conceptions, in bodily development, and in every department of life, all are inseparable with the sense of beauty." [16] In religion " the Greek custom is to represent the gods by the most beautiful things on earth, pure material, the human form, consummate art." [17] " Appollo signified the whole race purification from guilt and the voice of higher wisdom which spoke in the oracles, and that common paternity of Zeus gave to every one a standing of dignity in face of the unforeseen and scarcely comprehensible misfortunes and catastrophes of life." [18] In ethical conceptions, virtue was the free expression of a beautiful and harmonious soul.[19] The keynote of all Greek life was measure, order, proportion. This note found expression not only in ethical conceptions but in religion, science, art, and conduct.[20] The harmonious development of the whole personality, of the individual, intellectually, morally, physically, and æsthetically, is the ideal of Greek life.

The Dark Side of Greek Life. We have thus far selected what is best in Greek life. But the average of Greek life is not to be

---

[13] Dickinson, *Greek View of Life*, Page 132.
[14] Gardner, *Principle of Greek Art*, Pages 77–83 ; Mahaffy, *Greek Civilization*, Page 206.
[15] Dickinson, *Greek View of Life*, Page 187.
[16] *Id.*, Pages 187, 188.
[17] *Maxims of Tyre*, quoted by Gardner, Page 89.
[18] Gardner, *Principle of Greek Art*, Page 90.
[19] Dickinson, *Greek View of Life*, Page 200.
[20] Dewey and Tufts, *Ethics*, Page 112.

estimated by the genius of a few.[21] The existence of slavery caused a low standard of Greek morality.[22] The average Greek was selfish and cruel.[23] While the Greeks had learned to assert the rights of free men and to settle things by public discussions in the very early stages of development of Greek civilization,[24] the Greek constitution of the state was essentially unstable. Polybius told us that "the Athenian demus is always a ship without a commander." The people united together when peril came, but fought again when it was over. One party wished to continue the journey; another wanted to anchor.[25] In comparing Greek and Roman morals, Mahaffy told us that " if a Roman gives you his word you may trust him implicitly ; he will restore you a fortune if you trust it to him ; whereas sheaves of oaths and crowds of witnesses will not secure a single talent for you in the hands of a Greek." [26]

2. THE ROMAN IDEA OF THE LAW. While Chinese life can be enriched by the individual freedom, the intellectual activities, the physical perfectness, and the æsthetical ideals of the Greeks, in the field of institutional development we have to go to the Romans.

Roman Law, Chinese Li, or the " Principles of Propriety," and Penal Law. The principles of propriety are the foundation of Chinese society and the Chinese state ; law is the foundation of Roman society and the Roman state. In Chapter I, Part II, Development of Chinese Thought, we have made frequent references to the principles of propriety. Sin-tse took these as one of the two fundamental elements of the state. Kwan-tse took these as one of the four cardinal virtues of the state. Ton Tsonshu said that man carries out the heavenly idea by means of the principles of propriety and music. We have also used these as an equivalent term for the social system. To understand these better, more explanation is needed. As it was with law, the

---

[21] Mahaffy, *Greek Civilization*, Page 214.
[22] *Id.*, Page 150.
[23] *Id.*, Page 157.
[24] *Id.*, Page 87.
[25] *The Histories of Polybius*, selected passages in Fling's *Greek and Roman Civilization*.
[26] Mahaffy, *Greek Civilization*, Page 296.

principles of propriety were devised fundamentally for the regulation of human relations.[27] But they were extended to such a sphere that they regulated almost all and every kind of activities of life from birth to burial. They not only fixed the relations between parents and children, husband and wife, sovereign and ministers, elders and juniors; they also regulated marriage and burial ceremonies and worship and sacrifices to minute details. They also included the constitution of the state, school systems, international relations. In a nutshell the principles (or rules) of propriety are a " codification " of family traditions and social usages of the Chinese race. The basic idea is moral, the starting point is the family, and the enforcement of the principles (or rules) of propriety is the social opinion.

Now suppose an individual would dare to break the rules and violate them, disregarding social opinion, what would be the remedy? Sin-tse replied that the principles of propriety were to be supplemented by penal laws which were to suppress crimes and protect law-abiding people. Han-Hui-Tse went still further by declaring that the principles of propriety were entirely inadequate for maintaining social order, and the only means to that end was to enforce penal laws. Who was to make the penal laws?— The sovereign. There was no freedom for anybody but the sovereign.[28]

Thus we see on the one hand, the individual was restrained by social (or rather, family) regulations and on the other hand, he was suppressed by despotic penal laws. The individual was thus sacrificed for maintaining social order. The radical individual

---

[27] " The principles of propriety, by means of rules of propriety, are to regulate the relations of people to each other according to their appropriate positions, such as near or distant relatives, men or women, above or below; and to discriminate right and wrong." " By the principles of propriety, teaching is to be extended; cases concerning quarrels are to be decided; the relations of the sovereign and the minister, above and below, father and son, elder brother and younger, are to be fixed. . . . Therefore, by founding the principles of propriety and teaching them to the people, the sages enable men to understand the distinction between man and animal."— *Chu-Li, Book of Rites.*

[28] See Chapter I, Sin-tse and Han-Hui-Tse; Chapter XI, Penal.

school did not succeed in setting him free by attacking the social system of ancient China.[29]

When we come to a study of Roman law, we find a different conception of regulating human relations. Of justice and law, *Imperatoris Justiniari Institutionum* says: "Justice is the set and constant purpose which gives to every man his due. Jurisprudence is the knowledge of things divine and human, the science of the just and the unjust. . . . The precepts of the law are these: to live honestly, to injure no one, and to give every man his due."[30]

Then the distinction of public and private law is made. Law public is for securing the welfare of the Roman state; law private, for securing advantage of the individual citizen. Law private is of threefold origin. The first is the law of nature, which nature taught all animals, such as the union of male and female, called marriage and the rearing of children. The second is the civil law of Rome. Those rules which a state enacts for its own members are peculiar to itself and called civil law. Civil law is divided into written and unwritten law. Ancient custom with the force of statutes is called unwritten law. Written law is of several kinds. Statute is the enactment of the Roman people on the motion of a senatorial magistrate as a consul. Plebiscite is an enactment of commonalty on the motion of one of their own magistrates, as a tribune. Then there are senatusconsults, which is an ordinance of the senate; enactments of the emperor by virtue of the authority conferred on him by the people by *lex regia*, which was passed concerning his office and authority; edicts of magistrates; and answers of those learned in the law.

The third origin of law private is the law of nations, which is common to the whole human race. Under this comes wars, contracts, sales, partnerships, deposits, loans, etc.

Law is also divided into the law of persons and the law of things. Of persons, it is divided into freemen and slaves. Freedom, "from which men are called free," is defined as that which

---

[29] See Chapter I, The Naturalistic School, Chapter XI, Radical-individualistic.

[30] *Imperatoris Justiniari Institutionum, Libri Quattuor*, Book I, Title I, passages selected in Fling's *Greek and Roman Civilization*.

"is a man's natural power of doing what he pleases, so far as he is not prevented by force or law." Slavery is defined as "an institution of the law of a nation against nature, subjecting one man to the dominion of another." The law of things is divided into private ownership, which is acquired by various titles: things common to all, such as air, running water, the sea and the seashore, fishing rights in rivers, and things belonging to society and corporations, such as theaters, race courses as belonging to cities in their corporate capacity, and sacred things.

The Controlling Ideas of Roman Law.[31] Universality is one of the underlying principles of Roman law. It was first based upon the idea of universal reason of the Stoics. From the philosophy of the Stoics that the universal reason revealed itself in the law of nature, which operates both in the human mind and in the physical universe, the Roman lawyer received his inspiration and correlated this conception of universal reason with the general principles of the *jus gentium*[32] and served greatly to illuminate them. Secondly, it was due to the extension of Roman citizenship. As Roman citizenship was extended step by step, first to Latin towns, then to Italian cities, and then to favored outlying districts of the empire, the essential distinctions between the citizen of Rome herself and the citizens of her subject cities and provinces gradually disappeared. With Roman citizenship went Roman law. Therefore *jus civile* (civil law of Rome) and *jus gentium* (law of nations) advanced to meet each other. Thus Roman law grew to world-wide proportions and was more and more influenced by the principles of universal reason. Through the work of Roman lawyers, based upon universal reason and extended citizenship, Roman law was finally stripped of its local characteristics. "The recognition of the fact that there are common principles underlying all laws was a tremendous step in the direction of human unity."[33]

---

[31] Woodrow Wilson, *The State*, Chapter IV, *Roman Dominion and Roman Law*.

[32] "The *jus gentium* was not the law of nations, or international law, in modern sense, but a body of private and commercial law, chiefly the latter. It had nothing to do with state action, but concerned itself exclusively with the relations of individuals to each other among the races subject to Rome."—Wilson, *The State*, Page 149.

[33] Fling, *Greek and Roman Civilization*, Page 146.

Another fundamental principle of Roman law is that it is based upon the relations of individual to individual. One of the precepts of Roman law is "to give every man his due." The law of persons recognized the freedom of the individual, and the law of things, his property rights. Hence, Roman law was fundamentally to protect the private rights of the individual.

Development of Chinese Legal Principles. Chinese legal principles are of threefold origin. The first is the principles of propriety of the Confucian school; the second is the penal law of the penal school; and the third is the negative individualism of the naturalistic or radical-individualistic school. Based upon this first principle, the life of the people was conducted according to the traditions of ancient time; upon the second principle, the state maintained peace and order by codes of imperial penal laws by means of which offenders were to be punished and crimes to be suppressed; and upon the third principle, the state, as far as public safety was not menaced, adopted a *laissez-faire* policy that " the least governed is the best governed."

By the combination of the principles of propriety and negative individualism, the Chinese people have ever since very early times enjoyed such an extent of local self-government that the existence of state authorities is almost unnoticed by the localities. By the combination of the principles of propriety and penal law, the imperial penal law always gave cognizance to the social status of the individual as fixed by the rules of propriety.

A Comparison Between Chinese and Roman Legal Principles. There are three essential differences between Chinese and Roman legal principles. The first is the makers of the law. In China, it was the sovereign who made and proclaimed penal laws and it was the ancient sages who fixed the rules of propriety. In Rome, it wast he citizen who possessed " absolute power of passing and repealing laws." [34]

The second is central interest of law. The Chinese emphasized social stability, and the Romans, on the other hand, emphasized private rights. The unit of Chinese law is the family

---

[34] *The Histories of Polybius*, passage selected in Fling's *Greek and Roman Civilization*, Pages 79-92.

and that of Roman law is the individual. With Chinese law, the family may be responsible for the action of its members; with Roman law, the individual is responsible for his own action.

Third, the Chinese law drew its materials from traditions of the race. Roman law was, on the other hand, through the influence of *jus gentium*, the philosophy of the Stoics, and the extension of citizenship, based upon universal human experience.

Extraterritorial Judicial Rights in China. With the law that was based upon peculiar traditions of the race with the final aim to maintain social stability, it could not be expected that a foreign people whose law was fundamentally under the influence of Roman law, mainly to protect private rights, and whose military strength was far superior to China, should submit to the law of the land. Consequently, foreigners in China demanded and secured from China their extraterritorial judicial rights, thereby establishing consular courts which were to decide cases in which either the both parties involved were foreigners, or one of the parties involved was Chinese.

The existence of extraterritorial judicial rights in a country means the impairment of sovereignty of that country. But China cannot expect to abolish these rights enjoyed by foreign residents in her land until a reasonable length of time shall have elapsed during which she is to develop a judicial system that is based upon the universal principles now prevailing in the modern world.

In the discussion of the Greek view of life, we have come to see that the Greek idea of self-realization of æsthetic, intellectual ideals and the idea of physical perfectness of the individual, to the fullest extent, is the idea China must borrow from the Greeks. And in the discussion of the Roman idea of law, we have come to see that the legal principles, which are based upon universal human reason, the relations of the individuals to each other, and the protection of private rights, are what China has to learn in order to serve as a foundation to reform the Chinese judicial system.

The Greeks taught us the value of the individual; the Romans, the relations of individuals to each other. There is another point which a student of Western civilization cannot neglect—the Hebrew idea of the relation of man to supernatural power.

3. THE CHRISTIAN IDEA OF GOD. When we come to this problem, we are confronted with perplexed situations. The Christian idea of God as taught by Jesus has been, through the development of centuries, interpreted in various ways. The modern conception of God is a product of centuries.[35] Any attempt to present the conception of God in a short space would not only be inadequate, but would be misleading. There are different interpretations of God set forth not only by the Catholics and the Protestants, but also by different sets of the Protestant church. Furthermore, there are different interpretations of God among philosophers and scientists, nay, among different individuals.

For our purpose here, we are not so much concerned with Christian theology as with Christian ethics. We are not so much concerned with what is the supernatural power as with what is the relations of men to that power. For our purpose here, it would be enough for us to know just a general conception of God.

In spite of many interpretations and various conceptions of God, to the eyes of a Chinese, there seems to be a common ground—that there is only one God, one universal loving God, who is the source of truth and the creator of Man. If this interpretation is not entirely erroneous, it closely resembles the combination of the two Confucian ideas of Heaven and *tao*. Heaven is ever-benevolent and is the source of all truth. *Tao* (path or truth) is originated from Heaven, and that which reveals in the physical universe is *tao*, path or truth, of Heaven; and that which reveals in man, such as human relations, is *tao*, path or truth, of man.

The difference seems to lie in the fact that with the Confucian idea, God is metaphysical and with the Hebrew idea, on the other hand, God is personal. With the former, Heaven represents the supreme cosmic force; with the latter, God represents personal living force.

The central interest of the Chinese is the realization of the *tao* of man through the development of human relations. The central

---

[35] For the development of the Christian conception of God, see *Encyclopedia of Religion and Ethics*, God (Biblical and Christian). There is also an excellent article on the Chinese conception of God, see God (Chinese).

interest of the Hebrew, on the other hand, is the realization of the divine will through divine revelations and spiritual communications with God.

The importance of Hebraism in the development of Western civilization cannot be overestimated. As both Greek and Roman civilizations were fundamentally individualistic, the development of social ideas in the Western world was fundamentally under the influence of Christianity.[86]

Hebrew, Greek, and Confucian Ethics. " Hebraism and Hellenism,—between these two points of influence moves our world [Western world]," said Matthew Arnold.[37] In the study of Western civilization, an understanding of these two basic elements is indispensable. The foundation of Chinese civilization is Confucianism, supplemented with the teaching of Lao-tse and Buddhism. But Confucianism is the backbone of Chinese life. Therefore, a comparative study of Hebraism, Hellenism, and Confucianism is a study of basic elements of Chinese and Western civilization.

For the lack of space and time, we are simply to quote here Dewey and Tufts[38] on Hebrew and Greek ethics, but the essential points of Chinese ethics are to be supplied by the author.

Generally speaking, the Hebrew emphasized religion, the Greek, intellect, and the Chinese, morality. But there are also intellectual and moral elements in Hebraism, religious and moral elements in Hellenism, and religious and intellectual elements in Confucianism. The difference is rather in emphasis and focus.

We will now bring out the contrasting points of the three systems of ethics : " Conscientious conduct for the Hebrew centered in doing the will of God ; for the Greeks, in finding rational standards of good ; " for the Chinese, in observing the teachings of the sages. " For the Hebrew, righteousness was the typical theme ; for the Greek, the ideal lay rather in measure and harmony " ; for the Chinese, in filial piety. " For the Greeks, wisdom, or insight, was the chief virtue ; for the Hebrew, the fear of the Lord was

---

[36] Kidd, *Social Evolution*, Chapters VI and VII, *Western Civilization*.
[37] Matthew Arnold, *Culture and Anarchy*, Chapter IV, *Hebraism and Hellenism*.
[38] Dewey and Tufts, *Ethics*, Chapter VI.

the beginning of wisdom "; for the Chinese, benevolence was the chief virtue. " The social ideal of the Hebrews was the kingdom of God; of the Greeks, a political state "; of the Chinese, a benevolent paternal state. If we distinguish in conscience two aspects, thoughtfulness in discovering what to do and hearty desire to do the right when found, then the Greeks emphasize the former, the Hebrews " and the Chinese the latter." " Intellect plays a larger part with the Greek: emotion and the voluntary aspect of will, with the Hebrew "; duty, with the Chinese. " Feeling plays its part with the Greek largely as an æsthetic demand for measure and harmony; with the Hebrews it is chiefly prominent in motivation, where it is an element in what is called ' the heart,' or its functions in appreciation of acts performed, as the joy or sorrow felt when God approves or condemns "; with the Chinese it plays its part largely in mutual devotions between the sovereign and the people, the parents and the children, the husband and the wife, of brothers and of friends.

The Religious Problem in China. While Confucian ethics are centered upon human relations, such as the relations of parents to children, sovereign to subjects, husband to wife, etc., with supernatural power largely eliminated, the common people are worshiping what is called animism. They are not only worshiping earth-gods, mountain-gods, river-gods, but bridge-gods, door-gods, kitchen-gods, crop-gods, as well. With the extension of public education and the dissemination of modern knowledge, this animism of course will eventually disappear.

But man is not only a political animal, he is also a religious animal. With the introduction of Western civilization, Christianity will unavoidably force itself into Chinese life. Therefore, our problem is not to repel Christian teachings, but to understand them.

It is estimated that there are at present in China, a million and a half Catholics, half a million Protestants, and twenty-five million Mohammedans and most of the Chinese people are more or less believers of Buddhism. The Chinese people as a whole are rather indifferent to religious dogmas; or you may say, if you choose, that they are very liberal in matters of religious toleration.

The old religions will persist and Christianity must come in. The way to solve the problem is to let each religion exert its utmost energy and contribute to and enrich Chinese life with the best there is to each.

Confucianism must occupy the same position in China as Hellenism in the Western world. The future Chinese civilization will be the coexistence of Christian-Confucian-Hellenic, Mohammedan-Confucian-Hellenic, and Buddhistic-Confucian-Hellenic. The great old unifying forces are Confucianism, and the great new unifying forces in China will be Hellenism.

The old China was China of itself; the new China is China of the world. Politically, she has been transformed from a monarchy to a republic; therefore, socially, she must be transformed from a social system based upon patriarchy to that based on citizenship. The virtue of patriarchy is filial piety; that of citizenship is patriotism. The rise of modern Japan, besides other causes, is largely due to chivalrism, resulting from feudalism, which is called Bushido, combined with modern science; the future of China depends upon, besides other things, patriotism combined with modern science.

4. SCIENCE AND MODERN METHODS OF KNOWLEDGE. The development of the Western world during the last century is largely due to modern science and scientific methods. Modern science and its methods have permeated every branch of knowledge and every activity of life in the modern Western world. From the administration of national affairs down to the management of family kitchens, science has become an indispensable instrument. In commerce, transportation, education, medicine, surgery, or war, science is the chief weapon. History, philosophy, the fine arts, and even religion have employed scientific methods as the method of investigation. Science has conquered space and time by means of the aëroplane, the telephone, the wireless, and the automobile. In a word, what would modern civilization be if there were no science?

Owing to the lamentable lack of systematic method of knowledge, in spite of strong intellectual capacity and spirit of scholarship, Chinese thought has produced comparatively little result in proportion to the patient labor gone through by Chinese scholars for generations.[39] To compensate the lack of science, an immense amount of natural resources, which would make China the richest in the world, remains buried underground. In science China has the key to her future greatness.

---

[39] Why has China not developed modern science? See Chapter VI, The Problem of Science.

CHAPTER XIV

THE INDIVIDUAL, SOCIETY, AND THE STATE

The individual as conceived by the Chinese is a member of the family. Society is a combination of families. The state is a family on a large scale. There were city-states in Greece; there are family-states in China.

Under the influence of modern commercialism and industrialism, the family ties have been loosened. The new form of government has dethroned the patriarch, and enlisted the members of families to citizenship. The new Chinese is an individual and a citizen instead of a particle of the family. New freedom is fighting against the principles of propriety, and new citizenship against the family-membership. The older generation is lamenting over the passing away of the good old days. The very edifice of Chinese society is being rapidly torn down and the very foundation is rattling.

What shall we do then? In the preceding chapter, we have already discussed how the Greek idea of life is to point out to us our direction to new individualism; the Roman idea of the law, our direction to new idea of social institutions; science and modern method of knowledge are to give us new instruments to civilization.

In discussing Greek and Roman civilization, we do not mean that we are to go back to the good old days of the Greek and Romans for our models. The two ancient peoples passed away centuries ago, but the living forces of the two civilizations are embodied in the life and institutions of the modern Western world. We can find living models from the modern Western life. The modern Western civilization, however, finds its origin in the Greek and Roman civilizations. Upon the basic ideas of the two ancient peoples, as well as those of the Hebrews, the development and progress of modern civilization are based; just as upon the ancient

Chinese culture, development and progress of Chinese civilization are based.[1]

Moreover, the modern Western life has grown to such a complexity that no single study can possibly grasp the underlying principles. For the reasons given above, we have gone into a study of the two ancient civilizations in the preceding chapter in order to furnish basic materials for our study in this chapter.[2]

1. THE CONCEPTION OF THE INDIVIDUAL

Negative, Relative, and Positive Individualism.[3] No thinking man is not but conscious of the self. This consciousness is the starting point of individualism. When man is conscious of himself, he begins to see his native power. The assertion of the native power of the self may be called individualism. Now the assertion of the native power of the individuals will invariably result in conflicts or meet all sorts of obstructions and hindrances. Naturally various means will be devised either to adjust the individuals to such a condition that the conflicts of the individuals to each other may be avoided, or to remove obstructions and hindrances so that the individual may be free to live in the state of nature.

The scheme that aims at the removal of obstructions and hindrances of social organizations so that the individual may enjoy the free play of life in the state of nature, may be called negative individualism. The scheme that aims at the adjustments of conflicts of the individuals by means of social restraints imposed

---

[1] The Hebrew elements in Western civilization may be compared with the Hindu elements in Chinese civilization, in the sense that both were radically different from the native civilizations.

[2] Modern science, in a way, may be said to have found its embryonic idea and method in Greek philosophy. See Chapter VI, The Problem of Science.

[3] Individualism defined by Baldwin as:
"1. Exclusive or excessive regard for self-interest.
"2. The doctrine that the pursuit of self-interest and the exercise of individual initiative should be little or not at all restrained by the state, and that the functions of government should be reduced to the lowest possible terms."—*Dictionary of Philosophy and Psychology.*

upon the individual in order to maintain social stability, may be called relative individualism.

Negative Individualism. This type of individualism may be represented by Lao-tse and Tson-tse in ancient China and Rousseau in the eighteenth century. Both Lao-tse and Tson-tse claimed that all social institutions were bad and the only place that the individual could enjoy free activity of life was the state of nature.[4]

Rousseau claimed that "God makes all things good ; man meddles with them and they become evil." "Civilized man is born and dies a slave. The infant is bound up in swaddling clothes, the corpse is nailed down in his coffin. All his life long man is imprisoned by our institutions."[5]

Relative Individualism. Between the two extremes of the suppression of the individual by the penal school on the one hand, and the abolishment of social institutions by the naturalistic school on the other hand, the politico-ethical school (Confucian school) recognized the individual in relation to his fellows. He was recognized not as an individual to himself, but as a son to his parents, a subject to his sovereign, or as a compatriot to his fellow countrymen. The individual must cultivate his person. *The Great Learning* claims that the cultivation of the person, from the sovereign down to the general mass, is fundamental to all activities of life.[6] But the chief aim of this personal culture is directed towards the development of the individual in his knowledge and power to secure better relations with his fellow men.[7]

Mencius told us that all the good actions of man, such as benevolence and righteousness, were based upon man's social instincts. To develop the instinct of commiseration is the way to benevolence ; to develop the instinctive feeling of shame and dislike is the way to righteousness.[8] To Mencius, the development of moral personality was the chief aim of personal culture.

---

[4] See Chapter I, The Naturalistic School ; Chapter XI, Non-Confucian School, Radical-Individualistic.
[5] Emile, translation by Barbara Foxley.
[6] See Chapter II, Section 2.
[7] See Chapter II, Section 1, Virtue and Tao of Man.
[8] See Chapter XI, Confucian Schools, Naturalistic.

To the politico-ethical school, the individual is essentially a social being. By nourishing his social instincts, which are good, you will have a good individual. By starving his social instincts, you will have a bad individual.

Since man is a social being, his development or nourishment naturally lies in that of his social instincts. What is meant by " social " is the relation of men to each other. Therefore, to the Chinese, while the development of the individual is emphasized, individualism is but in a relative sense.

Here lie the merits as well as the defects of Chinese civilization. By emphasizing man's social nature, a stable society was built. Even though China had been invaded and conquered many times by alien races throughout the whole history, the social structure remained intact. Here seems to lie the secret why China, being one of the oldest civilizations in the world, is still living, while ancient Greece and Rome passed away centuries ago. On the other hand, while Western civilization, which is fundamentally individualistic in a positive sense, and essentially Hellenic, is in full blossom, Chinese civilization remains at a standstill.

Intellectual activity of the individuals seems to be one of the fundamental elements of a progressive society. Without free intellect, science and art cannot attain a high degree of development. And science and art are indispensable weapons to an ever-advancing civilization. There can be no free intellectual activity unless the full right of the individual to develop his intellectual power is granted to him.

2. The Development of Individualism

Positive Individualism is different from negative individualism in the sense that the one employs the method of abolishing institutions and adopting a *laissez-faire* policy as the means of freeing the individual, and the other employs the method of utilizing institutions to develop the individual and using conscious effort to develop all his impulses and powers. It is different from relative individualism in the sense that the latter emphasizes the development of social instincts of the individual to the sacrifice of his other impulses and powers.

THE INDIVIDUAL, SOCIETY, AND THE STATE   173

Positive individualism was born in the Hellenic world; undermined during the medieval ages; brought to the surface again during the Renaissance; widened in its magnitude during the Reformation; running to the extreme, it became negative during the eighteenth century; returned to its normal position in the nineteenth century; and since then, it has been seriously studied, critically examined, politically, economically, and socially adjusted under the influence of the theory of organic evolution and social progress. A study of the development of individualism is the key to Western civilization.

The Greeks. The free activities of Greek life, in intellect, in the æsthetic sense, in physical perfectness, and in ethical conceptions, have been fully discussed in the preceding chapter. It is unnecessary to repeat them. But I wish to point out here that the modern conceptions of individualism, however differently interpreted, are fundamentally Hellenic, though adjusted to modern conditions of life and institutions.

The Renaissance. In discussing the Renaissance, Paulsen characterizes this period of the development of Western civilization as "a passionate craving for freedom on the part of the individual: he was no longer willing to be bound by established opinions and institutions, but desired the complete and free exercise of all his impulses and powers; in the struggle for freedom he opposed nature to convention and tradition. But this was exactly what the Greeks had aimed at; the freest development of the individual; and for that reason Hellenism became the ideal of humanity." [9]

"In the Middle Ages," says Höffding, "man was valued according to his union with church and corporation. The natural man, with his purely individual, emotional life, was of no account, and was not regarded as authorized." In contrast to this, during the Renaissance, "the individual life of the soul was felt as a reality, and excited interest in and for itself, quite apart from anything to which it might be detached."[10]

---

[9] Paulsen, *System of Ethics*, Page 129.
[10] Höffding, *History of Modern Philosophy*, Volume I, Chapter II, *Humanism*.

As with the Greeks, the free intellectual activity during the Renaissance was limited to the few. The intellectual aristocracy was busy in its solution of intellectual and æsthetic problems. But as to the extent to which Humanism was to be extended to the people in general, it did not concern itself.

The Reformation. With the spirit of Humanism in Italy, the Renaissance of south Europe took the form of Reformation in the north which was to solve the social (or religious) problems—how to extend the sphere of intellectual activity from the few to the general mass. " It was the great merit of the Reformation that it would not be contented with an evasion of the religious question (as the Renaissance in the south was), but attacked it directly, proclaiming in the sphere of religion the same principle of personality which Humanism had already proclaimed in the other sphere of thought." [11]

Luther, in his struggle with the church, became the advocate of the natural man. " He especially emphasized the importance of the impulses and workings of simple human life." Religion was no longer an outer conformation to church, but a close personal union with Christ. Thus, individualism was carried into religion, which was then the strongest and most extensive social force, and its effect on general society was far-reaching.

The Eighteenth Century. It was not until the eighteenth century, known as the Age of Englightenment, that the spirit of individualism reached its highest tide. With all his vigor, Voltaire attacked the church, which to him was the chief stumblingblock to a free exercise of reason and reform and to all human progress.[12] Rousseau, with all his vigor, attacked the civilization of his time. " He declared that Europe was overcivilized, and summoned men to return to nature and simplicity." [13] In his social contract, he declared that every man had the right of participating in the government. The real sovereign of the state is the

---

[11] Höffding, *History of Modern Philosophy*, Volume I, Chapter VI.
[12] Robinson and Beard, *Development of Modern Europe*, Volume I, Page 170.
[13] *Id.*, Page 176.

people. In advocating the natural rights of man, he declared that " man is born free."

Although Rousseau's theory of the state was not the same as that of modern radical-individualists, who believe that institutions are fundamentally evil and seek to abolish them, nevertheless he looked at the past civilization with great suspicions and advocated that man should return to nature and simplicity. This spirit of individualism is negative because it lacks the idea of improving the native powers of the individual through men's conscious effort.

Rousseau's positive contribution towards individualism was his emphasis on the problem of worth—" the right of the great, simple, human values of life against every kind of aristocracy and refinement."[14] This right of the great, simple, human values of life is positively needed in China at the present, as against, not aristocracy of which China has none, but principles of propriety, from the overrefinement of which Chinese life and thought have been in chains for centuries.

The Modern World. The Greeks discovered the values of human life; the Renaissance thinkers rediscovered them after centuries of undermining; the Reformation leaders widened the scope of humanism; the eighteenth-century leaders knocked down the medieval institutions which were stumblingblocks to the freedom of the individuals; with the nineteenth century, under the influence of new biological and social sciences and industry and commerce, individualism received a new meaning. Thus we come to the modern world.

Individual and Society. Positive individualism, the prodigious child of Western civilization, permeated the thoughts of Western thinkers. Not only Mill and Spencer, defenders of the rights of the individual, emphasized the fact that the development of the individual is the foundation of civilization and progress,[15] but Treitschke, defender of state rights, declared that " only a nation which is imbued with strong sense of personal freedom can

---

[14] Höffding, *History of Modern Philosophy*, Volume I, Look V, *General Characteristics*.
[15] Mill, *Liberty* ; Spencer, *Social Statics*.

win and keep political freedom." [16] The values of individual life, and the development of the individual in all of his native powers, intellectually, æsthetically, and physically, are something inherent to Western thought. The difference lies rather in method and focus than in denial or defense of individualism.

Modern sociology has come to realize that society is not something which amounts to mere artificial aggregation of individuals, but it is an organism. In discussing social function, Giddings said that the ultimate end of social function is " social personality," which is " life in its higher developments, especially its moral and intellectual developments that society creates and perfects." All the public utilities are approximate ends of social function, which are the means to the ultimate end. Therefore the social institutions are not evils, but indispensable weapons to social progress. " In higher types of civilization," said Giddings, " individual freedom and well-being are continuously increased without necessary injury to the race." " Race maintenance and evolutions with diminishing cost of individual life, with increasing freedom, power, and happiness of the individual person—is progress." [17]

Social structure itself is neither good nor bad. Whether it is good or bad is conditioned by the function it performs. If a certain social organization is favorable to social progress, it is good. If it hinders social progress, it is bad. A progressive society creates and perfects individual freedom and well-being without necessary injury to the race. The individual and society are not opposed to each other, but react upon each other towards progress.

3. THE INDIVIDUAL AND THE STATE

Perhaps one of the most important modern ideas that China has to learn in order to construct her new state, is the relation of the individual and the state. There are two opposite types of the idea of state now prevailing in western Europe. One is German

---

[16] Treitschke, *His Doctrine of German Destiny and International Relations*, by Hausrath, English translation, New York and London, 1914, Chapter on *Freedom*.

[17] Giddings, *Descriptive and Historical Sociology*, Part IV, Chapter I.

which emphasizes state rights, and the other, Anglo-Saxon, which emphasizes individual rights.

Anglo-Saxon. " The least-governed is the best governed " is the controlling principle of the state according to the Anglo-Saxon idea. The free individuals are the foundation of the state. As long as the acts of the individual do not harm his fellow creatures, he must enjoy perfect freedom : " Liberty of thought and feeling," " of tastes and pursuits," and " freedom to unite " with voluntary associations.[18] " In proportion to the development of his individuality," said Mill, " each person becomes more valuable to himself, and is therefore capable of being more valuable to others. There is a greater fullness of life about his own existence, and when there is more life in the units there is more in the mass which is composed of them." [19]

The state is only a means by which the individual is refrained from " making himself a nuisance to other people." [20] " The only purpose for which power can be rightfully exercised over any member to a civilized community, against his will, is to prevent harm to others." [21]

Mill objected to the idea that the state had the right to make improvements upon the individuals against their will.[22] " Each [individual] is the proper guardian of his own health, whether bodily, or mental and spiritual. Mankind are greater gainers by suffering each other to live as seems good to themselves, than by compelling each to live as seems good to the rest." [23]

He was also hostile to state regulations. To him, " the regulation of every part of private conduct by public authority, on the ground that the state had a deep interest in whole bodily and mental discipline of every one of the citizens " was only admissible in a small republic surrounded by powerful enemies and in constant peril of being subverted by foreign attack.

---

[18] Mill, *On Liberty, Introductory.*
[19] *Id.,* Chapter III, *Human Elements of Well-Being.*
[20] *Ibid.*
[21] Mill, *on Liberty,* Chapter III, *Human Elements of Well-Being.*
[22] *Id.,* Chapter III.
[23] *Id., Introductory.*

The welfare of citizens is the first and last thing to be considered in the state. "In a society," said Spencer, "the living units do not and cannot lose individual consciousness, since the community as a whole has no corporate consciousness." "This is an everlasting reason why the welfare of citizens cannot rightly be sacrificed to some supposed benefit of the State; but why, on the other hand, the State is to be maintained solely for the benefit of the citizens. The corporate life must here be subservient to the lives of the parts, instead of the lives of the parts being subservient to the corporate life." [24]

German. In Anglo-Saxon countries "the State is almost always used to denote society in its more organized aspects, or it may be identified with government as a special agency operating for the collective interests of men in association." But in Germany, "society is a technical term and means something empirical and, so to speak, external; while the State, if not avowedly something mystic and transcendental, is at least a moral entity, the creation of self-conscious reason operating in behalf of the spiritual and ideal interests of its members. Its function is cultural, educative." [25] According to the German idea, the state is a living thing, it "lives quite as real a life as each of its citizens" and it "is an independent order, which lives according to its own laws." [26]

Liberty to the Anglo-Saxon is conceived as the free activity of the individuals in developing his own native powers. Freedom to the Germans is conceived as a supersensible realm where the individual enjoys his freedom of spirit, which they call *culture*.

The Germans live in two worlds: the outer world is bound by "the rules of necessity of space and time in which action takes place." The inner world is the supersensible not bound by the causal laws, the "ultimate freedom, the heightening of consciousness for its own sake, sheer revealing in noble ideals, the law of the inner world." [27] "The main thing is that Germany, more

---

[24] Spencer, quoted by Saleeby, C. W., in *Individualism and Collectivism*, London, 1906, Chapter IV, *Individual and the State*.
[25] Dewey, *German Philosophy and Politics*, Page 30.
[26] Treitschke, *Doctrine and His Life*, by Hausrath, chapter on *Freedom*, Pages 322, 323.
[27] Dewey, *German Philosophy and Politics*, Page 31.

than any other nation, in a sense alone of all nations, embodies the essential principle of humanity: freedom of spirit, combined with thorough and detailed work in the outer sphere where reigns causal law, where obedience, discipline and subordination are the necessities of a successful organization."[28] "The more the Germans accomplish in the way of material conquest, the more they are conscious of fulfilling an ideal mission; every external conquest affords the greater warrant for dwelling in an inner region where mechanism does not intrude."[29]

To the Germans, the state is an entity independent of other social institutions. Its highest function is to spread culture. All the detailed organizations of the state and the rigid regulations imposed upon the individuals by the state are regarded as a means to the ideal realm where freedom of spirit reigns supreme.

4. NATIONAL DEFENSE AND NATIONAL CULTURE

In view of the precarious condition that China is now in, her problems of first importance are naturally those of national defense; on the other hand, in view of the weakness of Chinese civilization in so far as a lack of positive individualism is concerned, her problems of first importance are those of national culture. National defense demands national solidarity; national culture demands individual liberty. The former requires emphasis on state rights; the latter, on individual rights. The former requires organization and efficiency; the latter, individual freedom and initiative. Bureaucracy is favorable for national defense; democracy, national culture. Therefore, on the one hand, China needs national solidarity, state rights, organization and efficiency, and bureaucracy; on the other hand, she needs individual liberty, individual rights, initiative, and democracy.

History proves that practical demands of the time will mold national policy. We must remember, as we have pointed out in the preceding chapter, that China's reforms aimed fundamentally at the solution of defense problems. Only through the failure of defense policy, we went on one step further, to cultural problems.

---

[28] Dewey, *German Philosophy and Politics*, Pages 36, 37.
[29] *Id.*, Page 30.

China first started to build a navy, but it proved to be a failure in the Sino-Japanese War. She built an army on modern plans, but it was no more than a national police. Then the Manchu government went to play the dangerous game of educational reforms. The result was the overthrow of the Manchu dynasty.

A reform of education meant an attack on cultural problems. Thus from the defense problems, it was shifted to the cultural problems. But the direct aim was still at the national defense. Because a direct reform of national defense was a failure, China turned her attention to the solution of the cultural problem, which was regarded only as an indirect means to national defense. " To save the country by means of education " became a national motto. " New education would produce new men," the leaders argued, " and it is new men that would be able to save the country by means of new methods."

To shift from the defense problem to the cultural problem would be nothing short of a defeat of the national purpose. We could not very well talk about individual liberty, rights, and initiative, while watching our national rights fast passing away into the hands of our " friendly " nations. The individuals would be no more if our country should perish!

However, unless a certain amount of cultural problems is solved, there would be no adequate national defense. Years ago we began to build a navy; but where is our navy now? We also built an army, which amounts to more than half a million men at the present time; can it defend our country in the face of an adequate force directed to attack us? Modern national defense does not depend upon the army and navy alone, but upon many other things as well. First of all we must have an efficient government, which is to organize the whole country into a workable system to transact the business of the state, to form and direct national policy, to extend public education, and to aid the development of natural resources. Then, we must have a national system of transportation to facilitate mobilization of materials and men. We must have all the material resources organized in order to furnish all sorts of supplies needed. We must have an adequate system of finance to mobilize capital and to transact business. These are necessary steps towards an adequate national defense.

We have to start all these things from the bottom. In speaking of an efficient government, our government is yet young: of a national system of transportation, we have only a few railroads; of organized material resources our national resources are yet buried underground; of an adequate system of finance, our finance is a mess. We must devote a major part of our attention to these problems. These may aim at the national defense, but the results would be much broader.

Railroads would quicken commerce and extend knowledge. Industries would enrich the people. A sound system of finance would aid business activities. Therefore, the material basis for national defense would serve at the same time for national culture. For culture cannot grow in an unorganized, chaotic, and poverty-stricken country.

In building railroads, fostering industry, and extending commerce by means of an adequate system of finance, we have the common basis for both national defense and national culture; and to these we must devote our time and energy.

The state should grant not only freedom to the individual to develop all his native instincts and powers; but also to provide adequate means to aid this development. For centuries the Chinese state has been maintaining a *laissez-faire* policy. Ever since very early times the people have enjoyed local government not interfered with by the state. Our lack of individualism was not caused by excessive state rights—too little of them—but by social traditions embodied in what is called the principles of propriety. It is the time now for the state to step in and force new culture upon the people, the chief weapon of which is a system of public education.

After all, the individuals are the foundation of the state. A strong, powerful nation is ultimately based upon powerful individuals. We cannot build a house on a foundation of shifting sand. We agree with Mill that "when there is more life in the units there is more life in the mass which is composed of them." Individuality, or a full development of all the native powers of the individual, is an invaluable asset to the state and civilization.

We cannot agree with Mill in his objection to the state's making improvement upon the individuals against their will.

There are no nations other than Germany where the state looks so much after the affairs of the people. Yet she has contributed no fewer scientists, thinkers, artists, musicians, and great writers than other advanced countries.

The Chinese idea of the state is essentially the same as the Anglo-Saxon. The idea that "the least governed is the best governed" is common to both peoples. Perhaps the idea that the state should claim authority to make improvement upon the people against their habits is repulsive to both the Chinese and the Anglo-Saxon. But in view of the practical social and national demands of the time, the Chinese people must realize that in this stage of international strife for power, they must sacrifice their individual inclinations for national good.

On the other hand, the state must recognize, as we pointed out a moment ago, that the foundation of the state is the individual, and that the powerful individual is a great asset to the state.

The state is not only an agent to maintain political independence of its people, but also an agent to spread national culture. The state should see to it that not only the individual rights should not be menaced by it, but should be protected from being menaced.

The people should realize that during these coming hundred years, their devotion to the state is absolutely necessary for their political independence, which is the foundation for future national culture, and they not only owe to themselves the full development of their native powers, intellectually, æsthetically, morally, and physically, but also their national consciousness, which is fun la-mental to patriotism. And patriotism is the chief virtue of a people who love political freedom.

Efficient government and industrial and commercial development are the common material basis for national defense and culture. Patriotism is demanded of the people by themselves for the protection of their political freedom, and it is the spirit of national defense. Positive individualism is to increase the values of life and to make life richer and more abundant. National defense and national culture—the happy medium of the two—

form the vital issue of China's national problem. This is at the same time the problem of national education of the young Republic, for national education is a means of solving national problems.

CHAPTER XV

SCIENCE AND ART OF EDUCATION

Education is threefold : spirit, ideal, and method. National spirit and ideal are the spirit and ideal of education. National spirit is the moving force of a nation and ideal is spirit visionalized. The method by means of which national ideal is to be realized is the science and art of education.

Education is an applied science based upon other sciences, especially natural sciences, such as biology and psychology, and social sciences, such as sociology and history. Education, like engineering, must utilize all that modern sciences are able to contribute. For the reason of the facts given above modern education is essentially different from old education.

Education is a practical art—the ability of applying sciences to attend a desired end. Education as a practical art means the skill or habit one has acquired to put into effect all there is in education.

There are distinctions between the teacher and the pseudo-teacher. The teacher knows the spirit, ideal, and science and art of education. The pseudo-teacher may or may not understand science and art of education, but does not understand the spirit and ideal. The pseudo-teacher teaches because he teaches. The teacher teaches because there is a spirit and ideal behind teaching. The pseudo-teacher teaches mechanically. The teacher teaches for animating the spirit and realizations of the ideal. Therefore, a true education is a living force and a false education is a lifeless mechanism.

The teacher is an interpreter of human spirits, and a bearer of human ideals. In other words, he is a personified ideal, a teacher of mankind, and a model of the human race. His thoughts represent the cream of intellect of the race, and his actions give inspiration to the people.

Then he must know the technique by means of which he is to execute his ideal, as an artist would do. This technique we here call the science and art of education.

Education as a Method to Spread Culture. The chief function of education is to spread culture. Civilization is not only to be measured by the amount of knowledge[1] the race possesses, but also by how extensive knowledge has been disseminated to the general mass. Civilization is to be measured both by depth and width.

Education as a Scientific Method. The old method of education was based upon speculations, and unorganized experience. The modern method of education is based upon inductive science and systematic experimentations. One of the most important factors by which modern science has influenced education is the theory of organic evolution—that is to say, life grows from simple to complex. The process of evolution brings about variations; and through the struggle for existence and natural selection, the fittest survives. From this theory, the problem of life and environment, nature and nurture, or heredity and education, extends to the field of education.

Evolution does not, however, mean progress. For progress implies the element of the conscious effort of man. Survival of the fittest does not necessarily mean survival of the most desirable according to human purposes. Education implies the conscious effort of man to create situations in such a way that they would favor the growth and survival of the most desirable in reference to purpose or purposes.

The method of inductive science has revolutionized the modern world. Not only in the field of physical and biological sciences, but also in the field of social sciences, such as history and sociology; the method of inductive science in its systematic way of gathering, controlling, and verifying data, and observation and experimentation, as the case may be, has discovered new truths by application of which to practical uses, life has become

---

[1] Knowledge is here used in a very wide sense,—it means the sum total of the achievements of the race.

enriched and happiness increased. Education, being a branch of applied sociology and psychology, is no exception. Modern educational sociology and educational psychology may be served as notable illustrations.

Education as a Means to Individual Development. Here in America, "individuality" and "initiative" are becoming the catchwords in the field of education. The native tendencies of the child are not to be checked but to be directed and developed. At least in theory, if not in actual practice, American education is attempting to produce a type of individual who dares to think independently and dares to act energetically. The conception of individual development in education is but a natural consequence of the idea of positive individualism. From the individualistic view of life, inherent to Western thought, modern Western education emphasizes individual development and values individuality and initiative.

Education as a Method to Social Progress. The organic view of society has come to stay in the modern Western world. As the individual and society react upon each other towards social progress, education for individual development is only one side of the whole problem. To a great extent, the richness of individual life depends upon that of community life. Therefore, the development of community life is but a different phase of individual development. The best type of individual not only represents his individual personality, but also social personality of the kind of society he lives in.

Moreover, modern civic life is the foundation of a modern democratic state. Community spirit is the fundamental force of civic life. His personality would be considered defective if the individual did not embody the community spirit. Why, is it not that the consciousness of the kind which is native to the individual needs also to be developed just as his other native tendencies?

Education as a Means to the Training of Citizenship. If the citizen has the right to demand from the state protection and assistance, the state has also the right to make demands upon the citizen for his defense of his country and devotion to her.

Citizenship implies both rights and duties. Nobody can enjoy rights permanently without the fulfillment of duties. Therefore patriotism is the supreme virtue of citizenship.

Education as a Means to the Training of Leadership. True democracy does not mean mediocrity, but leadership. The leader is the man who can think clearly and concisely, and who possesses genuine sympathy for his fellow men and has the courage to transfer his better feelings into deeds. He is a living force to his community and nation. He incorporates all the best there is to Culture into his personality and is *esprit de corps.*

BIBLIOGRAPHY

CLASSICS

The Thirteen Classics with Commentaries 十三經註疏

ANCIENT PHILOSOPHY

Tao Teh King, Lao-tse 老子道德經
Works of Kwan-tse 管子
Works of Tson-tse 莊子
Works of Me-tse 墨子
Works of Sin-tse 荀子
Works of Yang-tse 楊子
Works of Hui-Nan-tse 淮南子

SUN, YUAN, AND MING PHILOSOPHERS

Chun-Yi-Tong Philosophical Library 正誼堂叢書,清張伯寅
Hu Kuang's Collections of Philosophical Works 性理大全,明胡廣
Works of Elder and Younger Ch'ing-tse 二程遺書
Complete Works of Tsu-tse 朱子全書
Complete Works of Loh Shang-san 陸象山全集
Complete Works of Wong Yang-min 王陽明全集
Dialogues of Wong Yang-min 王陽明傳習錄
Chang Chiu-sao's Classified Collections of the Works of Sun, Yuan, and Ming Philosophers 理學類編,明張九韶

TS'ING (MANCHU DYNASTY) PHILOSOPHERS

Collections of Classical Commentaries and Researches by the Philosophers of the Manchu Dynasty 皇清經解,清阮元
Continuation to the above collections 續皇清經解,清王先謙
Works of Huang Tson-hi 黎洲遺著彙

History

Huang Sze-tung's History of Chinese Philosophy 道學淵源錄,清黃嗣東

Sun Chi-fung's History of Chinese Philosophy 理學宗傳,清孫奇逢

Huang Tson-hi's History of Philosophy of the Sun and Yuan Dynasties 宋元學案,清黃宗羲

Huang Tson-hi's History of Philosophy of the Ming Dynasty 明儒學案,清黃宗羲

Tang-chien's History of Philosophy of the Manchu Dynasty 國朝學案小識,清唐鑑

Tsu-tse's History of Elementary Education (published A.D. 1767) 朱子小學

Chen Yuan-lung's History of Physical Sciences (published A.D. 1733) 格物鑑源,陳元龍

Miscellany

Tsu-tse's Aims of Study (or Learning) 朱子學的

Chen Su-sai's Systematic Study of the Confucian Philosophy 聖學格物通,明湛若水

Tsu-tse's History of Philosophy of the Earlier Sun Period 伊洛淵源錄,宋朱熹

Courses of Studies, Ch'ing's Private Seminary (Yuan Dynsaty) 程氏家塾讀書分年日程,元程端禮

Chen Li's Records of Philosophical Fragments 東塾讀書記,清陳禮

Records of Tung-lin College (Ming Dynasty) 東林書院志

Chan Hung-mao's Regulations for Education of Boys 養正遺規,清陳宏謀

Chan Hung-mao's Regulations for Education of Girls 教女遺規,清陳宏謀

Deeds of Famous Men in History During Their Childhood and Youth 童蒙金鑑

Kuch Tsai Hsieh Pao, articles on : 　　國粹學報
    Origin of Chinese Culture 　　　國學原論
    Development of Ancient Chinese
        Philosophy 　　　　　　　　國學微論
    Development of Chinese Philosophy
        from the Han Dynasty to the
        Ming Dynasty 　　　　　　　國學通論
    Chinese Philosophy During the Manchu
        Dynasty 　　　　　　　　　　國學今論

ENCYCLOPEDIA

The Great Chinese Encyclopedia 　　古今圖書集成
Wen Hsien Tung Kao 　　　　　　文獻通攷

BIBLIOGRAPHIES

Index to the Imperial Library 　　　四庫全書總目提要
Hui Keh Su Mu 　　　　　　　　　彙刻書目
Bibliography of Chinese Books, Tokyo,
    1912 　　　　　　　　　　　　漢集解題

INDEX

Acquired characteristics, 50.
Aim of education, 35f., 94.
Ancient classics, method of studying, 25f.
Analytic method, or Mencian type of teaching, 121ff.
Archery, 95, 101, 102.
Aristotle, 36, 72.
Assimilation, 89.

Book-knowledge, 54.
Buddhism, 18, 167.

Cardinal virtues, 12.
Charioteering, 101, 102.
Chin dynasty (秦), 14.
Ch'ing-Tsu school (程朱派), 56f., 59, in comparison with Loh-Wong school, 57f.
Ch'ing tse (程子) (A.D. 1032–1107), on human nature, 43f.; acquired characteristics, 50; knowledge and conduct, 63, 133; concentration, 84; study of history, 86; thinking, 88; method of teaching, 120.
Chin-Sze-Huang (秦始皇), 14.
Comparative ethics, 148.
Concentration, 84f.
Conduct, 94f.; training of, 96, 105f.; as criterion of knowledge, 61f.
Confucian schools, 5, 15, 16, 47f., 80, 127.
Confucius (551–478 B.C.), 6f.; scheme of education, 32ff.; on knowledge, 52; conduct, 62; individual differences, 108ff.; method of teaching, 117f.; teaching of conduct, 136.
Conscience, 145f.
Cosmic reason, 141f., 144.
Culture, national, 179ff.
Curriculum, ancient, 94f.; of Wong Yang-min, 95ff.

Dancing, 95, 96, 102, 103.

Dewey, John, 54.
Discipline, 115f.
Duty, 1f.

Eclectic tendency, earlier period, 17; later period, 23.
Economico-ethical school, 12f.
Education, aim of, 35f., 94; meaning of, 31f.; problem of, 36; for personal culture, 33; for family, 33; for the State, 34; for the world, 34; to add something to nature, 45f.; to develop nature, 46f.; limit of, 47f.; and growth, 48f.; as practical art, 184f.; as method to spread culture, 185; as scientific method, 185f.; as means to individual development, 186; to social progress, 186; to the training of citizenship, 186; to the training of leadership, 187.
Elementary education, 93ff.
Emotions, 141f.
Encyclopædic tendency, 22.
Environment, forces of, 49f.
Epochs of Chinese thought, 5f.; the creative period, 6ff.; the period of restoration, 15f.; introduction of Hindu philosophy, 17f.; the Renaissance of Confucian thought, 18ff.; summary, 26ff.
Ethical and moral, 144f.
Ethico-cosmological tendency, 16.
Evolution, 185.
Extraterritorial judicial rights, 163.

Family, education for, 33.
Filial piety, or love for parents, 1, 34, 36, 94, 95, 96, 98.
Formalism, Wong Yang-min's attack on, 98f.
Froebel, 100f.

God, Christian conception of, 164f.;

INDEX

Confucian conception of, 165.
Good and bad, meaning of, 37.
Greek idea of life, 154ff.

Han dynasty (漢), 15.
Han-Hui-Tse (韓非子), 14; moral theory, 131.
Han Yu (韓愈), 19; on human nature, 42; function of the teacher, 107.
Happiness, Greek conception of, 154f.; Chinese conception of, 2,155.
Hebraism, Hellenism and Confucianism, 165f.
Hedonism, 18f.
Higher education, 93; also see Chap. II, 31ff.
Hindu Philosophy, 17.
Home, 3.
Huang Tso-hi (黃宗羲), 22f., 58f., 59f., n.
Hu An-tin (胡安定), 103.
Hu Chu-jen (胡居仁), 53f.
Huei-Nan-Tse (淮南子), 17.
Humanitarian school, 10.
Human nature, 37ff.; good, 37f.; neither good nor bad, 38; organic view of, 39f.; bad, 40f.; mixture of good and bad, 41; hierarchical, 42; intelligence and heredity, 42f.; quantitative view of, 43f.

Ideas, formation of, 143.
Individual and society, 175f.
Individual and State, 176ff.
Individual differences, 108ff.
Individualism, negative, 171; positive, 172f.; relative, 171f.
Instincts, 50.
Interest, 113ff.
Intuitive knowledge, 141f., 145.

Kanghsi Dictionary, 23.
Kaou-tse (告子), 37f.
Knowledge, problem of, 51ff; method of, 55ff.; process of acquiring, 56; use of, 91f.; criterion of, 61f.; relative values in, 78ff.; complete and partial, 64; aphorical as against systematic, 51, 74; interrelation of knowing and doing, 63f.
Ku Yen-wu (顧炎武) (A.D. 1612-?), 23.
Kwan-tse (管子) (5th cent. before Christ), 12f.; 130.

Lao-tse (老子), 10f., 130.
Learning, fundamental elements of, 83ff.; definite purpose in, 83f; factors in, 86ff.; organic growth in, 90f.; independent spirit in, 89f.
Legal principles, Roman, 161f.; Chinese, 162; comparison of the two, 162f.
Li Sze (李斯), 13.
Loh Shang-san (陸象山) (A.D. 1136-1193), 21; method of teaching, 122; moral theory, 129; will power, 134; teaching of morals, 138f., 144; criticism of, 58.
Loh-Wong school (陸王派), 57f., n., 60f.; in comparison with Ch'ing-Tsu school, 59ff.

Mathematics, 95, 102.
McMurry, 84.
Meaning of institutions, 2ff.
Memory and thinking, 86ff.
Mencius (?-282 B.C.), 7; education to develop nature, 46f.; environment, 49f.; human nature, 37ff.; concentration, 84f.; method of teaching, 118ff.; interest, 113ff.; will, 133f.; moral theory of, 128; teaching of conduct, 136.
Me-tse (墨子), 9; moral theory of, 130.
Mind, 57ff.
Moral conduct, 133f.; in reference to social value, 135; method of, 135ff.; accumulative or applicative method, 136f.; "Holding the fundamentals" as method to, 138f. reflective method, 140ff.; stages of, 140.
Moral problems, in China, 147ff.

INDEX

Moral theory, types of, 127ff.; Confucian schools, 128ff.; naturalistic, 128; corrective, 128; practical conduct, 129; fundamental human rights, 129; intuitive, 129; non-Confucian schools, 130f.; materialistic, 130; radical-individualistic, 130; humanitarian, 130; penal, 130; hedonistic, 131.
Moral training, 104ff., 132ff.; in schools, 149ff.
Music, 95, 101, 103.

National defense, 179ff.
Naturalistic school, 10f.

Particular experiences, in reference to universal ideas, 123ff.
Passions, 141f.
Penal school, 13ff.
Personal culture, 32f.
Philological tendency, 23ff.; value of the work, 25.
Physical training, 101ff.
Physical world, Chinese views of, 67ff.; speculations on, 69f.
Play, 99.
Politico-ethical school, 7ff.; meaning of, 75; aim of, 127f.
Principles of Propriety, or Li (禮), 9, 13, 17, 158f.; meaning of, 159f., n.; in comparison with Roman legal principles, 162f.

Reading, 97f.
Reason, 53, 60f., 77; as a panacea, 76; in reference to experience, 148.
Religious problem in China, 166f.
Renaissance of Confucian thought, 18ff.
Rituals, practice of, 97.
Roman law, 158ff.
Rousseau, 100, 175.
Russo-Japanese War, 154.

School, the, 4.
School age, 93.
Science, problem of, 67ff.; beginning of modern science in Europe, 72f.; in reference to modern Chinese education, 76; to modern method of knowledge, 167f.; as key to future greatness of China, 168.
Science and art of education, 184ff.
Self, true and false, 142.
Shan yang (商鞅), 13.
Singing, 96f. 99, 102, 103.
Sin-tse (荀子), 8f.; on human nature, 40f.; moral theory of, 128.
Social life during the Chow dynasty (1122-255 B.C.), 101f.
Spencer, 78f.
State, the, 3; education for the governing of, 34.
Summum bonum, 35f., 93.
Su Tun-pu (蘇東坡), 78ff.
Synthetic method, or Confucian type of teaching, 120f.

Tai Tun-yuan (戴東原) (A.D. 1723-1777), 24.
Tao (道), meaning of, 10f.; source of, 31; of Heaven, 31; of man, 32.
Teaching, psychological problem in, 108ff.; logical problem in, 116ff.; types of, 116ff.
Teh (德), meaning of, 10.
Theory and practice, 61ff.
Thinking, 88f., 89f., n.
Thorndike, 84.
Three things, teaching of, 95.
Ton Tson-shu (董仲舒), 16.
Truth, 57ff.
Tsing Teh-sher (眞德秀), on will, 134.
Tson-tse (莊子), 11f.
Tsu-tse or Tsu Tse (朱子) (A.D. 1130-1200), 20; human nature, 43; on education, 47; knowledge, 53; criticism of, 58f.; speculations on the physical world, 69f.; interrelation of knowing and doing, 63; relative values in knowledge, 78ff.; memory, 86; independent spirit in learning, 89f.; elementary education, 95; interest and discipline, 115f.; method of teaching, 120f.;

moral theory, 129; knowledge and conduct, 133; will power, 134; teaching of morals, 136ff.
Tse-sze (子 思), 31.
Tuan Yu-sai (段 玉 裁), 25.

Unitary ideal, 71f.
Universal ideas, 125f.
Universal love, 10.

Virtue, 11, 32.

Western thought, introduction of, 29f.
Will, 133ff.
Wong Yang-min (王 陽 明) (A.D. 1472, 1528), 20; on human nature, 43f.; theory and practice, 63f.; inner truth, 70f.; definite purpose in learning, 83f.; memory and thinking, 86; knowledge as instrument, 91; knowledge and life, 91f.; curriculum, 95ff.; principles of teaching, 98ff.; in comparison with Froebel, 100f.; individual difference, 111f.; method of teaching, 123; moral theory, 129; will power, 134; teaching of morals, 140ff.; rational morality, 147f.
World place, nine laws for, 34f.

Yang Hsiung (楊 雄), or Yang-tse, 16; on human nature, 41f.
Yu Cho-yuan (兪 曲 園) (A.D. ?-1906), 24.
Yun Lu Tai Tien (永 樂 大 典), 22.

英文擇業須知
FINDING YOUR JOB AND KEEPING IT

BY BRUNO SCHWARTZ

20 cts.

The author of this little book is a trained newspaper man and has had much experience in business. In this book he aims to help the young man who has just left school and is looking for a position. This is a critical time in the young man's life, and he needs guidance. Mr. Schwartz takes up such practical points as the choice of a vocation, directions for writing a letter of application correctly, hints for the personal interview, suggestions for keeping a job after it is secured, etc.

The book is written in simple and concise English, and contains more than twenty topics, each of which is interesting as well as practical. The young man who desires to achieve success will find in this booklet most valuable information and hints.

THE COMMERCIAL PRESS, LIMITED, PUBLISHERS

H 105

此書有著作權翻印必究

英文中國教育原理（一冊）

| 編纂者 | 蔣夢麟 |
| 發行兼印刷者 | 商務印書館 |

定價　大洋壹元伍角　外埠酌加運費匯費
初版　中華民國十四年二月

ALL RIGHTS RESERVED

A STUDY IN CHINESE PRINCIPLES OF EDUCATION

Author　　　　　　Monlin Chiang, PH. D.
Publishers and Printers　The Commercial Press, Ltd.
　　　Price:　$1.50　postage extra
　　　　1st ed., February, 1925

英文中國全國小學校概況
THE EFFICIENCY OF ELEMENTARY SCHOOLS IN CHINA

By E. L. Terman
Professor of Education, Yenching University

Published under the auspices of the National Association for the Advancement of Education

Pp. xvi + 202. $1.50

This volume describes the National Survey that Professor Terman and the people associated with him conducted under the auspices of the National Association for the Advancement of Education in 1923. It is divided into two parts. Part I gives the Story of the Survey, taking up the Background for the Survey, Its Conception, Its Reception, Its Tools (the Survey Tests), Its Organization, Its Operation, and Its Results. Part II deals with Technical Studies of the Survey—Interpretation of the Data, Regional Differences in Intelligence, Sex Differences in Intelligence, Type-School Differences in Intelligence, the Problem of Efficiency in Different Types of Schools, the Problem of Overageness, and Conclusions.

The book is illustrated with eight half-tone pictures, about twenty charts and graphs, and tables of figures. It contains a Foreword by Dr. E. W. Wallace, Associate General Secretary of the China Christian Educational Association, and an Introduction by Dr. W. T. Tao, General Director of the National Association for the Advancement of Education.

Educators in China are indebted to Professor Terman and his associates for the data they have collected and for the generalizations arrived at. This survey enables teachers to have a better understanding of the native ability and educational attainments of their students, and principals and superintendents a better knowledge of the standing of their schools and school systems. Each school can now study its score in the light of the final scores, and re-test its students to discover their position. This report is invaluable to persons interested in the nation-wide scientific measurement in Chinese education.

THE COMMERCIAL PRESS, LIMITED, PUBLISHERS
C453 Honan Road, Shanghai

图书在版编目(CIP)数据

中国教育原理 = A Study in Chinese Principles of Education：英文 / 蒋梦麟著.—北京：商务印书馆，2020.10（2021.11重印）
（北大教育学文库）
ISBN 978-7-100-18936-1

Ⅰ.①中… Ⅱ.①蒋… Ⅲ.①教育理论—研究—中国—英文 Ⅳ.①G520

中国版本图书馆CIP数据核字（2020）第151832号

权利保留，侵权必究。

北大教育学文库
中国教育原理
（英文本）
蒋梦麟 著

商 务 印 书 馆 出 版
（北京王府井大街36号　邮政编码100710）
商 务 印 书 馆 发 行
江苏凤凰数码印务有限公司印刷
ISBN 978-7-100-18936-1

2020年10月第1版　　开本 880×1240　1/32
2021年11月第2次印刷　　印张 7⅜
定价：46.00元